The Art of the Feud

The Art of the Feud

Reconceptualizing International Relations

EDITED BY
JOSE V. CIPRUT

PRAEGER

Westport, Connecticut
London

Library of Congress Cataloging-in-Publication Data

The art of the feud: reconceptualizing international relations / edited by Jose V. Ciprut.
    p. cm.
    Includes bibliographical references and index.
    ISBN 0–275–96854–5 (alk. paper)
    1. International relations—Philosophy. I. Ciprut, Jose V.
JZ1305.A78 2000
327.1'0121—dc21   99–045993

British Library Cataloguing in Publication Data is available.

Library of Congress Catalog Card Number: 99–045993
ISBN: 0–275–96854–5

First published in 2000

Praeger Publishers, 88 Post Road West, Westport, CT 06881
An imprint of Greenwood Publishing Group, Inc.
www.praeger.com

Printed in the United States of America

The paper used in this book complies with the
Permanent Paper Standard issued by the National
Information Standards Organization (Z39.48–1984).

10 9 8 7 6 5 4 3 2 1

For Marie-Jose, née Norrenberg

Courageous warrior and unrivalled partner.
With profound love and deepest admiration.

Listen as you will, pray do look around
From treetops on hilltops, late afternoon:
More than halfway closer to the moon,
Less than halfway farther from the ground.

[Upon further reflection on a Turkish poem]

Contents

Preface

Can international relations theory find new grounds on which to prosper within its core dimensions, along accountable pursuits through approaches reflexively attuned to the evolving realities of a globalizing landscape? If so, how so? And if not, why not?

In this book, we focus on the premises of past pursuits, on the promises of certain nascent rationales, and on the entailments of attendant changes and continuities—for social science theory in general and for international relations theory in particular. In our multifaceted concerns and pluridimensional explorations, we seek to elicit relevant insights permitting to imagine more inclusive practices of dynamic theory building. We examine the interlocking effects of language, mind-set, attitude, and method. We scrutinize the putative merits of interactive inputs within polyphonic settings and assess their alleged potential to impart capacity for adaptive selfemendation to theories-in-becoming: We compare some of the more likely reconfigurations and realignments anticipated in the domain of geopolitical economy, especially the ones expected to redefine fundamental concepts such as power, the state, the self, and the orders and borders of societal settings.

In a concerted effort, which in a better world could have gone even beyond the conversation it was designed to emulate, we embark on a series of complementary analytic syntheses in hopeful anticipation that richer understandings will unfold—without need for recourse to facile interpolations, ambivalent interpretations, or judgmental explanations, whether on the part of the reader or the writer.

The future of all social science theory resides in practices that are responsive, therefore responsible; reflexive, therefore self-redefining; accountable, therefore self-redirecting; and not least, ethical and trustworthy, therefore inclusive and open.

This book was inspired by a small cartoon. Depicted in that caricature were a couple of visibly agitated primates, seemingly for the first time erect on their hind legs and bewildered by the brusk discovery of two . . . "arms (?!)"—for which they were just now unable to imagine a use. "What now!?" read the caption, emulating an exclamation qua interrogation that could not have been voiced with such analytic precision and parsimony by life forms still incapable of complex teleological synthesis.

"What next?" we ask, as we invite our readers to join us on our exploratory journey across the pages ahead, now that—eons later—we know how to formulate the question . . . pending an answer.

INTRODUCTION

Making Sense of International Relations Theory in Global Context

JOSE V. CIPRUT

The art of theorizing culminates in a theory's parsimonious translation of the ephemeral and singular into the enduring and the universal. The science of theorizing triumphs when question, method, technique, and tool permit refutation or retention of the explanatory truths suggested by the empirical output legitimated by theory. If social and international theories rarely afford the parsimony and rigor that characterize the natural sciences, this is hardly for lack of trying. And there is good reason for some to regard such shortcomings as blessings in disguise.

International relations/politics seem to blossom best in the interstices that shield the latitudes of art from the constraints of science. And international theory offers its most when allowed to straddle a crossroads where art of explanation and science of understanding avoid collisions. After all, this is a terrain of inquiry where the exclusive and the exhaustive remain evasive, data are scarce, predictors are unreliable, and language meanwhile has become all too suspect of harboring ulterior motives.

Our ontological, epistemological, methodological headaches persist. The problem of nonadditivity among political variables (Alker, 1966) and myriad other technical challenges in converting verbal intricacies into mathematical equations when constructing theory in social science (Blalock, 1969) are very much alive. And as if this were not enough, disregard for a political economy of terms distorts what we mean to say when we speak (Bourdieu, 1982). At a moment when the very place of international relations inside the limits of political theory (Williams, 1996) is shifting, such conducts and contests only further dilute the state of dispersion in which the dividing discipline (Holsti, 1985) finds itself.

Before and since Lasswell and Kaplan (1950), Sabine (1961), Dahl

(1963), Eulau (1963), and Easton (1965), the state of theory in international relations/politics has been reviewed from myriad angles (Finnis, 1922; Russell, 1936; Kaplan, 1957; Hoffman, 1965; Butterfield and Wight, 1966; Morgenthau, 1973; Beitz, 1979; Waltz, 1979; Mayall, 1982; Holsti, 1985; Ferguson and Mansbach, 1988; Williams, 1991; Walker, 1993; S. Brown, 1996). Such have helped to reconsider historical, normative, empirical, methodological, and policy-related perspectives. They have neither dissipated doubts nor satiated cravings, however. And questions remain as theorists brace for yet another putative phase change in world order.

The complexities ensuing from increasing *inter*dependencies in national affairs, and the *intra*connectivities resulting from *trans*globalizations, are compounding the difficulties in making sense of international relations/politics. Many theorists are now weighing the merits and means of giving in to a postinternational mind-set (Rosenau, 1990) that would warrant jailbreaks, and escapes to newer freedoms, by way of novel premises and fresh inferences.

Respectful of the traditions of our discipline, we have many concerns about its fate as we enter an epoch when we will have to respecify, recontextualize, and ever more intimately interrelate the macro and the micro, the public and the private, the leaders and the followers, the governing and the governed, using holistic lenses. This is why we take in the next pages a much closer look at the altered character and changing nature of some concepts of critical import to theoretical thinking in our discipline. These include power and the state, territoriality and the self, war and peace, development and ecology, sovereignty and globalization. We attempt thereby to encourage a reassessment of the depleted value of their classic factors as variables for theories not yet built and as predictors or determinants for models still in the making.

We take stock of past shortcomings, current dilemmas, and future challenges in international relations theory building, not toward facile criticism but in an effort to explore how better to design our theoretical pursuits in transnationalizing settings that are likely to resuscitate severally embedded units of analysis and to reaccommodate fuzzy borders of actor and of domain identity across concomitantly changing yet competitively globalizing landscapes. As extant models fail to provide guidance, we find reason to ask ourselves whether our fragmented international relations theories can continue to make sense for much longer of the transformations that proceed diversely to integrate our universe and to threaten the succor of our worldviews in significant ways. Why, how, which of our theories should be rethought or replaced? And if so, what fresh mentality, which new priorities, should prevail toward what novel directions? Could classic units of analysis and conceptual building blocks continue to serve well the evolving discipline, even after epistemological self-reexaminations and corresponding theoretical rearticulations under way allow theorists to distill the promise of newer destinies from the human condition itself?

Elsewhere, we dealt with the import and implications of the fears and foes engendered by the complex interactive dimensions of insecurity in an evolving global political economy (Ciprut, 2000). Here, instead, we concern ourselves with what we see as a pressing need for dynamic theories capable of coming to grips with emerging realities. And this is why we examine the role of language, narrative, and mind-set in the making of social science theory in general and of political and international relations theory in particular. We begin by scrutinizing the contextual and substantive exigencies for the "languaging" of theory in holistic modes. We review attitudinal impediments to understanding before even considering the evolving connotations of foundational terms as globalization saturates these with newer denotations. Finally, we link our reconceptualizations to a theoretical framework more dynamically attuned to the newer inter-entity relations that may transform the destinations of human societies in the years ahead.

LANGUAGING AND UNDERSTANDING IN SOCIAL AND INTERNATIONAL THEORY

The discipline of "international" relations has developed into an ocean in which distal archipelagos, themselves subdivided into islets of theory, provide abode to aborigines who speak with each other in their local tongue, using mutually reassuring code. This obliges outsiders to interpret meaning—not to gain a direct understanding indispensable for firsthand "criticism" [authority "to show how it is what it is, even that it is what it is, rather than to show what it means" (Sontag, 1982)]. Whom and what should theory building in "global" politics speak to? And why and how?

If a science of *global* politics needs to be built gradually from the bottom up, in a cooperative fashion, and in a manner to cast light for new empirical pursuits, where are the relevant theories and data—on which such science must increasingly depend—to come from? Even more important, from where will the global scientific community arise, and how will it converge into an entity that will share a code of rules and stipulations as to what qualifies to be a scientific question and what constitutes an equally scientific answer: a code on which "normal science" (Kuhn, 1962) may depend? And absent that, who and what else can consolidate and defend the paradigms that seal identity, (re)define loyalties, (re)direct commitments, and thereby enable the global scientific community to choose problems and to select priorities? In a Kuhnian world, science's *globally* respectable authority should result not from a rule-governed method of inquiry selected to liberate a particular scientific knowledge but from the specific scientific "community" that actively obtains, willfully interprets, and doggedly spreads that very knowledge. What ought the organizational principles of a "global" scientific community be, and how could they come about in always participatory if not necessarily fully consensual ways?

Our metatheoretical concern with epistemology dwells on the nature of international relations theory in globalizing contexts. It is complemented by our empirical interest in practical issues of rigor and relevance—including the shifting locus and evolving meaning of the key concepts that have this far fueled theoretical output and directed the empirical thrust of the discipline. In a world where the continuity-preserving forces and vital patterns of structure (such as norms, regimes, states, castes, classes, roles) may become less externally imposed on (exogenous to) and more explicable from within (endogenous to) transglobal voluntary associations, issue circles, and reflexive societal institutions, choice of function, process, and tongue may become more deliberate and responsive and thereby also more responsible for actors' own destinies. In such dynamic complexity, is there a "proper" place for the theorist? Ought that place be on the side of structure or action? Of neither and both? Elsewhere or in between? And who may say so? Might not globalization in and of itself simply dissolve the long-unresolved dilemma (Merton, 1973; Latour, 1987; Woolgar, 1988a, 1988b) of "structure versus action" through far-spreading avowals of the profoundly political nature of theory building in all fields—inter-entity relations and world politics included?

If the reach and reward of our theories are affected by the extent of our techniques and tools, and if "languaging" is such a tool, how is the social scientist and the international relations theorist to normalize grammar, vocabulary, and voice in an attempt comparably to explain amorphous units of analysis and fuzzy links within the complex and compound heterogeneities of globalization? A theorist draws meaning from factual and normative information by ordering one's questions and answers in ways that accommodate and comfort one's underlying beliefs about what is or is not very important and how the important facts and values interrelate. How, then, will the intermingling of cultures, mentalities, and personal propensities affect patterns perceived and inferences drawn, with requisite assurance that conclusions are intrinsic to that which is being observed and do not stand for what is being unwittingly imposed? In other words, in what sense and to what extent might globalization facilitate or impede the ability to distinguish "fact" from "truth" in value-dependent intersubjective observations that are likely to become frequent when greater numbers of individual and societal biases begin to intersect and affect acts of theory-making as "periphery" and "center" form one scientific community?

Owing to its preference for exclusive control over territory as an attribute of wealth and power, the state finds itself all the more disempowered to administer deterritorialized authority in an age of global telecommunications that transcends the traditional limits of statist controls. As international affairs continue to globalize, will not the theories of science as well as those of the professionalization of modernity that base themselves on how the state operates (Avineri, 1972; Galbraith, 1974; Wilson, 1977; Donelan, 1978; Skocpol and Amenta, 1986, etc.) need to reinvent themselves? And what voices would contribute to such an overhaul?

In light of these crisscrossing questions and perspectives, should greater attention not be paid to polyphony and speech act (Bakhtin, 1993) if globalization in theory building is imaginable?

In Chapter 1, Klaus Krippendorff of the Annenberg School for Communication at the University of Pennsylvania elaborates on an earlier theme for us (Ciprut, 2000) on the perilous shortcomings and the fearful consequences inherent to the routine practices of theorizing in social and political science. Here he outlines a way of introducing polyphony into theory building in an approach that tends to put the ideas of Ricoeur (1976, 1986, 1992, 1995) and his own interest for ethics (Krippendorff, 1986) in evidence. "Ecological narratives" help create room for the voices of those that constitute the object of our theories. They help empower the contextual meaning intrinsic to theory by bridging the chasm that has opposed contextuality based on ontology (Feyerabend, 1960) to contextuality based on usage of language (Wittgenstein, 1953). They also help appease time-honored concerns over the liberation of theory from itself (Albert et al., 1986); over the elaboration "in ordinary language [of] the variability of turbulent processes if their underlying patterns are to be uncovered and assessed" (p. xiv in Rosenau, 1990); and over the regrettable practice of self-contained syllogisms that impede further analysis and that sustain a particular ideology in an elusive quest (Ferguson and Mansbach, 1988: 215–22) for scientific theory in international politics. And all this without even claiming to offer more than a disposition, let alone a method or substitute for good theory. In virtue of ecological narratives, may it become possible for a science based on ideas, not facts, to be constructed on phronesis (intuitive judgments reached via discerning reasonings) and not on institutionalized "frozenness" (Bunge, 1962), one would think? Integrity remains paramount here.

ON OTHER IMPEDIMENTS TO GLOBAL COOPERATION IN THEORY BUILDING

Besides "languaging" in responsible theory building, there are many other categories of hindrances to understanding—between theorizer and theorized but among theorizers as well. Some of the sources of misunderstanding are institutional. Others may be individual, as in the matter of intellectual intolerance—a form of misunderstanding that unfortunately exists today in the ranks of practitioners. Professor Kalevi J. Holsti of the University of British Columbia explores the few sources and many faces of this "monopoly syndrome" in Chapter 2. He analyzes its materialization in the ethical and political problems that drive theoretical work and in the link between partisanship and scholarship, as well as in the long-standing effort to create a single, all-encompassing theory of international relations. The issue of incompatibilities of roles, the tensions between the normative and the theoretical, and the merits of pluralism and tolerance among theory builders are also examined. Holsti's insights update and complement issues raised by others (Wight, 1966; Lijphart, 1974; Morse, 1976; Kent and Nicholson, 1980; Collins, 1982; Rosenau, 1992) over the obstacles that retard the evolution of good international theory.

ON POWER AND GLOBAL RELATIONS THEORY

Long before the political division of the world into spheres of influence, religious partition of the globe into thresholds of war (Dar-ul Harb) and peace (Dar-ul Islam) and zones of goodwill on earth (North to South, by the Treaty of Tordesillas in 1494; Westerly, by the Treaty of Zaragosa in 1529) had already created latitudes for abuse in the name of secular and spiritual "power."

In 1512, Niccolò Machiavelli's *Il Principe* would place power on the shoulders of the virtuous and mighty prince who, unlike a medieval ruler, would not need to command his subjects' loyalties in order to secure the state's success by any means at any price. In 1890, Alfred Mahan's *The Influence of Sea Power upon History* would make German geopolitics and British hegemony understandable to all, legitimating the imperialistic cravings for spatial power and martial force that Sir Halford Mackinder's *Democratic Ideals and Reality* would endow with the expediency of modern governance. Thus, in 1946, with innocent precision, Wight's *Power Politics* would come to define a "world power" as "a great power which can exert effectively *inside* Europe a strength that is derived from resources *outside* Europe" (Wight, 1978: 56). But history would soon prove otherwise. And since the collapse of the Soviet Union, paradoxically, "power" has not been a game of "winner-take-all."

The literature on power is extensive. The concept has been studied from many angles (domestic, foreign, political, economic, commercial, social), in different contexts (anarchy, conflict, cooperation, peace, war), and relations (N-polar, balance) as well as in its underlying logic. Its future, too, has led to much conjecture, following the dismemberment of the Soviet Union.

In Chapter 3, Professor Barry Buzan of the University of Westminster, in London, critically surveys the past uses and present meanings of the notion of "power" in international relations, with an eye to the future. He speculates about what the very concept may come to denote and what purposes it may end up servicing in a globalizing international arena. His power-theoretical scenarios point toward a divided world, the processes of globalization notwithstanding. Buzan's contribution sets the stage for the chapters that follow on the changing meaning of state, self, territory, and ecopolitical-economic development.

THE ROLE OF THE STATE AND THE FUTURE OF INTERNATIONAL RELATIONS

In Chapter 4, Professor Ronnie Lipschutz of the University of California at Santa Cruz investigates the moral authority of the state in an evolving global political economy. His critique redirects the scrutiny of power from the global to the local. He surveys the present practices of state power in the light of the moral implications of past exercises of state authority. He goes on to interrogate the state's future capacity for legitimacy. He examines its various efforts to restore (b)orders and speculates on the potential meaning and the implications for theory of such an impossible task in a twenty-first-century context for global politics.

The role of the state in national and international affairs has commanded a vast literature since the days of the *Politea*, a Platonic dialogue—better known as the *Republic*—on stability and justice in the order of power at the *polis*, the Greek city-state. The evident and implicit interconnections among state, individual self, governance, justice, equality, order, and peace are subtle. For Plato, justice is a "surface concept," an "index" of Hellenic discursive formation and practices that "demarcate Greek man" and "differentiate his civic space" (Ofir, 1991: 47). In Plato, the "problem of justice" is an "overcivilized" man's problem; so long as civil life does not lead man "to overstep his humanity," such an "undercivilized community may contain no source of instability." It is the "transition from undercivilized to civilized life" that "brings with it a source of social instability, together with the possibility of delineating justice and injustice" (p. 83). A sheer "desire for more than is needed for human existence" is lust for surplus. "Excess leads both to civilized life and to war." Though a "just city presupposes both excess and war," excess is a source of inner instability . . . not only of expansionism and war." But in any case, "war creates the best type of citizen and prepares the ground for philosophical activity" (p. 83). If Plato's Socrates "exemplifies the impossible combination between the rational and the political in the deteriorating corrupt city" (p. 50), Plato's Plato embodies the "intense conflict between reason and power" (p. 52), knowable only to those who have "experienced the tension between a will to power and a will to knowledge" (p. 50).

For Aristotle, justice means "maintaining a certain equality by correcting inequalities in the distribution of those things shared among men in a political system, mainly power, money and goods"; and even though "equality defines justice," the different types of equality that exist "are not comparable as to their justness" (p. 54). In Aristotle's *Politics*, justice "is the bond of men in states (*poleis*)." But the "administration of justice," which is solely "the determination of what is just," is merely the "principle of order in political society"—not "justice as such" (p. 54). And the "determination of what is just" "depends upon an existing socio-political order" that "itself cannot be judged as just or unjust" (p. 55; cf. Ackerman, 1980).

Plato's model of community evolves from a frugal one, "fit for pigs" (in which individuals cooperate to produce physical necessities that they neither own nor stockpile but consume in leisure; and wherein there are no desirable surpluses to steal, let alone properties to protect), to a luxurious state (in which luxuries and surpluses create "inflammation"; collusions between political, military, and private interests generate inequality and disorder; and misgovernance by powerful, self-serving, and corrupt individuals in positions of authority sow the seeds of conflict). Tightly held by a self-designating political and military elite, which neglects its duties, divides its people, disactivates its citizenry into political apathy, and institutes special lifestyles and ownership privileges for itself yet is Spartan in its rule, Plato's "civilized" city-state was highly criticized in classical Athens for its two-tier communist mentality (Carver, 1994: 24–27).

Like Plato, Thomas More "shielded himself behind various narrative and dialogical devices, so that it is more than usually difficult to attribute to him an authorial view" (p. 28). More's alternative model for communism was "utopia"—a primal and frugal society comparable to Plato's primitive society in which nothing that is material is private and exclusive; practical experience and seniority take precedence; sexual division of labor and high emphasis on religion apply; population is planned; incentives for individual accumulation do not exist; military training is dispensed, but wars are fought only in self-defense or for morally justifiable reasons; and luxury is deemed a conduit to corruption and shunned. Absent the sources of want and penury, temptation and greed are theoretically nonexistent. Consequently, the authority structure is deemed to be politically not overburdened (pp. 28–29).

Communist and socialist ideas and experiments (ranging from "schemes to be managed by authoritarian 'scientists of society' " to "democratic plans for national workshops" intended to equalize "disparities between effort and reward") mushroomed between the mid-seventeenth and mid-nineteenth centuries, only to yield their place to Marxism at a time when, by the beginning of the twentieth century, the modern means of communication and growing literacy made "the activity of pursuing communism . . . itself an intellectual endeavor" (p. 32).

When industrialization and commercialization took root in Europe and opened markets across the world, the "social question" (prevention of poverty, unemployment, backwardness, imputable to unequal development imposed by commercial economies on agrarian societies) became the purview of the state. The "socialist" state tried to substitute itself for the capitalist economy by adopting opportunistic measures ranging from mild redistribution of income and wealth to ultra-egalitarian, fully revolutionary, sometimes even conspiratorial schemes to institute workers' control of the international economy (Carver, 1994: 30). The "communist" state sought to humanize the work environment, to minimize daily hours of worktime, to augment productivity, to foster solidarity among workers at home and abroad, and to encourage innovation and advanced technology, placing an emphasis on the central use and control of material resources by the state in an attempt to bar individualistic economics and politics through government regulation and control. Both socialism and communism went bankrupt by stifling the self. But no capitalist or communist state, whether led by a democratic or by an authoritarian government, and not even the countries of the European Union plan to relinquish their sense of territoriality.

Lipschutz's query on the legitimacy of the state raises for global theory an issue that international theory has not resolved (Connolly, 1984; Keating, 1988). He submits that while the borders separating state from state may be rigidified by army, navy, and police armed to the teeth, the borders of passionate moralities drawn in the minds of nations always have been and are likely to remain fluid and difficult to demarcate. Carried to its extreme, he submits, the very "market" that challenges the "state" may now have to transform each of us into a particle and all of us into a global nation of 10 billion atoms before our descendants consider inaugurating a borderless world. His thoughts intersect those of Richard Mansbach, who detects some use for newer maps in world affairs.

ON ORDERS AND BORDERS IN GLOBALIZING INTERNATIONAL THEORY

In the quasi three decades that separate Jaspers (1951) from Taylor (1979), and the 20 years since, much has been written over the borders of the self in the physical, political, civic, and moral space of others (L. Brown, 1972; Brown and Shue, 1981; Hoffman, 1981; Rokkan and Urwin, 1982; Raz, 1986; Linklater, 1990; Posen, 1993).

In Chapter 5, Professor I. William Zartman, of the Nitze School of Advanced International Studies at the Johns Hopkins University, proposes to place that very question in perspective and context. Identity and territory are essentially zero-sum concepts, both well defined and distributive. They were so in the post–World War II era of nationalism and the Cold War. But they need not be so under a globalizing world order. They can be made soft and positive-sum, therefore loose and accommodative. The post–Cold War era opens up the possibility of softer, integrative solutions to problems of self and space. Nested identities and permeable space are traits of present times; negotiations on conflicts involving self and space can create flexible outcomes rather than rigid resolutions and can lend themselves better to the management of change. How, then, can one put such wisdom to use in the too often disruptive developmental logic of globalization, in practice as in theory?

TOWARD A THEORY OF THE DEVELOPMENTAL LOGIC OF GLOBALIZATION?

In Chapter 6, Professors Henry Teune, a political scientist at the Univeristy of Pennsylvania, and Zdravko Mlinar, a sociologist at Ljubljana University, consider these questions. For them, the process of globalization is integral to social development. They see in "globalization" a reference to processes that integrate and regenerate diversity. Theories of developmental change and a logic of differentiation and integration explain these within the limits of a continuum, with the individual at one end and the world at the other. This has a number of serious implications for the structures of a budding world system, some of which are already apparent. Teune and Mlinar's outlook is in fact that of a world transforming into a different kind of system (cf. Bury, 1955; Kindleberger, 1962; Lewis, 1970; Falk, 1977; Nisbet, 1980; Attir et al., 1981; Gilpin, 1981; Rosecrance, 1986; Kennedy, 1987). But inside a coincidentally expanding and retracting worldwide span, and within the turbulent dynamic generated by the developmental logic of globalization, what means exist for humanity to sustain global civilization in an evolutionary pursuit? And what does this mean for theory?

TOWARD AN EVOLUTIONARY ECOPOLITICAL ECONOMY OF GLOBALIZATION?

The "Essay on the Principle of Population" (Malthus, 1798) appeared at a time when London boasted 864,000 residents, Paris, 547,000, and the New York figures did not affect debates over an overheating Europe. If T. R. Malthus were alive today, would he have turned to "the local" (say, to China, India, or Indonesia) in order to press his thesis or, rather, to "the global" in ways permitting him to reword his sweeping premises and somber inferences?

Concerns over the damaging effects of uninhibited industrial growth on wellness, longevity, and milieu but principled (ethical, political, or ideological) postures on ecopolicy as well, have a way of attaining the crest of their up-cycles in times of malaise (the 1973–1974 oil embargo) or disaster (the meltdown of 1986, in Chernobyl). And the field of environmental research illustrates the import of languaging in theories conducive to policy making. After assimilating acid rain, global warming, and ozone depletion, our vocabulary—flooded with acronyms of harmful chemicals—can now etymologically distinguish between conservation/preservation and ecologism/environmentalism without necessarily unveiling the political-ideological nuances that divide *the greens* themselves on the means and ends of their pursuits. An as of yet unanswered crucial question concerns the discovery of a practical way of favoring development over growth without the necessity to adopt a dehumanizing, overprincipled, system-worshipping model of ecofascism; an overgoverned version of ecocommunism that can stifle progress in the name of pseudo-equalitarianisms based on zero-growth or steady-state development; or an untamed pursuit of blind greed that can only sow the seeds of its own ultimate obliteration.

It falls on Professor Dennis Pirages of the Department of Government and Politics at the University of Maryland, who also heads the Harrison Program on the Future Global Agenda, to supply a detailed answer to that question in Chapter 7. Pirages's model is grounded on less-than-perfect past behaviors. His ameliorative conception relies on other than naive or utopian future pursuits.

The international system is evolving into a global one. The technological innovations, demographic changes, and environmental shifts are combining to accelerate change, to create ecological challenges of global import, and to merge previously isolated human societies into a global community. Many of these wrenching shifts are creating numerous global issues. Most of the violent clashes that have accompanied the modernization process, though often disguised as class or ethnic conflict, are but collisions between agrarian and industrial paradigms—two different ways of perceiving reality and defining a good life. Pirages's worldview is original (cf. Meadows et al., 1972; Ingelhart, 1977; Bramwell, 1989; Eckersley, 1992; Goldsmith 1992; Meadows, Meadows, and Randers, 1992).

Industrial development and modernization are twin processes. They are characterized by world wars, revolutions, and large-scale bloodshed. But they beget unprecedented abundance, rising living standards for much of the world's population, and increased human mobility. Pirages finds mounting evidence that material-intensive industrial civilization may no longer be sustainable—that still another, a third, major transformation may well be under way.

Compared to the last "revolution," there is at hand greater accumulated knowledge of the dynamics involved. Should it not be therefore possible and desirable to make some intelligent policy choices in an effort to "smoothen" the period of transition? This leads Pirages to rethink "sustainability" in theoretically manageable terms and in environmentally practicable approaches.

But a globally sustainable and ecologically secure societal development can take root only in peaceful contexts of voluntary participation. How, then, are we to "manage the unknown" to desired ends in an insecure world where international relations are being currently redefined? And how may theory help capture the dilemma?

MANAGING TOMORROW TODAY: THE CHALLENGES
TO THEORY FROM PRACTICE

In the final chapter, Chapter 8, Professor Richard Mansbach of Iowa State University undertakes to "probe the unknown" and to expose some of the changing visions in the field of international relations theory and practice. He offers us a critical rereading of some of the recent literature bearing relevance to the linked issues and concerns raised in the preceding chapters. Mansbach's chapter examines what fundamental lacunae need to be confronted toward building theories likely to display sensitivity to change. For one thing, theory would have to take account of the changing nature of political organization (cf. James, 1986; Riggs and Plano, 1988; Jackson and James, 1993). Theory would need also to avoid the "territorial trap" (cf. Zartman, this volume) and remain attuned to the changing nature of space and time. It would also have to focus on the forces simultaneously promoting fragmentation and integration in global politics (cf. Teune and Mlinar's chapter). Not least, theory would have to rethink the nature of its own normative content (cf. our chapters by Krippendorff and Holsti).

Mansbach suggests that, among theories, the most in need of reconsideration are those on nation-state, domestic politics, and territory. Yet he cautions against hasty cleanups. Criticism is facile; theory building, not necessarily so: "Where we destroy by plan, we must rebuild by design." Moreover, theory does not only echo reality; it also helps to reshape truth. And more often than not, it ends up assuming a verity of its own. Thus, while foes of realism have sought to substitute such constructs as "the state" and "the national interest" with "international organizations" and "international law," realists have advocated the virtues of the "sovereign state" and upheld its status in global politics—each infusing one's homegrown analysis with normative fervor.

What key issues does Mansbach see arising before us? Like Buzan in this volume and Singer and Wildawski (1993) in the recent literature, Mansbach sees two worlds of global politics emerging: One is a pluralist security community made up of the world of industrially and societally advanced nation-states for which organized violent conflict has become a remote contingency. Here, theory would gain in being informed not by disintegration or collapse but rather by transnational concerns, international institutions, globalized understandings, and supraterritorial alliances.

By contrast, in much of the developing world, and especially South Asia and Africa, violence remains a distinct possibility. But here, too, the usual place of interstate explanations in international relations theory has been long taken over by intrastate conflict. In addition, notwithstanding their Westphalian trappings, a disquieting number of states in the developing world are still unable to face the large-scale socioeconomic forces that create domestic dislocations and unrest. Often dismissed as "quasi-states" by some, as "failed states" by others, the chronic incompetence and corruption that surrounds the world from islands in the Carribean to regions in Europe, Africa, and Southeast Asia will be able to threaten the more advanced peoples of this world with dangerous burdens, extending well beyond daily sustenance of their peripheries. Here the question of the moral authority of the state so eloquently raised by Lipschutz acquires a whole new meaning, calling for truly novel and swift theoretical insights.

In a vast epicenter of sorts, two very different worlds meet also in East-Southeast Asia, where China and Taiwan, the Koreas, Vietnam, and Laos/Cambodia provide their very own idiosyncrases. And the legacies of Western colonialism are fast catching up with the newer realities of a world boasting 200 independent states of which the many with virtual sovereignty, tribal organization, and fluid borders lie alongside the few with guarded hard boundaries.

The bipolar world opposing two superpowers, which redefined global affairs between them following World War II, precipitated profound transformations in the political institutions and in the conventional behaviors of many. A wedge developed between theory and practice whereby prediction became impossible when inadequate understanding had to resort to interpretation where explanations failed. What, then, will the future offer to globalizing theory?

Like Mansbach, we see at least three intellectual hurdles to building theories of global politics: (1) the false dichotomy that severs international from domestic politics; (2) the static nature of much of theorizing in global politics; (3) and the dominance of an obsolete territorial conception of the world and the absence of a vocabulary and grammar that might get us beyond obsessions based on strictly proprietary claims to ecopolitical-economic spaces.

Regarding the inside/outside dichotomies, the walls—erected to separate the international and intranational areas—once very crucial to the definition of the sovereign state, are crumbling in many parts of the world. As to the need for dynamic models, it is time for theory to come to terms with the disintegration of a number of political communities and the integration of some into larger polities. And in the matter of sharing space, as political configurations begin to interpenetrate, it will become necessary for all to redefine "territory" in nontraditional ways. In doing so, theorists will have to reconceptualize space and think also of time as creating and/or eliminating distance between peoples. New theory will have to recognize that the interstate system of exclusive territorial authority is losing ground to a growingly deterritorialized present. A future is becoming imaginable in which geographic boundaries might begin to be eroded by the logic of economic markets and by megalopolistic agglomerations of human beings with multiple identities.

We live in a world that is continually dying and aborning—and this reality calls for a genuinely historical perspective to be adopted in scholarly research. But memory by way of narrative is contingent on languaging. Languaging cannot altogether afford to ignore preexisting theoretical context. Thus, a vicious circle catches the discipline unprepared and unqualified for new theory.

The disparities between the developed and developing regions conduce us to revisit the question of change and the processes of expanding/contracting authority. Since it is almost impossible to know with any certainty whether events augur fundamental change or promise simply to provide more of the same, answers ultimately depend on the theoretical framework that one chooses to employ.

Do recent changes in global politics augur more than a simplistic reshuffling of interstate relations? Realists, whose vision of global politics is that of a world congealed in deep insecurity, anarchic conflict, and struggles for power, might see confirmation in the sporadic violence that continues to consume the developing world. Their theoretical premises help them to expose conflictual aspects in global politics. This, in turn, props their worldview. They are decidedly less comfortable with a world integrating away from "anarchy." Power theorists deal with change condescendingly, in the conviction that continuity by definition forever prevails.

Liberals, in contrast, like to perceive striking differences between a humanizing world and the congealed universe of realism. Mansbach suggests that they mistake belief for reality of ongoing change, often at the cost of ignoring the endemic violence that devours the developing world. Realists err by belittling change to favor continuity. Liberals mistake locomotion for change, as if moving on were always better than standing still. As Mansbach sees it, they confuse change with progress and—as realists also do—they prefer to pick and choose what they want from history.

It is the belief of all of us in this volume that neither realists nor liberals have approached the question of change with the gravity that it merits. Short of treating events as if they were devoid of values, how is theory to provide an understanding of the realities of the world even as they are in the making? The time seems right for global theories to cease to create new facts by reshuffling the old, and to address the newer realities through holistic lenses that discern change in time, space, units of analysis, actors, roles, contexts, and composite relationships as well.

REFERENCES

Ackerman, B. (1980). *Social Justice in the Liberal State*. New Haven, CT: Yale University Press.

Albert, Michael et al. (1986). *Liberating Theory*. Boston: South End Press.

Alker, Hayward R., Jr. (1966). The Long Road to International Relations Theory: Problems of Statistical Nonadditivity. *World Politics* 18 (June).

Attir, Mustafa et al. (1981). *Directions of Change: Modernization Theory, Research and Realities.* Boulder, CO: Westview Press.

Avineri, S. (1972). *Hegel's Theory of the Modern State.* Cambridge: Cambridge University Press.

Bakhtin, M. M. (1993). *Toward a Philosophy of the Act.* Trans. and notes by V. Liapunov; ed. M. Holquist and V. Liapunov. Austin: University of Texas Press.

Beitz, C. (1979). *Political Theory and International Relations.* Princeton, NJ: Princeton University Press.

Blalock, Hubert M., Jr. (1969). *Theory Construction: From Verbal to Mathematical Formulations.* Englewood Cliffs, NJ: Prentice-Hall.

Bourdieu, Pierre (1982). *Ce que Parler Veut Dire: L'Economie des échanges linguistiques.* Paris: Fayard.

Bramwell, A. (1989). *Ecology in the 20th Century: A History.* New Haven, CT: Yale University Press.

Brown, L. (1972). *World without Borders.* New York: Random House.

Brown, P. G., and H. Shue (1981). *Boundaries: National Autonomy and Its Limits.* New York: Rowman & Littlefield.

Brown, Seyom (1996). *International Relations in a Changing Global System: Toward a Theory of the World Polity.* Boulder, CO: Westview Press.

Bunge, Mario (1962). *Intuition and Science.* Englewood Cliffs, NJ: Prentice-Hall.

Bury, J. B. (1955). *The Idea of Progress: An Inquiry into Its Origins and Growth.* New York: Dover.

Butterfield, Herbert, and Martin Wight (eds.) (1966). *Diplomatic Investigations: Essays in the Theory of International Politics.* London: Allen & Unwin.

Carver, T. (1994). Communism. In *Ideas That Shape Politics.* New York and Manchester: Manchester University Press.

Ciprut, J. V. (ed.) (2000). *Of Fears and Foes: Security and Insecurity in an Evolving Global Political Economy* Westport, CT: Praeger.

Collins, Hugh (1982). Problems of a Fragmented Field. In Coral Bell (ed.), *Academic Studies and International Politics.* Canberra: Australian National University.

Connolly, W. E. (ed.) (1984). *Legitimacy and the State.* Oxford: Basil Blackwell.

Dahl, R. (1963). *Modern Political Analysis.* Englewood Cliffs, NJ: Prentice-Hall.

Donelan, M. (ed.) (1978). *The Reason of States: A Study in International Political Theory.* London: Allen & Unwin.

Easton, David (1965). *A Framework for Political Analysis.* Englewood Cliffs, NJ: Prentice-Hall.

Eckersley, R. (1992). *Environmentalism and Political Theory: An Ecocentric Approach.* London: UCL Press.

Eulau, H. (1963). *The Behavioral Persuasion in Politics.* New York: Random House.

Falk, R. A. (1977). Contending Approaches to World Order. *Journal of International Affairs* 31 (Fall–Winter): 171–98.

Ferguson, Y. H., and R. W. Mansbach (1988). *The Elusive Quest: Theory and International Politics.* Columbia: University of South Carolina Press.

Feyerabend, Paul K. (1960). Patterns of Discovery. *Philosophical Review* 69: 247–52.

Finnis, J. (1922). *Studies in Political Thought from Gerson to Grotius, 1414–1625*. Cambridge: Cambridge University Press.

Galbraith, J. K. (1974). *The New Industrial State*. 2nd ed. Harmondsworth: Penguin.

Gilpin, R. (1981). *War and Change in World Politics*. Cambridge: Cambridge University Press.

Goldsmith, E. (1992). *The Way: An Ecological World View*. London: Century.

Hoffman, S. (1965). *The State of War: Essays on the Theory and Practice of International Relations*. New York: Praeger.

Hoffman, S. (1981) *Duties beyond Border: On the Limits and Possibilities of Ethical International Politics*. Syracuse, NY: Syracuse University Press.

Holsti, Kalevi J. (1985). *The Dividing Discipline: Hegemony and Diversity in International Theory*. Boston: Allen & Unwin.

Ingelhart, R. (1977). *The Silent Revolution: Changing Values and Political Styles among Western Publics*. Princeton, NJ: Princeton University Press.

Jackson, R. H., and A. James (eds.) (1993). *States in a Changing World: A Contemporary Analysis*. Oxford: Clarendon Press.

James, Alan (1986). *Sovereign Statehood: The Basis of International Society*. London: Allen & Unwin.

Jaspers, Karl (1951). *Man in the Modern Age*. New York: Anchor Books.

Kaplan, Morton (1957). *System and Process in International Politics*. New York: Wiley.

Keating, M. (1988). *State and Regional Nationalism: Territorial Politics and the European State*. New York: Harvester Weatsheaf.

Kennedy, P. M. (1987). *The Rise and Fall of the Great Powers: Economic Change and Military Conflict from 1500 to 2000*. New York: Random House.

Kent, R. C., and G. P. Nicholson (eds.) (1980). *The Study and Teaching of International Relations*. New York: Nichols.

Kindleberger, C. P. (1962). *Foreign Trade and the National Economy*. New Haven, CT: Yale University Press.

Krippendorff, K. (1986). *Information Theory: Structural Models for Qualitative Data*. Sage University Papers, Quantitative Applications in the Social Sciences, No. 07-062. Beverly Hills, CA: Sage Publications.

Kuhn, Thomas (1962). *The Structure of Scientific Revolutions*. Chicago: University of Chicago Press.

Lasswell H. D., and A. Kaplan (1950). *Power and Society: A Framework for Political Inquiry*. New Haven, CT: Yale University Press.

Latour, Bruno (1987). *Science in Action*. Cambridge, MA: Harvard University Press.

Lewis, W. A. (1970). *Theory of Economic Growth*. New York: Harper & Row.

Lijphart, A. (1974). The Structure of the Theoretical Revolution in International Relations. *International Studies Quarterly* 18 (March): 41–74.

Linklater, A. (1990). *Men and Citizens in the Theory of International Relations*. London: Macmillan.

Machiavelli, Niccolò (1512). *Il Principe*. See, among many others, Rome, Italy: Antonio Blado d'Asola, First Edition of 1532.

Mackinder, Sir Halford (1942). *Democratic Ideals and Reality* New York: H. Holt and Company.

Mahan, (Captain) Alfred T. (1890). *The Influence of Sea Power upon History, 1660–1783.* Boston: Little, Brown and Company.

Malthus, Thomas R. (1798). *Essay on the Principle of Population as It Affects the Future Improvement of Society.* London: printed for J. Johnson.

Mansbach, R., and J. Vasquez (1981). *In Search of Theory: A New Paradigm for Global Politics.* New York: Columbia University Press.

Mayall, J. (1982). *The Community of States: A Study in International Political Theory.* London: Allen & Unwin.

Meadows, D. H., D. L. Meadows, and J. Randers (1992). *Beyond the Limits: Confronting Global Collapse, Envisioning a Sustainable Future.* Post Mills, VT: Chelsea Green.

Meadows, D. H. et al. (1972). *Limits to Growth.* New York: Universe Books.

Merton, Robert K. (1973). *The Sociology of Science.* Chicago: University of Chicago Press.

Morgenthau, Hans (1973). *Politics among Nations.* New York: Knopf.

Morse, Edward (1976). *Modernization and the Transformation of International Relations.* New York: Free Press.

Nisbet, R. A. (1980). *History of the Idea of Progress.* New York: Basic Books.

Ofir, Adi (1991). *Plato's Invisible Cities: Discourse and Power in the Republic.* Savage, MD: Barnes & Noble.

Posen, B. (1993). The Security Dilemma and Ethnic Conflict. *Survival* 35, 1 (Spring): 27–47.

Raz, J. (1986). *The Morality of Freedom.* Oxford: Oxford University Press.

Ricoeur, P. (1976). *Interpretation Theory: Discourse and the Surplus of Meaning.* Fort Worth, TX: Christian University Press.

Ricoeur, P. (1986). *Du texte à l'action.* Collection Esprit, Essais d'Herméneutique. 2. Paris: Editions du Seuil.

Ricoeur, P. (1992). *Oneself as Another.* Trans. Kathleen Blamey. Chicago: University of Chicago Press.

Ricoeur, P. (1995). *Le juste.* Paris: Editions Esprit.

Riggs, R. E., and J. C. Plano (1988). *The United Nations: International Organization and World Politics.* Chicago: Dorsey.

Rokkan, S., and D. W. Urwin (1982). *The Politics of Territorial Identity: Studies in European Regionalism.* London: Sage.

Rosecrance, R. (1986). *The Rise of the Trading State: Commerce and Conquest in the Modern World.* New York: Basic Books.

Rosenau, J. N. (1990). *Turbulence in World Politics: A Theory of Change and Continuity.* Princeton, NJ: Princeton University Press.

Rosenau, P. M. (1992). *Post-Modernism and the Social Sciences: Insights, Inroads, and Intrusions.* Princeton, NJ: Princeton University Press.

Russell, F. M. (1936). *Theories of International Relations.* New York: Appleton-Century.

Sabine, G. H. (1961). *A History of Political Theory.* New York: Holt, Rinehart and Winston.

Singer, Max, and Aaron Wildavsky (1993). *The Real World Order: Zones of Peace, Zones of Turmoil.* Chatham, NJ: Chatham House Publishers.

Skocpol, Theda, and Edwin Amenta (1986). States and Social Policies. *Annual Review of Sociology* 12: 131–57.

Sontag, Susan (1982). *Against Interpretation—and Other Essays*. New York: Octagon Books.

Taylor, Charles (1979). *Sources of the Self*. Cambridge: Cambridge University Press.

Walker, R.B.J. (1993). *Inside/Outside: International Relations as Political Theory*. Cambridge: Cambridge University Press.

Waltz, K. (1979). *Theory of International Politics*. Reading, MA: Addison-Wesley.

Wight, Martin (1966). Why Is There No International Theory? In Herbert Butterfield and Martin Wight (eds.), *Diplomatic Investigations: Essays in the Theory of International Politics*. London: Allen & Unwin.

Wight, Martin (1978). *Power Politics*. Ed. Hedley Bull and Carsten Holbroad. 1946. Reprint, London: Royal Institute of International Affairs; New York: Holmes and Meier.

Williams, H. L. (1996). *International Relations and the Limits of Political Theory*. New York: St. Martin's Press.

Williams, Howard L. (1991). *International Relations in Political Theory*. Milton Keynes, UK: Open University Press.

Wilson, Elizabeth (1977). *Women and the Welfare State*. London: Tavistock Publications.

Wittgenstein, Ludwig (1953). *Philosophical Investigations*. Trans. G.E.M. Anscombe. Oxford: Basil Blackwell.

Woolgar, Steve (1998a). *Knowledge and Reflexivity*. Beverly Hills, CA: Sage Publications.

Woolgar, Steve (1998b). *Science: The Very Idea*. New York: Tavistock.

CHAPTER 1

Ecological Narratives: Reclaiming the Voice of Theorized Others

KLAUS KRIPPENDORFF

INTRODUCTION

The urge to theorize has been a driving force of Western intellectual tradition. It underlies academic discourse, giving the scientific enterprise its vitality. Without systematic theorizing, much of contemporary culture, particularly technology, would be virtually unthinkable.

Naturally, theorizing has not been without critics. The skeptics have raised their voices against the ability of theory to describe anything at all. Radical empiricists such as Francis Bacon and even some logical positivists have had stories to tell of the "blindness of abstraction."

Now, postmodernists, poststructuralists, constructionists, deconstructionists, and others are questioning the intelligibility of master narratives and the ability of unifying theories or of logical/mathematical systems to represent reality. From their perspective, science, literature, and law are just three of many literary genres, each cultivating its own reading of texts.

The most recent critique comes from feminist scholars. Feminism is not a unified perspective. Feminist thought has grown far beyond its early advocacy of equal rights, by conceptualizing patriarchal society, exploring gender differences, and contributing scathing critiques of male rationality, of technological world constructions, and of the oppressive consequences of theory itself. Along its path, feminism has emphasized the embodied nature of knowledge, for example, by accounting for voices instead of texts. Feminism advocated relational epistemologies, insisted on the participation of emotions, and discovered validation in practical actions that could lead to personal liberation.

Narrower in scope, but no less important, is the opposition to theory by philosophers concerned with ethics. Dwight Furrow (1995), for instance, influenced by a rereading of Aristotle, questions the capacity of normative ethical theory to provide guidance on normative questions and challenges its relevance to the lived experience of moral agents. Such critiques are fueled by a need to understand the Holocaust and all other atrocities committed since World War II by people with theories to live by.

Within literary scholarship, writers continue to reexamine their own foundations by questioning the intelligibility of texts in terms of the theory-driven distinction between meanings and an author's intentions. To them, there is nothing in a text that could point to the difference between the two and no method that could shed light on what this distinction creates. For Knapp and Michaels (1985: 30): "[Theory] is the name for all the ways people have tried to stand outside [the] practice [of reading and interpretation] in order to govern [that] practice from without. . . . [N]o one can reach [such] a position." This leads them to propose that "the theoretical enterprise should therefore come to an end."

The foregoing critiques have very different histories and little in common with each other except for their opposition to systematic theorizing. Often they even oppose each other. For example, feminists have been criticized for essentializing the very gender differences they oppose; proponents of postmodernism, for being silent on moral questions that significantly undermine the intelligibility of moral experiences.

Many of these critiques rely on what I would call *deficiency arguments*—a rhetorical strategy that seeks to expose the failure of a theory by showing what it blatantly omits or surreptitiously distorts, without recognizing that such critiques are based on another theory—usually one closer to these critics' hearts and therefore more "real" to them. Critiques of ideology, Marxist, for example, excel in this. They argue against theories of knowledge from a perspective that is assumed to be "free" of ideological biases, more encompassing in scope, capturing broader territory, or offering a greater number of distinctions. Yet, using one theory to criticize another remains entirely within the practice of theorizing and cannot therefore reveal the blind spots of theorizing. Worse, unable to recognize these blind spots makes theorists blind to their own blindness.

The following summarizes the social role of theory and the particular relation that theorizing entails between theorists and the theorized others who are in fact the natural focus of social scientific inquiries.

SOME ENTAILMENTS OF THEORIZING

Etymologically, *theory* comes from the Greek *theoria*, the meaning of which comprises not only the process of "looking at," "viewing," "contemplating," or "speculating" but also the very object perceived, "a sight," "a tableau," or "a spectacle." These meanings imply a distinct attitude vis-à-vis what is theorized. Spectacles are created to be seen and discussed, not to be altered. Spectacles are in front of the viewer's eye. In such accounts of theorizing, the use of ocular metaphors entails a tacit *preference for sight* over sound, touch, and feelings, and it assigns secondary importance to voices, to stories, to oral traditions, and to practical knowledge. It is no accident that we speak of scientific "observers," not of scientific listeners. There is no auditory or tactile analogue to "observation," and although reading and writing would be difficult without sight, we tend to exclude them when we speak of observing things.

As spectators, theorists observe but do not allow themselves to *enter* their domain of observation. Consequently, theorists endow facts naively conceptualized as residing outside of us with the power to determine which theories are valid. It is the belief in this ontology, if nothing else, that ultimately justifies claims of being able to theorize facts for what they are, without bias or preconceptions and without accountability to those who may be affected by these theories.

Since the seventeenth century, science has become increasingly "successful" in disconnecting theory from facts and observation from practice, notwithstanding that etymology links "fact" to manufacture. Perhaps with the exception of hermeneutics and constructivism, all scientific methods operationalize the derivation of theories from observational data. Aside from the rare admission that data depend on theory, I know of no formalization of this reverse dependency or of interactions between the two (see Woolgar, 1993: 36, 53–66).

Ethnographic analyses of scientific practices reveal the cherished unidirectionality in proceeding from observations to theories to be a myth (see Garfinkle, 1967; Garfinkle, Lynch, and Livingstone, 1982). But overcoming this unidirectional conception would seem impossible as long as theories are stated in terms of extensional logic such as the logic of propositions or modeled by computers, which are sequential machines that embody the very same logic. To preserve this unidirectionality of scientific discourse against the threat of vicious paradoxes, Bertrand Russell invented his famous Theory of Logical Types, which has the effect of outlawing self-reference. It is this restricted notion of logic and of language that places scientific observers at the top of logical hierarchies, that conceptualizes description top-downwards, and that leads theorists to believe they could observe their world *without* being observed by the objects of their observation.

The ocular metaphor is so prevalent within the scientific community that theorists are encouraged to keep their distance not just to the observed but to their theories as well. A case in point is the distinction between theory and belief. In scientific texts, theories appear as more or less confirmed hypotheses—each having a calculable probability, however small, of being invalid. Not so for beliefs. When we theorize, we do so *about* something. When we believe, we do so *in* something. In beliefs, the emotional detachment that theorists claim to have vis-à-vis their theories is erased in favor of the virtual certainty that things are the way they are *seen* and *spoken of.* For Stanley Fish (1985: 116):

A theory is a special achievement of consciousness; a belief is a prerequisite of being conscious at all. Beliefs are not what you think *about* but what you think *with.* . . . [I]t is within the space provided by their articulations that mental activity—including the activity of theorizing—goes on. Theories are something you can have—you can wield them and hold them at a distance; beliefs have *you,* in the sense that there can be no distance between them and the acts they enable.

The truths of theories may be pondered, but the truths of beliefs are held.

Contrary to popular conceptions of theories as very accurate representations, theories are attractive because they can exceed their domain of observation in at least five ways: (1) Theories *generalize* to cases claimed to be similar to those observed. Yet, without further observations, no assurance is available that the unobserved cases would support a theory's claim. Therefore, their generalizations rely on a good deal of belief. (2) Theories also *predict* under the assumption that the patterns observed in the past will persist into the future. Beliefs in such continuities have much practical value, but, as Francis Bacon already noted, they are ascertainable only in retrospect. (3) Theories also *integrate* several propositions into a single coherent network and (4) *generate* empirical hypotheses from very few quasi-axiomatic propositions. (3) and (4) are predicated on the belief that the logic of propositions corresponds to the logic of the world. For Carl Hempel (Mitchell, 1985: 7), moreover, (5) theory tends to be taken as "a complex spatial network [that] floats, as it were, above the plane of observation and is anchored to it by rules of interpretation." Yet rules of interpretation always are the rules of a theorist or of a community of theorists, not of an observed nature. They allow theorists to justify omitting details deemed irrelevant, accidental, unique, inconsistent, or subjective; filling in the gaps of missed observations; and smoothing the rugged curves—none of which are derivable from observation and measurement.

Politically, the more territory a theory covers, the more it is preferred, the better it will be remembered, the more likely that it will be applied. Thus, theorizing supports a *conceptual imperialism*—the urge to oversee, predict, control, and govern ever-expanding territories (Krippendorff, 1993)—an inkling that science shares with other forms of government in national, spiritual, or commercial spheres of life. True, by themselves, theories neither reign nor rule. Once institutionalized, however, they do empower their users to "survey," "capture," "represent," "monitor," and ultimately "manage" if not "discipline" what they claim to describe. The underlying logic of propositions, and in particular its Theory of Logical Types, favors the construction of logical hierarchies of ever-increasing levels of abstractions, from objects to language to metalanguage to meta-metalanguage, and so forth, with theorists being comfortable only at the top.

Foucault's (1977) metaphorical use of the *panopticon*, to show how knowledge works in society, is telling. The panopticon is an ideal prison design that enables centrally located guards to monitor the behavior of all inmates, who in turn can see only the guards observing them but not each other. Here discipline is assured by the efficiency of observation. In taking this design as a metaphor to explore power relations in society, Foucault equates knowledge and theory and carries the built-in ocularity to its ultimate socio-logical conclusion: the government of one view at the expense of all others (see Holsti, this volume).

Theories are also expected to be rational and consistent, ideally in the form of mathematical expressions, as systems of equations, for example. Formalizations of this kind have the double advantage of being computable in principle and of sparing one the complications of context and meaning. Mathematical theories provide the backbone of the natural sciences but have made inroads also in efforts to explain social and political phenomena, in economics, linguistics, psychology, and systems science, for instance. While rationality and consistency are seen as twin values in scientific explorations, they also provide two different aspects of the monologism that theory implies. Being "rational" is tantamount to expressing oneself in the voice of one's community, a voice that is assumed common to all of its members and sanctioned as such. Rationality defers one's own voice to a fictional authority. Being "consistent," on the other hand, is tantamount to avoiding contradictions among the propositions of a theory. Consistency entails the belief that a single overarching logic could govern the phenomena a theory claims to be about. The requirement that theories be both rational and consistent thus reduces them to *monological* constructions in the dual sense of being the product of a single voice and of being cast in terms of one (coherent) logic. This has considerable implications for both social theorizing and theory building in international relations.

THE LANGUAGING OF THEORIES

Consider the following rather typical propositions, which could be found in any social science writing:

(a) Institutions have four functions.

(b) Nationalism is an outgrowth of modernism.

(c) Terrorism is caused by a breakdown in political structures.

(d) Unemployment feeds crime.

In the context of the foregoing, these four propositions should be troublesome: None of them indicates whose truths they state, attesting to their complete disembodiment. All hide that they are fundamentally about what people do. Institutions, nationalism, terrorism, unemployment, and crime do not exist without their performers. Yet their voices are silenced in each of these generalizations. There is no indication of how their behaviors end up being so categorized. Even the voice of the theorist remains, perhaps deliberately, hidden in objectivist parlance. Language is implicated here in even more fundamental ways, however: Of the four propositions, (a) asserts that a concept "has" or is "in possession of" properties, which lends an almost physical existence to this concept, to institutions as it were. Proposition (b) applies an agricultural metaphor to two rather high-level abstractions from a complex nexus of human behaviors without referring to any particular group of people or locale—even though metaphors reside in language, not in nature. Proposition (c) claims two abstractions, a category of human behavior and a stable pattern abstracted from a process, to be causally related. How could that be? And (d) accounts for what is likely a statistical correlation between two variables in terms of nutrition—one being an agent, the other its target. A casual reading of these propositions gives the impression that they state facts. However, such a reading overlooks their metaphorical nature. How could concepts cause anything analogous to how billiard balls bounce against each other? How could measurement variables act or interact? In what sense could nonmaterial structures break? The failure to recognize the metaphorical nature of language even in our most rigorous scientific discourses attests to remarkable unawareness of how language directs the world that we theorize.

Theories are formed in language, but they must be languaged into being in a manner to be fit to survive in processes of human communication. In the context of their communication, the notion of theory suffers from two illusions:

(1) The first stems from the belief that the form of theory could be separated from what language makes available and that, by the same token, human communication has no influence on how and where theories come into being. Theories are not merely found. They are constructed, proposed, promoted, published, discussed, and either adopted or rejected. Their reality lies in stating them (see also Mansbach, in this volume), in understanding them as such, and in enacting them into actual practices. These are the acts of real people, actors who see some virtue in promulgating what they speak of. It follows that theorizing cannot be understood from a notion that language is a neutral medium of representation (as formalized in propositional logic) nor from the corollary that theories may be justifiable solely by observations (of objects outside language). The notion of languaging as a dialogical process permits us to recognize theories as mediating between their stakeholders, as residing in processes of communication (as in Pirages, this volume). From this perspective, theories cannot be found in the contents of statements nor inside individual minds but in processes of their contin-

uous rearticulations. Theories that fail to compel people to reproduce and recirculate them within their community simply fade away.

As communications, theories serve various social functions. They can define a theorist's identity. They can form the basis of particular research programs or schools of thought. They can also become institutionalized in disciplines that require adherence to or belief in them from its practitioners. Linguists, biologists, psychologists, all academic disciplines, distinguish themselves by the theories they believe in. Sometimes, theories may take the form of abstract paradigms that privilege particular scientific explorations. At other times, they certify practitioners and protect them against criticisms from other disciplines. In either case, theories are political phenomena.

(2) The second illusion arises from the conviction that social theories have invariant and single meanings. Unlike natural scientific theories, social theories, once published, can reenter and touch the lives of the very people about whom they speak (Krippendorff, 1996). When such a reentry occurs, theories and those theorized in them begin to interact and modify each other in ways that violate the idea of theory as a descriptive account of stable facts, as a representation of an unintelligent world. Those who find themselves theorized might use this publicity as a way to enhance their status or perceive such as a threat to their very identity. When known, a theory can affect the behavior of the theorized by either strengthening or invalidating it: Black Power and feminist movements, for example, effectively countered prevailing theories about them by theories of their own. Theories may also be adopted by people who discover new meanings by way of living through their propositions, acting out their stereotypes, preserving their distinctions, and making them truer thereby. The mass media, by catering to audiences who are conceptualized in terms of their size and attractiveness, "mainstream" the public, causing more people to become similar to each other and thus enhancing their attractiveness to advertisers. Taking theories, especially predictive ones, as prescriptions for action can turn them into self-fulfilling prophecies. In social reality, which depends on the knowledge that people have of it, this is typical, not exceptional. Thus, theories of social phenomena do not merely represent; they also *transform* their objects in the process of their communication. Positivists have reasons to worry that the reentry of theories into their domain of observation could well undermine their validity: They take considerable methodological precautions to protect their ontology from such challenges. But if theorizing is a political process and if the dissemination of social theories does change their validity, one might think that political science would have much to say about the politics of theorizing and that the theories created in the social sciences would at least *account* for their own social consequences. This, however, seems not to be the case.

Inspired by the triumphs of the natural sciences, convinced that the social sciences, too, could discover and accumulate a body of theories, social theorists have effectively succeeded in rendering social theory "unsocial," political theory "apolitical," and so forth. The widespread practice of theorizing the social (see Holsti and Mansbach, this volume) conceals its communicative and political nature.

Theorizing the social seems to work only where theorists, the institutions using their theories, and the theorized others collude, if only by holding the theorized reality constant while collectively denying that they had anything to do with it. This grand self-deception correlates well with the myth that theorists could stay outside of the language that they use in explaining the world as inhabited by people without linguistic intelligence of their own and taking a "God's eye view" (Putnam, 1981) of the universe. Scholars who have dared to question such monological practices have been seriously sanctioned. This has happened to several philosophers of science—including Popper, Lakatos, and Kuhn—among whom physicists chose to single out the late Paul Feyerabend as "The Worst Enemy of Science" (Horgan, 1993).

It would seem that the foregoing offers us a choice. We can continue practicing natural science methods when theorizing our domain of observation, hide behind an objectivist language, and lose touch with the social world that we unwittingly transform. Or we can deliberately and responsibly involve ourselves in the very politics that our inquiries set in motion. To underscore the urgency of this choice, let me explore how fellow humans fare in theories about them, as I have done elsewhere (Ciprut, 2000), before submitting a proposal for an alternative theoretical path.

THEORIZING THE OTHER

(1) *Theorizing Gives Birth to Distant Otherness.* As generalizations, theories classify observations and theorize people in terms of third-person plural. "They" are the subjects of experiments, the interviewees of surveys, and the respondents to mail questionnaires. "They" are the observed, the conservatives, the unemployed, the Catholics, and the terrorists. All of "them" are labeled and assigned to particular classes on account of characteristics that all members of such classes are assumed to share. Classification begins at the data-generating stage of social research. In interviewing, neither the identity of the interviewee nor that of the interviewer becomes data. For fear of biasing the data, personal knowledge, which could emerge when experimenters come too close to their subjects, is repressed systematically. In the theater, spectators would have no problems distinguishing between actors and the characters that they play on stage. In social research, individuals *are* the very categories that a theory provides for them. Where individuals do identify with a group, belief, or trait, theorists are not prohibited from dismissing such declarations as subjective, lacking abstraction, or irrelevant to their theory. When quoted, individual voices are taken to exemplify the voice

of a class. This is achieved when a polyphony (a multitude of voices) is channeled into a single synthesized voice—one for each class or category of the theorist's choosing.

Classes never speak, however; only individuals do, albeit always to others, even when they are virtual. In the reality of everyday life, collective monologues, choruses, for example, are extremely rare. To take such exceptions as a norm for social scientific insights is to avow the artificial unsocial nature of theorizing.

In everyday languaging, third-person pronouns refer to those absent. Theorizing makes this absence a virtue that bestows on theorists the freedom to characterize others in ways radically different (and inferior) to themselves. Whether one calls this a professional disability (a deafness to individual voices or an institutionalized disrespect for otherness), theorizing ends up being responsible for estranging others from ourselves.

(2) *Theorizing Trivializes Others by Reducing Them to Obedient Mechanisms.* As spectators, when social theorists observe human behaviors, including verbal interactions, they do so from outside the spectacle. From this perspective, behaviors appear as linear sequences, temporally ordered chains of events, or trajectories in a Cartesian space within predefined coordinates. To understand trajectories, natural scientists seek to discover their patterned regularities. Here, talk of "regularities" assumes that these are followed without choice in the matter; talk of their "discovery," that they existed prior to observation and measurement. Note that such assumptions are not only built into mathematical theories of behavior and inscribed into computational techniques for analysis of behavioral data—they can also penetrate less formalized talk of social causation. For example, plays are usually scripted, and scripts explain much of what theater audiences end up seeing. For the strict determinacy of machines, scripts are to performances much as computer programs are to computations, however. They are in control of the plot. Thus, describing human behavior in terms of scripts, rules, and grammars, even as reactions to messages, conjures the determinism of obedient mechanisms. Since spectators can never be sure of whether, when, and to what extent an observed behavior is minutely scripted, responses to unobserved conditions or improvised or deterministic accounts have no observational basis. They are a matter of preferences—unless theorists step out of their observer's role to ask pertinent questions. However, even the Turing Test, designed to distinguish machine from human intelligence, is never quite conclusive. Its use has taught us that interaction is a necessary but not sufficient condition to determine the presence of human intelligence or agency. Yet theorists cannot afford this interaction since it would shift the authority for theorizing to the subjects being observed and thus erode the theorists' objective observer status.

Thus, theorizing remains stuck in causal and mechanistic explanations of human behavior, from which that of the theorists is excluded. Without engaging theorized others in conversations on the theories being developed about them, social theorists are remarkably free to explore any theory that would be of interest to their community. Although novel conceptualizations may not come easy, from the convenient position of an outside observer it is quite all right for sociologists like Goffman (1959, 1963) to describe social interactions in dramaturgical categories; and for psychologists like Schank and Abelson (1977) to interpret a same behavior in terms of individuals following rules and scripts; for literary scholars like Hirsch (1967) to extract intentions from authors' writings; for cognitive scientists to develop algorithms that are presumed to govern individuals' processing and exchange of information; or for economists and political scientists to measure the efficacy with which actors apply available resources: Without consulting the constituents of the social phenomenon of interest, almost anything goes.

(3) *Theorizing Inscribes Its Monologism into Its Observational Data and Creates the Very Unsocial Conditions in Which Theories Can Survive.* At moments of contact between the theorist and the theorized, social research invariably depends on collaboration and dialogue. Only by informed consent may human subjects be used in scientific experiments. Yet after signing their consent form, their ability to understand the nature of their involvement and to say no to practices they might consider unconscionable is rarely ever called upon again, does not enter the data, and has therefore little chance to inform a theory that speaks to these subjects' capabilities. In order to uphold the notion that theory is responsive to observations only, the dialogical nature of the actual contact must be hidden, and the collaboration needed to conclude an experiment, concealed.

Or consider interviewing. In this asymmetrical interaction, the interviewer asks questions, and the interviewee is expected to answer them. Interviewees are allowed to speak only within the narrow confines of what is relevant. In effect, interviewees are being *used* to support the point that researchers intend to make, and in the course of this exploitation, the asymmetrical power relations are necessarily and irretrievably inscribed in the data on which theories are constructed.

The deception of informants as to the main purpose of their participation in a research project, the myriad questions that are irrelevant to interviewees' lives, the contrived stimulus conditions to which subjects are asked to respond—all affirm the essential asymmetry, artificiality, and unsocial conditions that spawn the data for social and psychological theories. These power relations creep into the data-making process in obvious violation of the idea of theory as observer-independent. Yes, theorizing does subject its subjects. It renders them *serviceable* (Sampson, 1993) to theories that end up demonstrating little more than *how well theorists have managed to disable the social nature of human beings.* True, submitting to authorities, following instructions is part of what we can do. But replicating such undesirable human conditions, at the expense of human agency, for the mere sake of theorizing, amounts to political suicide for the social sciences.

(4) *Theorizing Nurtures a Culture of Blindness to the Political Nature of Theory—for Theorist and Theorized Alike.* The social sciences are concerned with the ways that human beings *can* live together (see Teune and Mlinar, this volume); sociology, with how people organize themselves into larger wholes and coordinate their actions in ways that sustain these wholes (see Pirages's chapter, this volume); political science, with how people create publics, arrive at some consensus on agendas, and mandate their leaders to form governments (see Lipschutz's chapter, this volume); international relations, with how the peoples of the world perceive, and deal with, each other across national boundaries (see Buzan's chapter, this volume), resolve international conflicts (see Zartman's chapter, this volume), and regulate the innumerable interactions between the diverse constituencies of nation-states; and communication research, with how people construct, sustain, and transform their social universe by communicating with each other.

But none of these social phenomena can be understood by straightjacketing people into mechanistic conceptions and removing from them the spaces in which they interact with one another. The celebration of theory, the use of ocular metaphors for knowing, the reliance on extensional logic, and the naturalness with which people accept confinements during datamaking processes all have become part of a culture that suppresses the awareness of the political nature of theories—not only for theorists but also for all those who see each other in these terms. The very culture of theorizing makes it difficult for the social sciences to reflect on its social nature.

This self-defeating consequence of theorizing in the social sciences is not recognizable from within a representational sense or notion of language that philosophers such as L.J.J. Wittgenstein, R. Rorty, M. M. Bakhtin, J. C. Austin, and J. R. Searle have so systematically challenged in preference to less abstract and dialogical conceptions. Their critiques center largely on the fact that words are actions, too, and that languaging accomplishes things beyond describing them. Reentry adds a cybernetic spin to their critique, showing that languaging is recursive. Where language informs action, theories are likely to become self-validating. Under these conditions, our generalizations of others, whether published as scientific papers, in journals, or disseminated in the mass media, provide fertile ground for social prejudices to arise and to become truths that can easily subordinate, discipline, marginalize, and criminalize others for their otherness.

It is always possible to contest and reject a claim. But in view of the authority that scientific theories do conjure in our culture, contesting them would go against a whole complex of deep-rooted cultural beliefs—among them, that theories have but one legitimate interpretation and that theories are shaped by observations, not by theorists. The latter belief leaves no real target for challenges; the former makes political considerations seem irrelevant.

Whenever scientific accounts concern specific populations—be they the homeless, women, homosexuals, African Americans, Arabs, Catholics, consumers, or teachers—they can achieve two things: In the immediate, they can entice "us" to treat "them" in the very categories that these accounts employ. In the long run, this treatment can transform "them" into the homogenous groups that we claim "they" are. Self-validation, or reification, is typical in the social sciences. As Giddens (1984) observed, has not the mere metaphorical use of the term *market* in the academic writings of the nineteenth century about economic activities ended up materializing that reality in ways that, today, neither economists nor chief executive officers would dare to question? Has not our conception of "the public" shifted from what was discussed in salons and side-street cafes to what scholars theorized as public opinion and then encouraged polls to measure? Has not the use of hydraulic and archeological metaphors in Freud's writing of the human psyche produced a whole industry of psychotherapists and clients for all of whom mental disorders have become as real as they can be? And have not the theories of consumer behavior and of mass media consumption, so avidly embraced by advertising agencies, brought forth the very consumerism that these theories needed in order to survive—by creating precisely the passive audiences that theories of mass communication are so good at describing? Do not correlations reported between intelligence, ethnicity, and crime, together with genetic explanation, inform our educational policies and hiring practices that keep such correlations real, well beyond published data? Do not statistics of cultural, racial, sexual, and national population characteristics inform and reify the very distinctions that statisticians initially build into their survey instruments and then naively "discover"? Is it then not likely that theories, which cannot but describe human nature in mechanistic terms, help create the very cultural dupes that television requires, abet the very behaviors that enable institutions to persist, discourage people from contesting scientific theories about them, and create obedient citizens who might differ as to whom they vote for but not as to how they could be influenced?

This is the reality we face. I am not suggesting that the project of the social sciences is doomed. I am submitting that if theorizing does continue to dominate our understanding of other human beings, it unwittingly installs an intellectual imperialism in our social world that silences the voices of the theorized, that prevents us from engaging in meaningful conversations with those who constitute the social phenomena we wish to understand, and that risks depriving us therefore of our primary source for understanding how social phenomena come to be.

A PROPOSAL FOR ECOLOGICAL NARRATIVES

Much of scientific theorizing, it must be emphasized, is manifested not in talk but in writing. Many of the entailments of theorizing that I have sketched may not be entirely attitudinal or epistemological but traceable to what the medium of writing makes (un)available to the theorist. In writing this chapter, I, too, feel the pull of monologism: After all, I am conceiving of social phenomena in the absence of those I am writing about. I, too, stand to be accused of theorizing about theorizing. But after considerable deliberations, what I am proposing here is a form of writing that might circumvent the old practice. I am calling it an *ecological narrative*, a manner of writing a story of social phenomena that embraces the stories of its human constituents and in so doing can be reembodied in their lives.

An *ecology* of diverse plants and animals, human populations explicitly included, can be said to arise in the interactions among its many constituents who, by distinguishing among kinds of interactions, organize themselves into families, cultures, and species and enact their own local and positional understandings of their worlds (Pirages's, Teune and Mlinar's, Zartman's, Buzan's, and Lipschutz's chapters, each in its own way, deal with ecology). An ecology is always more encompassing than the world of any of its constituents. Hence, an ecology is neither wholly theorizable (comprehensible) from any one position within that ecology nor fully exploitable (controllable) by any one of its species, all possible dominance relations (see Buzan, this volume) among them notwithstanding.

By stark analogy, a *narrative* can be said to arise in the stories told or written in the expectation of being understood and rearticulable by active listeners or readers—constituents of that narrative—who, by sharing certain stories and not others, especially of themselves, form numerous narrative communities. Their individual members understand these stories as giving meaning to their lives within these communities. Narratives are always incomplete. They cannot carry their full history into the present, and they preserve the possibility of being extendable by rearticulation, commentary, recomposition, or the addition of other, heretofore unheard, voices.

For a start, one could liken an ecological narrative to the written records of a conversation whose readers can distinguish between several voices responding to each other, can understand what is going on in the exchanges, and could carry the process onward—ideally by feeling invited to join the conversation as participants and to prolong the ongoing process in real time. Like ecologies, conversations are not manageable by any one party and the interpretation of what is said cannot be expected to be the same for each participant. They are not theorizable from any single position. Consensus can neither be expected nor demanded. Conceptual diversity and conflicts, even struggles over correct interpretation—over conceptions of the whole, for example—are constitutive of the multiple and ever-emerging conversational realities, precisely because these conceptions live in processes of communication. Should alien conceptions, theories, for example, enter from outside a conversation, their viability would depend on nothing simpler than being rearticulable and meaningful to its constituents. Ecological narratives have to foster such readings.

An ecological narrative is not social, political, or international because it *represents* social, political, or international phenomena (as theorists must claim for their theories) but rather because its distinctions are an acknowledged part of what is being narrated, enacted, and hence *experienced* by its participants. Such a narrative cannot be modeled on or emulate a mechanistic, organismic, or mentalistic system. Instead, it may be understood in terms of a *dialogical concept of language*—namely, through *languaging* or conversation.

An ecological narrative mitigates natural tensions between social and individual explanations. On the one hand, social realities are brought forth in dialogue, in interactions that involve language, which is a social phenomenon as well; and on the other hand, such realities constitutively depend on and are informed by the conceptual, narrative, and conversational skills and abilities of its individual constituents. What does this mean for writing social science? I state my proposal in six points:

First, to narrate ecologically means to recognize that *observational accounts do not exist without their narrators*. Observations are made by observers. Narratives are made by narrators capable of being observers as well. And this entails a particular *standpoint* or *perspective* from which each speaks. Positionless accounts divert the attention of their readers away from the narrator, as the source of such accounts, to contents outside of the process of giving accounts to each other. It is the latent consequences of positionless rhetoric that renders scientific discourse so troubling. To overcome this rhetoric, I am recommending that we, social scientists, actively assert our responsibilities for what we write—for example, by adopting the first-person pronouns "I," or "we"; by using verbs that elucidate our active involvement; by assuring our readers that the path we happen to be taking need not be theirs; and by explicitly acknowledging that our narrative constructions might affect unknown or unintended others as well. In ecological accounts, since even theories should be regarded as *someone's* theories, they should be considered to lead to manifold interpretations, scientific insistence on single readings aside. Not least, ecological narratives have to acknowledge explicitly their positional and polysemous nature.

Second, in ecological narratives, we *must grant others their voices as well*. We need to let the constituents of social phenomena speak for themselves, of themselves, from positions of their own choice and in situations in which they can feel comfortable and at home. Listening to what people want to say and taking their narratives seriously open us up to worlds otherwise unthinkable, even when uncomfortable or troublesome at times. Ecological narratives must acknowledge the agency of others and the spaces that they have created in order to move about and to take standpoints different from ours. Otherness is our most important challenge (see Zartman and complement with Holsti's, Buzan's, and Mansbach's chapters, this volume).

Reporting the stories of those whose worlds we wish to learn to understand is done by several research traditions, especially *ethnography*. But unfortunately, even ethnography has acquired the flavor of being applicable to ordinary folks only. Their method does not prevent (the often anthropological) ethnographers from floating above their informers, much as theorists seek to stay above their facts. The voice of the ethnographer should be considered neither uncontestable nor superior to ethnographical research. This does not speak against abstractions. Politicians do not shy away from conceptualizing their political realities in abstract, positionless, and often stereotypical terms. Since an objectivist rhetoric can provide power and influence to its users, its use is likely to continue. Rather, by always acknowledging the source of such abstractions, ecological narratives will not capitalize on this rhetoric. Those who use them—politicians but also certain analysts who interpret political speeches and analyze political climates, structures, or events of which politicians speak—merely add their voices to political processes, voices that should not be taken more seriously than those of other participants. Often, the voices of social scientists, as important as they may be in the social scientific literature, might mean nothing to those directly engaged in the events being written of. Thus, merely reporting on what others say or do, assembling a kaleidoscope of parallel ethnographies, recording a polyphony of sorts, writing a polyphonic novel—as Bakhtin would say—is simply not enough.

Third, I suggest, therefore, that ecological narratives try not to take the stories that they record at face value. Everything said or written (a) *should be qualified* in terms of how their readers or listeners respond to it and (b) should be approached with *as few theoretical presuppositions as possible*. The first part of this recommendation is not entirely new but rarely heeded. It takes seriously Bakhtin's notion (see Todorov, 1988: 41–60) that any utterance implies at least two voices, that of the speaker and that of the addressee. The meaning of an utterance—the speech act it performs, for example, or the sense it makes to someone—critically depends on the relation between what we hear a speaker say and how we observe its listeners respond (see Holquist, 1990). What we hear being said, the stories we read and quote, should not be considered "inherently" meaningful, as "containing" meanings or "conveying" its author's "intentions," even when they mean something definite *to us*. For "containing," "conveying," and "intending" invoke metaphors that objectify meanings as entities and seemingly dispense with the need for our reading: Semiotics has largely followed this line of theorizing. But, in ecological narratives, we must refrain from vying to be the sole authority on meanings, on others' understandings. We must instead find ways of listening to how others take what we may hear differently, to how they respond in ways we would not. This calls on us to locate meanings in the responses and rearticulations that they trigger, in the relations between writers and readers or between speakers and listeners. For we, too, assume merely one of these positions. Only in the last instance would meaning be our interpretation—but not forever, because the narratives that result from ours are as important as the narratives that we incorporate in our own. To narrate ecologically means to curb the self-arrogating assumption of our being the only reader/interpreter/respondent of note. To show what something means is to embed it, where possible, within the networks of its responsive (re)articulations.

In scholarly writing, to be sure, we do quote our sources, often extensively, but mostly in support of the point we hope to make. By contrast, in an ecological narrative, we must resist censoring the voices of others. This calls for our not dismissing the stories we hear being told—unless they are dismissed within the conversations from which they stem. It calls for avoiding the temptation of presuming to know what others "really" intend— even without consulting them. In particular, this calls for renouncing our self-celebratory "hermeneutics of suspicion," which elevate us to a position of knowing what we deny others to be aware of—hegemony, for example, or our systematic doubt in the sincerity of others, or conspiracy theory, for instance, unless "hegemony" or "deception" occurs in the conversation we are attempting to enter. In this regard, terrorism provides a good example. Terrorists tend to hold well-worked-out constructions of reality that make their actions meaningful to them. It is our own normative theory of how all good citizens should behave that justifies our dismissal of their world as a distortion of reality, a reality whose self-serving construction we fail to acknowledge as such. In this (our own) reality, our actions tend to drive uncomfortable-others from being mere deviants to becoming active dissenters or terrorists, to fall into the very categories that we may fear and to which we require that disabling punishments apply. In effect, fighting terror preserves a world without need to grant spaces for alternative realities to coexist.

In order to minimize the constraints of theoretical presuppositions, our approach to ecological narratives should be as naive as possible, offering a deliberately open mind, from a position of "not knowing," as the therapist Harlene Anderson (1997) recommends—this, in order to overcome the ever-present temptation of projecting our own theory onto others and, instead, to take in and to echo what others tell us, including who they are. True, this could well make ecological narratives more complex (and possibly less elegant) than the more current monological theories or the extant undigested collections of individual ethnographies. But public policy decisions, international events, political debates, social problems, and even family happenings—when seen through such narrative networks—are rarely more complex than the stories that their constituents can tell of these —events, of each other's stories of these events, and of their responses to them. Whereas ethnographers assemble individual stories, ecological narrators will have to weave them (back) into social fabrics, as the examples further below may demonstrate.

Fourth, inasmuch as *social realities* do arise in the *co-enactment of the understandings that participants have of their worlds*, of themselves, and of each other in them, understanding the worlds that others occupy and how they define themselves in relation to one another is key to *understanding the dynamics that unfold in the interactions across these worlds*. In ecological narratives, what would matter most is how the various constituents of a social phenomenon perceive each other's stance, capabilities, intentions, views, and probable responses to what happens or is being said. In classical systems theory, it is the theorist who specifies the relations between the components of a system before attending to their consequences. Systems theory, like all theories, makes no room for human agency. It does not provide options among which the "components" of a system may select their system's conceptions. It leaves no spaces for the human constituents of social systems to act on the awareness of each other's choices. Game theory would have come close to such an awareness, were it not theorized from outside of the players. The game theorist assumes that all players face each other in a shared world of payoffs, a world that is of the theorist's own construction. In contrast, narrating ecologically means a priori respect for the potentially unlike worlds of those who language each other into being; who give each other accounts of the paths they are pursuing; who coordinate their stories; and who thus find themselves codirecting a social dynamics from inside the process being narrated by them. Ecological narratives require and therefore must esteem the agency of their narrators. Conceding the necessary openness of narratives, ecological narrators have to make some effort *to extend the network of recorded stories by articulating their possible continuations,* ideally in ways that would make sense to' those being narrated in them.

I suppose one might slip here into speaking of predictions. But this is precisely what would deny those narrated their agency and dismiss the possibility of their accepting or contesting the narratives of concern to them. An ecological narrative would not assign agency to abstractions, to systems, for example, or to the physical environment, but would presume its narrators' ability to act on their understanding of what they see, of each other's stories and of each other's understandings of these stories. Respectful communication requires such a recursively embedded understanding. Mechanistic explanations unable to acknowledge this understanding may indeed arise in narratives, although not from the ecological narrators for whom such an understanding is wholly constitutive.

Fifth, as all other participants in a dialogue, ecological narrators have to live with the humbling experience that *social realities are profoundly unpredictable*, that all accounts of them therefore must remain *open-ended, incomplete*, and *constitutively incoherent much of the time*. This may prove disturbing for outside observers who must struggle with great numbers of seemingly contradictory accounts that may make a lot of sense from within and also with generalizations that appear arbitrary and shallow from without. In everyday life, people communicate with each other selectively, creating parallel conversational realities. Taken together, these realities form loosely connected "multi-versa" that supplant the construction of a singular and coherent system or "uni-verse."

The purported globalizing effects of mass media technologies are far from converging toward a unified world. Their reality is complex, multifaceted, fractionalized, tentative, and continually reconstructed and maintained. Narrators cannot be in these multiversa all at once. Even a simple construction such as terrorism, sweeping and judgmental as it may be, survives only in particular networks of told stories—for example, the network of manifestos issued by revolutionaries seeking to change the world; of stories told by the members of an establishment facing an unexpected wave of disrespect or of violence from a previously unknown group; of police reports generated by officers trying to fulfill their duty in apprehending criminals; of narratives by victims and by their grieving families; of speeches by politicians seeking to cash in on an instance of public uncertainty; or of accounts that TV viewers and newspaper readers obtain by attending to the news. Each acknowledges, or connects to, some of the other stories, and all compete for attention in a public space within which terrorism is defined, politicized, even as it thrives and eventually recedes into history. This offers the ecological narrator much to work from. Readers of such narratives may have to tolerate at least as much diversity, inconsistency, and contradiction as is evident in the multiversity of the interwoven worlds being narrated. One can hardly start from the assumption that the worlds, which such stories bring forth, are either similar or complementary to one another. Yet it is the very discrepancies and discontinuities of these worlds that enable their narrators to extrapolate a dynamic of what might happen, should these narratives come in contact. Stories evolve in the very dynamics they individually inform. And in these interactions, stories rarely ever stay the same.

As dialogical accounts, ecological narratives cannot but be incomplete: (1) They present no more than one discursive moment in the process of their continual rearticulation. (2) Efforts to embrace the narratives of all of its constituents can be at best fair, at worst illusory, but always contestable by anyone present. (3) And the telling (communication) of these narratives can be responsive to only some of the many voices that, together, inform their multilogical self-producing future.

And sixth, if politics means acting in the belief of knowing others' intentions, being cognizant of the history of one's individual participation in the political process, remaining mindful of how one's own languaging might enable, constrain, or (re)organize the public lives of others including one's own, then *a social science that recognizes its own politics offers two ways of understanding its phenomena.*

The first way is more in line with our established scholarly tradition. I like to see it as a mere step toward the second. It involves *sitting back and analyzing* the network of narratives heard, then *extrapolating* from them all *conceivable continuations* without getting personally involved. This is what journalists claim they do when reporting an event through the stories of its participants, witnesses, and stakeholders. This is also what most political activists do when discussing requisite strategies with their advisers before going public.

The second, largely neglected way of understanding becomes evident in one's *active participation and discursive intervention in the social processes of concern.* This is achieved by tuning narratives and actions to their possible effects; inviting others to voice their concerns, even to comment on each other's stories, and to collaborate with us in writing of what is happening. This means collectively weaving and reweaving available narratives into each other until the process reflects the manifold stakes claimed by its participants and allows the process to continue without precipitous need for a definite conclusion.

Active involvement in the collaborative rearticulation of ongoing social processes is probably also the best assurance that our narratives remain viable within the very constituency of our choosing and that our role as narrator remains acceptable to that constituency. I believe all human beings are endowed with this fundamentally social ability. An example is how politicians in a democracy manage to preserve their role as such. It involves the ability to narrate compelling stories that rearticulate and braid the stories of their constituents in ways that these constituents could accept as their own. It surfaces in the ability of setting agendas, of involving political bystanders in one's project, of encouraging everyone to voice their concerns—while preserving the possibility for the process to continue, even in some other form. Ecological narratives, too, should engage their readers in just such a process. Hopefully, readers' responses invite us—the writers—back into the kind of involvement we find challenging. This second kind of understanding is thus not propositional but all too evidently dialogical.

The criterion for the first way of understanding is that our *narratives can reenter the social processes that they narrate.* This means that they must be understandable and reproducible by their constituents and hence respectful of them. The criterion for the second way of understanding is that, *upon reentry, these narratives can contribute to the social life of those that they narrate,* enabling the latter to direct the social phenomena being narrated *without becoming an embarrassment to us, as ecological narrators.*

To say that ecological narratives can, were it in principle, reenter and inform the processes they narrate is not to suggest that they require consensus or need to satisfy everybody. On the contrary, the inevitable inconsistencies among stories within ecological narratives (see fifth point) and the suggestion that all meanings be ascertainable mainly through their consequences (see third point) are unlikely to please everyone equally or always. Since ecological narratives typically provide larger contexts for their individual contributors' stories, they typically recontextualize and display the propensity to challenge and even provoke existing conceptions and practices. This can prove uncomfortable to some though liberating to others. And therein lies a clear invitation for critical scholars to question constructions of reality that are deemed suspect and to alter the conditions that give rise to them—not from the position of a godlike judge, nor in the voice of omniscient spectators/interpreters/experts, but as sincere participants who not only treat all of their narrated others, and especially those that critical scholars need to challenge, with due respect but who also act in the knowledge of being held accountable for their critiques. Ecological narrators' sincerity spares embarrassment, attracts respect, prolongs their activity.

EXAMPLES

Perhaps an example would be useful here—not of a complete ecological narrative that would exceed the scope of this chapter but of a story familiar enough to be merely referred to: the 1993 human tragedy in Waco, Texas. The narratives that defined that sequence of events have ancient roots. The term *tragedy*, since then commonly used in describing the event, ties this story to a classical dramaturgical form of Hellenic origin. The apocalyptic discourse of the Davidians has been identified as the ideology of an embattled minority. It goes back to early Christian experience of Roman persecution—as reflected in the Book of the Apocalypse (or Revelation) by St. John. But these narratives acquired new realities in the voices of people that found each other at real discursive moments.

As the tragedy unfolded, numerous narrators could be heard reporting what they saw and responding to what they heard others say. Reporters were eager to interview participants, to dramatize their stories. And without their involvement, we might never have heard of the event. Agents of an antiterrorist (U.S. Bureau of Alcohol, Tobacco, and Firearms—ATF) force, later joined by Federal Bureau of Investigation (FBI) personnel, were set to arrest a criminal and eager to speak of how difficult that mission was proving to be. The U.S. attorney general, trying to assure that the actions taken were demonstrably legal and politically correct, added yet another voice. Then there was David Koresh and his fellow Branch Davidians who, having modeled themselves according to their readings of religious texts, sought to live their way of faith, best achievable within the bounds of a fenced compound.

At any one moment, most of the players spoke of themselves, of those they saw themselves as facing, and of why they responded to each other in the ways they did. Commentators, scholars of religion, sociopsychological experts, and militant rightists also entered the public discourse. Even the voice of God was roped into the process, speaking to Koresh through the latter's reading of the Old Testament. Each of these narratives brought forth different worlds with little, if anything, in common except that they could not easily ignore each other. It was these differences that set the stage for the events that would unfold with a most terrifying determinism.

The Davidians inside the compound had constructed a world premised on the coming of either a golden age or a fiery end to their universe. They saw unquestionable "signs" for the latter. Koresh, as the Lamb of Revelation, worked hard at opening The Seven Seals, which would enable him to foresee what would happen. The world of the government agents outside the compound became determined by the pursuit of a strategy that had most recently proved effective during another siege at Ruby Ridge. It was designed to confine the movement of identified criminals and to force them to choose between surrender or violent death. Perhaps unwittingly, the Davidians reinforced the ATF/FBI's conception of the situation as a military siege by using firearms against a forceful intrusion into their compound. For the ATF/FBI, David Koresh became an armed criminal; for the public, he became the charismatic leader of an obscure, hence potentially dangerous, cult and a psychopath. These perceptions gave those outside the compound no reason to take Koresh's words seriously. Religious scholars surfaced in the mass media, interpreting Koresh's teachings, warning that his story anticipated someone to play the role of the evil forces that would bring about the end of the world by a disastrous inferno, an apocalypse—a role that the FBI would soon play, unknowingly. These experts advised the FBI about the role it occupied in Koresh's mind and tried to engage Koresh in dialogues aimed at dissuading him from his course of action. From what we know, these efforts failed to enter the narratives of either party.

The ATF/FBI, seemingly unable to take seriously Koresh's different rationality, continued to dismiss him as an armed psychopath. They stuck to their military narrative and continued their siege, adding psychological warfare techniques—beaming bright light and broadcasting loud music and messages toward the compound—with the intent to weaken the resolve of the besieged. Seeing themselves surrounded by "noisy forces of evil" and becoming increasingly suspicious of these unknown mediators, Koresh and his group became less and less inclined to consent to the kind of conversations suggested. For all sides, time became of the essence, albeit in diverging directions. Koresh sought to buy time before surrendering, ostensibly to finish writing a treatise he was inspired to leave behind. The ATF/FBI, under increasing public criticism for their lingering operation, sought instead to shorten the siege—by force if necessary—and added equipment to this effect. Thus, a world of military strategy, weapons, and logistics, driven by the public demand for quick and decisive action, interacted with an equally closed if differently oriented world in which the Davidians not only foresaw their own fate but accepted it as such. The proof of the validity of their story came to them with the inferno that would end the siege.

Increasingly evident to those of us less attached and therefore able more carefully to see how these narratives responded to each other is that these narratives differed in *content* while neatly *complementing* each other in the behavioral *responses*, which they entailed. As the tragedy unfolded, the dialogical space narrowed to a single path, eventually leading to the very end that Koresh had prophesied but also to the ultimate solution that the ATF/FBI had considered. Each side had maintained a frightful consistency within its own worldview. The death of 80 people, killed in the fire that consumed the compound, terminated their voices. In the course of telling and retelling these narratives, there emerged a single story with a dramatic ending and a place name of reference. Although this now neatly bracketed story no longer commemorates the logic of the less fortunate others, varied versions continue to travel below the surface. As militia movements in the United States and the Oklahoma City bombing would indicate, these narratives are still able to reproduce themselves into incidents that, although separated by time and geography, hang together by the stories that continue to fuel them.

I could have chosen other examples, the recent events in the former Yugoslavia, for instance. In this case, too, grand political theorizing proved quite powerless when compared to the efforts of bringing into interaction the stories that people told each other and of each other. These stories rearticulated historical events (of Turks invading the Balkans, of local heroes challenging the Austrian empire into World War I, of atrocities by Nazi collaborators in World War II) that sufficient numbers of people could relate to, that politicians could use to reconstruct present episodes as though they were historical continuities, that a univocal mass media system could compellingly dramatize and widely disseminate under immunity from competing versions with the help of the government in Belgrade. The resulting ethnic war arose entirely from within these stories. It is best understood in terms of where it took place, which stories came to be retold and enacted, and how the multiplicity of individual behaviors unfolded into unspeakable ethnic atrocities that we read of but can hardly imagine. These stories withstood the new names, places, means of delivery, and narrators and went on to recreate the network of much earlier, if not less heinous, interactions.

I could have exemplified ecological narratives also by way of therapeutic conversations. Published psychoanalytic theory notwithstanding, therapeutic discourse is largely shielded from public scrutiny. The stories that patients bring into a session are all that therapists have available to begin the intervention. Initially, the narrators are the actors in their own stories. Soon, however, the therapists have to enter these narratives, albeit by different paths and in different roles as well. The patients' stories are as real to them as any reality can ever be. The therapists' intervention consists of conversing with their patients in ways that would enable the latter to rearticulate their stories into more livable ones—until they feel competent to continue narrating their lives on their own, not only to themselves but, more important, in collaboration with others.

CONCLUDING REMARKS

Each of these examples accounts for social situations that while vastly different from each other are driven largely by the stories that their participants bring to them and enact in view of each other. We theorists, too, participate in social processes as narrators, regardless of where our topics may come from. No sooner than we abandon the God's eye view of social theorists and adopt an ecological perspective, do we come to realize that in the social process that we are narrating *all* participants are competent conceptualizers, narrators, and even "theorists" of their *own* local worlds—and, as such, quite capable of offering situationally adequate accounts of the reasons for their actions. We are all alike in this respect, except that our commitments to narrate ecologically as scholars and theory builders encourage us to acknowledge the possibility of diverse worlds, to attribute them to those who narrate them into being, and not least, to accept professional responsibilities for our own narratives.

Narratives always leave much unsaid. Narrating unattended dimensions in the lives of others seems easy enough, especially in the absence of interaction with them. But unlike theorists—whether experimental psychologists or observers of hegemony—no ecological narrator may claim the authority to speak for others without the latters' permission. Narrating what others do not (yet) understand should amount to no more than an invitation to dialogue, without attempts to purport one's superior abilities.

Ecological narratives can expand the understanding of their participants continually by including the narratives of each within the context of all others. This expansion requires access to as many narratives as is practical. Above all, it depends on a participant's openness to expand one's horizon. Superior postures and perspectives, completeness, accuracy, and finality are anathema in ecological narratives.

Ecological narratives attempt to account for ongoing social phenomena in terms of all participants' understanding. As such, they can provide early warnings in the most demanding contexts. The tragedy at Waco demonstrated that accounts of unfoldings that fail to embrace the narratives of their constituents, at least of the leading players, are ultimately self-destructive. In former Yugoslavia, the principal actors enacted their own single-minded accounts of whom they "knew" they faced and created ruin for all.

All social processes, I would argue, are self-directing, and even autopoietic, while being mediated by the stories that their constituents revive, tell each other, co-enact, and even live by. Placing these stories in ecological interaction is one way for us to make the dynamics of the ongoing social processes analyzable. Encouraging ecological narratives to reenter the processes that we claim to narrate assures us of their autonomous viability—except where distinctions between *my* superior and objective accounts and *their* inferior and subjective stories enter that process (see Holsti's chapter, this volume). Where such distinctions come to dominate any discourse, they can easily destroy its ecological nature by erasing the very ground on which human communications can take place. This self-destruction is analogous to the one that Gregory Bateson (1972) observed in his *Steps to an Ecology of Mind*. Bateson had searched for ways to overcome the Cartesian construction of mind as the master over matter—the cherished ideal of transforming nature in the service of exclusively human self-interests and the reliance on validity and on instrumental criteria for human communication.

We cannot prevent social theories from reentering and, yes, transforming their domain of observation. Observations involve both the theorists and the theorized in a recursion. Ecological forms of narrating are ways of accounting for social phenomena collaboratively, without the self-serving presumption of superior abilities to theorize others. Privileging a single description as accurate is one manifestation of a claim to superiority in that a priori it disregards the voice of others and the content of their readings. In therapy, historical accuracy comes second to getting the lives of troubled patients on a better track. Meaning does not reside in references to external facts but in the viability of continued narration. The possibility for our narratives to reenter the social processes that they address provides not only a fortuitous test of their viability but also a benefit to all involved: It honors all of its human constituents' understanding, it conserves the diversity of their perspectives, it assures the continuation of the process of narrating social reality, and it reserves a space for our participation.

Ecological narratives could have therapeutic effects on a social scale. To be sure, the terrible stories that resurfaced in the former Yugoslavia lay in waiting for a long time. However, had the mass media retold these stories in ways remotely resembling our ecological narratives, especially in Serbia, where the press and television enjoyed an uncontested monopoly, had its principal actors been encouraged to appreciate the stories of the other side as complementing theirs, and had these actors been able to put them together and see what their braiding had in store for them, perhaps the mindless horror that resulted from unwavering pursuits of the theories that each held of the other could have been avoided.

Perhaps a last distinction is in order here: that between narratives *lived* and narratives merely *heard of* or *read*. Their difference results in two very different kinds of understandings. For those who live their story, the latter is indistinguishable from reality. The Davidians in Texas lived their story as much as the ATF/FBI did theirs. And the consequences of their interaction were real for both sides. But this may not be so for the stories that we read or hear others tell. An other's story may be heard, listened to, visualized, empathized with, perhaps even retold. But whether such a story comes to be lived and enacted by its listener is another matter. A major problem of therapy is that it is always easier to listen to advice and to rearticulate what was said than to live an earlier-heard narrative. Hence, ecological narrators, too, can live only their own part of the story, which they narrate: Heard stories never have the reality of lived ones. Social scientists who do research on records (data) from a past without a present are concerned with stories heard. They are free to adopt any criterion for those of their articulations welcomed by their community—consistency with certain privileged stories, or novelty, for example. This might be all that historians can do. Justifiably perhaps, this also is the situation that invites theorizing. However, as long as the social processes of interest remain observable and retain constituents who could tell their stories and comment on ours, we as social scientists should feel obligated to reinsert our narratives into these processes, lest their viability in the lives of others remain an open issue.

To abandon our comfortable role as social theorists with well-honed observational abilities, and to acknowledge that our stake in any social reality that we construct is always only one of many, could be viewed as an act of courage. However, because this would also render our inquiries into our social worlds socially responsive and permit us to see each other as the political actors we have always been, it would also constitute an act of candor.

Reclaiming the respect for the otherness of others, which theorizing systematically undermines, has become of pressing importance. Ecological narratives could help us achieve this commonly preferred mode of being and becoming.

REFERENCES

Anderson, Harlene (1997). *Conversation, Language, and Possibilities.* New York: Basic Books.

Bateson, Gregory (1972). *Steps to an Ecology of Mind.* New York: Ballantine.

Ciprut, Jose V. (ed.) (2000). *Of Fears and Foes: Security and Insecurity in an Evolving Global Political Economy.* Westport, CT: Praeger.

Eco, Umberto (1976). *A Theory of Semiotics.* Bloomington: Indiana University Press.

Fish, Stanley (1985). Consequences. Pp. 106–31 in W.J.T. Mitchell (ed.), *Against Theory.* Chicago: University of Chicago Press.

Foucault, Michel (1977). *Discipline and Punish: The Birth of the Prison.* New York: Pantheon Books.

Furrow, Dwight (1995). *Against Theory: Continental and Analytic Challenges in Moral Philosophy*. New York: Routledge.

Garfinkle, Harold (1967). *Studies in Ethnomethodology*. Englewood Cliffs, NJ: Prentice-Hall.

Garfinkle, Harold, M. Lynch, and E. Livingstone (1982). The Work of a Discovering Science Construed with Materials for the Optically Discovered Pulsar. *Philosophy of the Social Sciences* 11: 131–258.

Giddens, Anthony (1984). *The Constitution of Society*. Berkeley: University of California Press.

Goffman, Erving (1959). *The Presentation of Self in Everyday Life*. New York: Doubleday.

Goffman, Erving (1963). *Behavior in Public Places*. New York: Free Press.

Hirsch, E. D., Jr. (1967). *Validity in Interpretation*. New Haven, CT: Yale University Press.

Holquist, Michael (1990). *Dialogism: Bakhtin and His World*. New York: Routledge.

Horgan, John (1993). The Worst Enemy of Science: Paul Karl Feyerabend. *Scientific American* (May): 36–37.

Knapp, Steven, and Walter Benn Michaels (1985). Against Theory. Pp. 11–30 in W.J.T. Mitchell (ed.), *Against Theory*. Chicago: University of Chicago Press.

Krippendorff, Klaus (1993). Conversation or Intellectual Imperialism in Comparing Communication (Theories). *Communication Theory* 3, 3: 252–66.

Krippendorff, Klaus (1996). A Second-Order Cybernetics of Otherness. *Systems Research* 13, 3: 311–28.

Mitchell, W.J.T. (1985). Introduction: Pragmatic Theory. Pp. 1–10 in W.J.T. Mitchell (ed.), *Against Theory*. Chicago: University of Chicago Press.

Putnam, Hilary (1981). *Reason, Truth and History*. New York: Cambridge University Press.

Sampson, Edward E. (1993). *Celebrating the Other: A Dialogic Account of Human Nature*. Boulder, CO: Westview Press.

Schank, Roger C., and Robert P. Abelson (1977). *Scripts, Plans, Goals, and Understanding*. Hillside, NJ: Lawrence Erlbaum.

Todorov, Tzvetan (1988). *Mikhail Bakhtin: The Dialogical Principle*. Minneapolis: University of Minnesota Press.

Woolgar, Steve (1993). *Science, the Very Idea*. New York: Routledge.

CHAPTER 2

Hindrances to Understanding in International Relations

KALEVI J. HOLSTI

INTRODUCTION

The academic field of international relations has developed through many diverse routes: as an art (e.g., diplomacy, war), as a philosophy (e.g., theories of international law), as history, and as science, broadly conceived. International relations, compared, say, to economics or psychology, has always been a synthetic field combining insights, concepts, and methodologies from diverse sources. Its "truths" and understandings thus necessarily diverge depending on the theoretical and epistemological perspectives brought to bear on a particular problem. The world examined through the lenses of demography will look different than the world scrutinized by social psychologists. We have accepted these diverse perspectives for decades. But discussions of epistemologies seem to generate much more controversy. We should, however, acknowledge that positivist, hermeneutic, and critical perspectives may all contribute to understanding—depending on what we want to know—but if debates are conducted on the assumption that only one may make a legitimate claim to scholarly authority, there is going to be a good deal of misunderstanding arising from the resulting polemics. Because the discipline's epistemological, historical, and ontological sources are so varied, we will always have "perspectivism" and theoretical pluralism.

Pluralism is also the product of the vast domain that has to be made sensible. Whatever the units of analysis—whether they be individuals, genders, groups, nations, states, organizations, or their literally billions of historical and contemporary ideas, activities, transactions, and relationships—these units have to be simplified into types, patterns, trends, and significant anomalies. Without attempts at such intellectual "compression," there could be no coherent field of study.

ON UNDERSTANDING

The task of this chapter is to examine hindrances to *understanding*. The latter term is itself contested—it has no fewer than nine major lexical meanings—thus, a few words of interpretation of it are in order. Martin Hollis and Steve Smith (1991) have provided us with a valuable excursion of the differences between explanation (causation) and understanding, between formal scientific explanation and social construction. In my view, both are necessary components of a more general understanding of the entities, structures, and processes of international relations. Both empirical-positivist and social constructivist research strategies may pay off. Whether one form of analysis is more appropriate than another depends to a great extent on the nature of the materials examined and on the purposes of the inquiry. What they have in common is their concern to make complexities more intelligible, or to impose some type of intellectual order on phenomena that seem, at first glance, to be chaotic or lacking pattern or devoid of underlying similarities. An analogy may illustrate my thought here:

To the proverbial person from Mars, or even to the average citizen in most countries in the world, the game of cricket when observed for the first time makes no sense. That is, we cannot understand it except for the vague knowledge that because it is a competitive game the purpose of it must be to win. But without knowledge of rules, the hundreds of distinct activities in the field may appear senseless if not totally chaotic. While there may not be precise analogues to the rules of the cricket game and international relations, we can make international relations intelligible (understandable) only if from the welter of distinct activities we begin to observe patterns, repetitions, regular processes, as well as some similarities among and across actors. In international relations studies, as in cricket, we must make classifications; classifications make sense only if there are repeated and patterned behaviors. This is fundamental. Without classifications, we could not identify statics, changes, trends, and anomalies. The act of classification of course imposes some sort of order on "facts," but if the facts themselves did not suggest some sort of order in the first place, the classification probably could not be made. It is only because the players in cricket repeat their activities that we can begin to infer what is going on. And by observing, we can begin to make sense; there is a bowler, hitter, and fielders, and although the trajectory of the ball changes with each pitch or hit, certain things repeat. Our understanding increases.

But if a fan of the game had told us at the beginning all the rules of the game, not only would our understanding of it have been achieved more quickly and with more authority, but we would also have been able to identify the unusual—the anomaly—that may make the game more interesting. In seeking understanding, then, we search not only for patterns, repetition, and rules but also for the exceptional event.

However, the game itself may not be all we want to learn. We may also want to explore the "meaning" of the game as a social phenomenon, as a metric of class divisions, or as one of imperialism's many exports. We may want to raise such questions that are not made obvious from the data of the game.

These are mundane observations, to be sure, but in many of our scholars' excursions into epistemology, ontology, and metatheory, we sometimes lose sight of one of our common purposes as international relations scholars: to make a seemingly difficult and often chaotic field of ideas, activity, and practice more intelligible through the process of classification and, moreover, of contextualization. Philosophical analysis may help identify biases, alert us to the political and social implications of our findings, focus attention on things we did not examine—the famous "silences" of postmodernism—and render problematic assumptions and concepts that we tend to use uncritically. These are all pluses. But philosophy (or metatheory) is not the purpose of the study of international relations; it is an aid to understanding, as are statistics, knowledge of foreign languages, research funds, travel and first-hand experience abroad, adequate acquaintance with the historical and contemporary literatures of the field, familiarity with bodies of knowledge, reliable data and evidence, and many other supports of scholarship. Thus, metatheoretical discussion should not be privileged over the numerous other necessary components of intellectual competence.

These introductory words reflect my personal views toward some of the issues that have generated debates and polemics in the so-called crisis of international relations of the past decade. In these discussions, one often sees the roots of misunderstanding, with scholars engaged in lengthy debates that seem ever more distant from the subject we purportedly wish to understand better. How do we know there is misunderstanding? There are at least two indicators: lack of mutual awareness and intellectual closure. The first is demonstrated in the institutional limitations to learning and dissemination of knowledge. The second is revealed in the intolerance that sometimes pervades debates in the field. The first problem is relatively simple because it refers to practices, habits, and constraints that can be ameliorated through communication, determination, and funding. The second is probably insoluble, although awareness may help bring more mutual tolerance and understanding to the theoretical diversity that is a necessary characteristic of the field.

INSTITUTIONAL HINDRANCES TO UNDERSTANDING

Some of the institutional barriers to mutual understanding are not always acknowledged in many of the theoretical debates that surround the field today. Knowledge of a foreign language, for example, may open up new worlds that help create or develop understanding and insight.[1] Lack of such knowledge necessarily restricts a universalist understanding. Research funds help provide access not only to information but also to time for speculation and introspection. Disparities of such resources help to explain the continuing gaps in qualities and quantities of scholarship around the world (cf. Holsti, 1985: ch. 6).

Travel and firsthand experience increase the probabilities of enhancing understanding—understanding in the sense both of intelligibility/causation and of making us aware of the extent to which our perceptions, theories, and other means of organizing observations and knowledge may be bounded by space and time. The inductive generalizations generated by policy makers are an often necessary antidote to the abstract theoretical formulations of academics who occupy offices and libraries and form their visions of the world through the *New York Times* and television news. The tensions between theorists and practitioners are well known and need no repeating here. Suffice it to say that communication between them ends when the one is unable to make any sweeping generalizations from vast experience in the field, and the other engages primarily in epistemological and lofty metatheoretical argument. The one drowns in a sea of hyperfactualism, the other in an ocean of metaphysics. Caught in the middle, the student learns little of lasting value about international relations, and one social role of theory—pedagogy—becomes compromised and, in some instances, maybe even impossible.

In wealthy societies, almost all these institutional and practical hindrances to understanding can be overcome by funds, determination, and time. In poorer societies, the working conditions of academics are such that it is difficult if not impossible to travel and to launch sustained research programs, which have as their main purpose the increase of knowledge and understanding, as distinct from explaining, justifying, or buttressing the policies of the governments of the authors.

DISAGREEMENT AND MISUNDERSTANDING

Academics read each other's works, they cite each other, and some of them even engage in coherent research programs. Numerous authors write of "progress" in the field, there is some evident cumulation, and occasionally research dead-ends are acknowledged and abandoned. There are, of course, lengthy debates and some fundamental disagreements on whether the field is a discipline, whether it can or should develop along trajectories similar to those of the physical, natural, or other social sciences, and which methodologies are most appropriate. I know of no field in which such debates do not exist. Such disagreements lie at the heart of all scholarship and are often essential for creating understanding. They indicate that the parties at least agree on the questions, even though they may have different answers or strategies for locating answers. Disagreement is not the same as misunderstanding. The latter is indicated when people speak past each other. When is this the case? Usually, it is when people believe they are right and all others are wrong. It is seen in the habit or stance of arguing that my methodology or, worse still, my metatheoretical preference is valid, whereas yours is not; that my school of thought (or, as current jargon has it, my project) offers the only way to approach the field, whereas yours does not (cf. Brecher, 1995: 5). We can call this the "monopoly syndrome." Why do such attitudes exist?

Numerous explanations are possible. In an age when one's "identity" appears so important, scholars may wish to pigeonhole themselves and others as means of creating both distinction and distinctiveness. Other explanations derive from the sociology of academic life. Those who launch or introduce a new "school" of approach to the subject may garner the greatest reputational and status rewards. The exclusiveness, authority, and validity of a particular approach are of course compromised when other schools or approaches claim equal status. In some ways, the academic enterprise, particularly in North America, is a zero-sum game. We should also mention faddism, the need for one generation to make its theoretical mark in order to distinguish itself from its predecessors; and the appeals of intellectual constructs that are more complex, sophisticated, and suggestive than, for example, the relatively simple desiderata of the scientific method.

But perhaps the greatest source of the "monopoly syndrome" in international theory is the fact that theory involves value choices. Whatever methodologies, approaches, or epistemologies are employed, ultimately the theoretical enterprise is normative. Why is this the case?

THE PROCESSES OF THEORETICAL INNOVATION

To get some clues, perhaps the best way to proceed is to chronicle what theorists of international relations do and for what purposes. What theorists *should do* is another matter and—given the nature of the materials with which we work and the very different social contexts for different academics—one upon which we can hardly expect agreement. The scenario described below is a simplification in that it offers only a rough representation of the main types of activities of the theoretical enterprise.

Theory usually begins with the identification of a problem. A problem is often a social construct. Depending on era or some particular culture, the condition may be seen as a preordained act of god(s), a regular force of nature, or a case of historical inevitability. This is how war was seen through most of recorded history. For as long as war was inevitable, it was not seen as a "problem" in the sense that one could or should analyze it and/or do something about it.

The study of international relations as a distinct field of inquiry developed as a response to the problem of war. Until war was socially perceived as a "problem," whose sources resided in human agency (and which could be managed, controlled, eliminated by human design), there was little systematic study of it as a phenomenon. The problem of war, and its derivatives of peace, stability, security, and/or order, has come to form the core intellectual question of international relations over the past 300 years or so. Elsewhere (Holsti, 1985), I have termed this the "classical tradition." Whatever the methodologies, the perspectives, or the schools of international relations, writing, research, and pedagogy focused on this problem. More recently, analysts have begun to identify other, and sometimes competing, problems. These include trade, commerce, and technology; they also include international governance (though it is not a new field), quality of life as influenced by environmental destruction, and relations between peoples, nations, genders, and "identities."

To claim that these problems require systematic inquiry is to make a value choice reflecting moral and ethical concerns. The focus on war expresses an abiding priority with the security of independent political communities and with saving lives. The problems of trade, commerce, and technology reflect values of efficiency, equity, and reciprocity, as well as of the quality of life. Theorizing about environmental problems indicates similar priorities but also adds both ethical and aesthetic dimensions. Relations between individuals, classes, groups, genders, and "identities" are templates of more general concerns surrounding power, equity, and justice. When we enter into these realms, our debates about the ultimate value of particular subjects, and over particular approaches or "schools," are likely to become intense and often exclusionary.

Is it the case that all inquiry begins with the analysis of a moral/social/political "problem"? No. Curiosity is also excited by the unexpected, the unusual, the unknown and novel, and the dramatic. We enter the realm of theory when deviations from standard patterns or expectations appear. Witness the explosion of theoretical studies on the end of the Cold War, the explorations of the "democratic peace," the fate of the state in an era of "globalism," the resurgence of "regionalism," and other topics that deal with current anomalies and trends. Notice also, however, that because these studies converge on an identifiable problem around which there is reasonable consensus, the debates are rarely exclusionary.

Finally, theory itself drives theory. Theory develops from the identification of logical, empirical, or epistemological problems in existing renderings of international relations. Epistemological debates, the tensions between theory and praxis, and methodological concerns stimulate efforts to correct, improve, or replace existing bodies of knowledge or theoretical perspectives. Lack of isomorphism between conventional theoretical constructs and frequent/common observations of international practice may spawn new perspectives. Many will challenge "truths" dear to the leaders of the profession. Currently, for example, the appearance of critical and postmodern perspectives has stimulated significant debates at the metatheoretical level but also some robust polemics that betray bruised egos on all sides.

Most important, certain new perspectives, such as those emanating from critical theory, may broaden the parameters of the field by problematizing that which is ordinarily taken for granted. Robert Cox (1986: 201) summarizes it well:

[Theory] is critical in the sense that it stands apart from the prevailing order of the world and asks how that order came about. Critical theory . . . does not take institutions and social and power relations for granted but calls them into question by concerning itself with their origins and how and whether they might be in the process of changing. It is directed toward an appraisal of the very framework for action, or problematic, which problem-solving theory accepts as its parameters.

Cox here attempts to broaden the perspectives of the field and to increase understanding. It is a strategy of addition. There is no claim to delete what is known from previous scholarship. But some approaches have less constructive dimensions. They often adopt exclusionary and denunciatory coloration. The zealots of science during the 1950s and 1960s, like some contemporary poststructuralists, signaled intolerance by the copious overuse of invented vocabulary and complex jargon and also by requiring a mastery of the works of a pantheon of intellectual heroes who may be obscure in the field and who usually had no expertise in the subject. A multitude of boundary-marking code words distinguish insiders from outsiders. All that went on before is dismissed as wrongheaded and valueless. Scholars sometimes deliberately use such exclusionary strategies to distinguish (and also distance) themselves from others and to support their claims of having found the ultimate truth.

Theory may also arise from almost pure acts of creativity. New conceptualizations of the world, as Quincy Wright's (1955) development of Kurt Lewin's field theory or Morton Kaplan's (1957) elaboration of Ludwig von Bertalanffy's general systems theory, do not emerge from identifiable or demonstrable moral/political problems or from epistemological or philosophical critiques of existing theories. They are *sui generis* and demonstrate the capacity of humans to imagine purely abstract representations of complex phenomena. Because they are often radically different, unusual, abstract, and detached, they face difficulties of operationalization and conversion into research programs. But even in these, a moral/political purpose may lurk; often the purely abstract rendering of complexity hides an imagined better world.

FROM PROBLEM IDENTIFICATION AND CHOICE TO DIAGNOSIS

Once a topic is selected—and I repeat that, often, this is implicitly or explicitly a moral/political choice—the diagnosis begins. The purpose here is, first, to identify the nature and dimensions of the problem and, second, to locate its sources, that is, its necessary and/or sufficient causes or conditions. In the case of war, we have a rich literature that, as Kenneth Waltz (1959) has summarized for us, locates sources at different levels of analysis and with different degrees of explanatory authority and validity. Since there are significant differences of authority and validity, there are also numerous analytical/explanatory systems that compete with each other. Rousseau's explanation of war, via the stag hunt analogy, is a brilliant analysis if we are content to understand why wars recur in an anarchical system. But it cannot account for the variation in war incidence and participation by different countries and regions of the world, and hence it may pass only the test of sufficient explanation, without specifying the necessary conditions. For these, we have to turn to different analytical levels.

Dependency theories demonstrate the same patterns. Once a problem (inequality) is identified, its essential characteristics and dimensions are described, often empirically rather than narratively, and then accounted for at different levels of analysis and using different methodologies. The theory remains contested, however, because of significant anomalies, lack of consensus on the main explanatory factors, and different diagnoses of those factors.

FROM DIAGNOSIS TO PRESCRIPTION

Implicit or explicit within diagnoses is a "solution" to the problem. The solution may be epistemological, historical, political, or social; it can be realistic or utopian; but if the diagnosis is sound—and there is rarely consensus that it is—then there seems to be things individuals, groups, or governments can do to manage, alleviate, control, or eliminate the problem. I take this as one of the meanings that Robert Cox (1986: esp. 207) conveyed in his famous statement that theory is always "for" someone or something.[2]

This observation, then, takes us to the final step: offering solutions to the problem. It is at this point that the theorist may become a partisan. Rousseau, Bentham, Mill, Wilson, Carr, and Waltz were all, in their own fashion, policy advocates. They offered solutions to the problems they had analyzed. Some, like Wilson, were in a position to change the world, to accommodate their diagnoses and prescriptions (and in the case of Wilson, they demonstrated how the theories were flawed); others became publicists and even propagandists, with variable influence on policy makers.

Is it possible to reconcile partisanship with scholarship? Were we to acknowledge that the selection of problems for analysis is often a moral/political/social choice, how could we go about diagnosing them in such a manner that our preferred or assumed solutions do not take precedence over high-quality diagnosis based on reliable evidence? Whatever the shortcomings of science, at least there is an explicit concern with questions of the quality of evidence. Such is seldom the case with partisan pursuits. Woodrow Wilson's championing of the concept of national self-determination as a just solution to the problem of European wars, for example, was—as Wilson himself later did acknowledge—based on an erroneous, possibly expedient estimation of how many "nations" there really existed in post–World War I Europe. Wilson's worldview affected his search for reliable data to the point of ultimately conducing to poor policy. Many other examples are readily available. The limits at which the various priorities served by partisanship conflict with the obligations demanded by the rigors of scholarship may be too quickly reached.

Is prescription a necessary result of diagnosis? Apparently not, for there is a strong tradition of creating or gaining knowledge for its own sake or, as I will argue below, for pedagogic reasons such as improving professional competence, citizenship, and broadening understanding for those whose perspectives are limited by lack of education and experience. Some exemplars? It is hard to see how, for example, Frank Russell's survey of international thought (1936), Quincy Wright's monumental study of the discipline (1955), Jim Rosenau's foray into social trends affecting states' autonomy (1990), or Fred Halliday's outline for a neo-Marxist perspective on international relations (1994: ch. 3) necessarily offer "solutions" to basically moral/political problems. Their justification for these works, and their intellectual contribution, is foremost in the domain of knowledge itself. This, because their purposes were essentially intellectual, not moral or political. They wrote, among other reasons, so as to enhance our knowledge of the field's genealogy (Russell) and conceivably also to avoid repeating the claim that everything we read is new; toward bringing order to a discipline characterized by intellectual chaos (Wright); toward identifying significant new trends and anomalies and to note the theoretical significance (Rosenau) of these; seeking to fashion analytical categories and perspectives that have not but might enhance understanding of some significant questions within the field (Halliday). Only in the very broad sense are these major theoretical efforts "for" someone or something. They are certainly not justifications for identifiable state or class interests. They are for knowledge and pedagogy, for which no one should be made to feel guilty or inadequate.[3]

It follows that if prescription is not a necessary consequence of diagnosis, then neither is partisanship in the political sense. One can be partisan toward one's theories, perspectives, and/or methodologies without taking on advocacy of a political program or a policy solution to a problem. In other words, what I question is the necessity for a connection between the theoretical diagnosis of a problem and partisanship toward any particular political order. It is easy for those who believe in such necessity to slip into the "monopoly syndrome," be it out of fear or belief that all scholarship must promote or sustain a political order—no matter how oppressive, lacking, or repugnant.

MORE SOURCES OF MISUNDERSTANDING: DEFINING THE FIELD

So far, I have discussed primarily *how* we do things in international theory. Misunderstanding also arises from *what* we do. Two practices are particularly notable: (1) the search for a general, all-encompassing theory of international relations and, related to it, (2) the failure to acknowledge the distinction between international politics and international relations.

The Search for a Grand Theory

There has been, particularly in North American circles, an abiding expectation that scholars can eventually develop an overarching, single theory of international relationships. This is the idea of a "grand theory," one of the centerpieces of the behavioral persuasion but certainly not confined to it. Such a totalizing project—similar in faith and hope, if not in form, to Marxism—still underlies the field. Yet, as I have sought to demonstrate, the normative palette of problems today is large—and growing. There are also too many significant anomalies and new trends that have to be explained. There cannot be a single, all-encompassing theory of international relations, a point I stressed more than a quarter-century ago (Holsti, 1970). Different moral discourses and problems lead to different forms of diagnosis and to different prescriptions (see Krippendorff and cf. Teune and Mlinar, Lipschutz, and Pirages, this volume). The world of international relations is multifaceted. This has been acknowledged and underlined by theorists since at least the time of E. H. Carr. Yet the presumption of a single explanatory system for these diversities continues to drive much theoretical debate, even if the resulting efforts to combine or synthesize theories encompassing diverse moral/political problems have had, indeed, rather limited results (Crawford, 1996).

The search for "the" theory of international relations creates misunderstanding and is one of the roots of the "I am right/you are wrong" intellectual posture. Efforts to explain all socially constructed "problems" through a single analytical structure or framework are bound to create misunderstanding and heated debate that could be directed more profitably to other projects and research programs. A good example of wasted energy is the almost mantralike denunciation of neorealism, and particularly of Kenneth Waltz's *Theory of International Politics* (1979), on the grounds that it does not explain a whole host of problems such as international governance, economic competition, quality-of-life issues, gender relations, among others. While even in its own terms Waltz's effort may be lacking, the author specified exactly what he wanted to explain: some big questions in the field, such as recurrence of wars and balances of power, propensity of the system to duplicate itself, inability of states to accept relative gains in security issues, and the search for autonomy in situations of interdependence. That it does not explain other problems should be irrelevant. Yet critics continue to chastise Waltz for not developing a "total" theory. This criticism assumes both its desirability and possibility. I believe that such a goal is a chimera and logically impossible. Instead of opening every article, or devoting entire books (cf. George, 1994) to denouncing neorealism, why not get on with the task of developing alternatives that explain the same phenomena better or of building theories that explain other matters well? A few analysts have used Waltz's effort as the platform from which to launch better explanations for security problems (cf. Wendt, 1992; Buzan, Jones, and Little, 1993), but criticism devoid of seminal proposals for the development of original alternatives remains a nonconstructive academic practice.

The lively enterprise of denouncing neorealism is founded on a misunderstanding of what that theory is all about. It is an attempt to explain regularities and anomalies in a circumscribed issue area or domain. This misunderstanding may also illustrate the influence of social context on scholarship. It may be no accident that the most robust critics of realism and neorealism toil in Phoenix, Canberra, Victoria, B.C., Des Moines, and London—none of which is located close to zones of long-range rivalry, periodic militarized crises, and occasional war. In contrast, such criticism rarely arises from Jerusalem, New Delhi, Belgrade, or even from Athens, where security dilemmas, profound mistrust, misperceptions, and preparations for wars are part of daily life.

These comments do not, however, absolve some Realists from bringing telling criticisms upon themselves. An analytical device that has been successful in helping to explain some big, but not all-encompassing, questions in the field can also become an ideology that is insensitive to changing historical, economic, and social conditions. In particular, it fails to acknowledge that ideas, epistemic communities, and reigning political assumptions, as often as power and power distributions, can drive international politics (cf. Holsti, 1994). Some Realists' view on the future of Europe, best summed up in Mearsheimer's (1990) famous analysis, is a good example of the employment of an analytical device without adjusting for altered conditions or ideas. Mearsheimer argues that with the end of the Cold War,

Europe will revert to classical balance of power politics, meaning that there will be chronic conflict and war. While power determinism may be a good analytical device for explaining or understanding eighteenth-century European international politics, it is of questionable utility for explaining parts of the nineteenth century and most of the period since 1945.

An important source of misunderstanding in international relations thus remains our expectation that there can be a single explanatory system encompassing international politics and international relations. There are two versions of this problem: (1) the view that there should be a single "grand" theory describing and explaining all international phenomena or (2) the view that there can be a massive synthesis of contending, even if incommensurable, "schools" of thought into a single megatheory (cf. Neufeld, 1993; and for partial fusion, Groom, 1995: 74–77). But specialization is a natural result of the identification of different moral/political problems in social life. If a field develops from concerns with different normative problems and issues, it follows that there will be proliferation of theory. Yet the myth of a "grand theory," a residue of nineteenth-century positivist hope and twentieth-century notions of progress defined in terms of science, continues to underlie and frame significant proportions of the field's debates. The quantity of books and articles that denounce various schools, perspectives, and approaches to the study of international relations, and then argue that there is another, single, proper way to do things, suggests a fundamental misunderstanding of what it is that drives theoretical work in the first place. At risk of repetition, it is the diagnosis of socially constructed problems— of which there are already several in the field, with their numbers growing.

If we wish to argue the relative merits of various schools and theories, then the place to start is not so much with their inferences as it is with their premises. This is a normative exercise. I believe that the problem of war, an activity that has cost on average more than half a million lives annually since 1945, should command our attention. Others are justified in arguing that the problem of economic inequality in the world should command similar or greater attention. There are many who can make a convincing case that international collaboration, governance, and the management of environmental problems require systematic thought. Some, persuaded that the state can no longer serve its main purposes of defense, welfare, and prosperity, wish to problematize it to try to develop a theory explaining the rise and anticipated decline or transformation of the state. Women's "silence" in almost all renderings of the field is now a problem that is drawing increased theoretical attention, and we can well expect that in an age of increasing concerns with "identity," attributes other than gender will also stake out a claim for a "problem" in an international context that requires theoretical analysis. While there may be connections between problems, it is unlikely that we will ever develop, or that we should even seek to develop, a single perspective, approach, or theory that will account for the character, sources, and dynamics of all of them. The problems of feminist scholars in fashioning a distinct theory of international politics demonstrate the difficulties involved: Having identified gender biases in the construction of analytical concepts, they have not been able to construct an alternative to any of the main theoretical schools in the field. Some day there may be a theory of feminism *and* international politics, of women *in* international relations, but a feminist theory *of* international politics/relations is not possible, because the *problématique* of the role of women in international life differs fundamentally from the *problématique* of the security of states.

International relations began as a synthetic field of diverse perspectives, methods, and theories and will continue to be so. No intellectual knockout punch will establish any single moral/political problem as exclusive, although under particular social conditions, one or more may predominate at any given time. Nor will epistemological crusades or anti-Enlightenment polemics result in a single, new metatheoretical orthodoxy. As I have often reiterated (Holsti, 1985, 1989), intellectual pluralism and large doses of incommensurability are inevitable consequences of the normative bases of our investigations.

International Politics and International Relations: Distinctions

The second aspect of *what* we do—or in this case, what we fail to do— is to state or acknowledge the differences between international politics and international relations. Realism is an explanation of the security problems that arise from time to time between states. It is no more than that. It does not claim to explain or solve other problems—be they of equity; quality of life; relations between individuals, groups, genders, or classes.

It is one of the puzzles of our field that the distinction between international politics and international relations is seldom acknowledged in theoretical discourse but is a fairly standard practice in the classroom and among textbook authors. If we examine textbooks, starting with samples from the 1930s and extend the search to today, we will note that most include chapters or sections on various forms of transnational relations and that they clearly characterize the field as one encompassing both the conflictual and cooperative aspects of relations between states and societies. Similarly, any well-rounded undergraduate program in international relations contains courses in security issues as well as in international law and organization. This is because international relations encompasses *all* forms of units, actors, and activities between societies, whereas international politics focuses on the *problématique* of war/peace/order.[4]

DIFFERENT MOTIVATIONS, DIFFERENT UNDERSTANDINGS

Yet other hindrances to understanding derive also from the proliferation of authors' motivations in theoretical writings on international relations. The diversity of purposes is already apparent in the brief characterization of what theorists do. This has revealed, for example, that some people are driven by creativity, some by curiosity, and yet others by a determination to help "fix" a problem or to change the world in fundamental ways. I have a strong impression, but no solid body of evidence to support it, that some of the most bitter debates in the field also reflect a poor understanding of implicit motivations and social roles. Instead of stating their social and/or pedagogical purposes explicitly, authors tend to fight their battles on an intellectual turf, on the plane of ideas, whereas the sources of their differences may derive from different intellectual stimuli and contending conceptions of roles (see Krippendorff's chapter, this volume).

What are these competing motivations? A nonexhaustive list would include the following: (1) pedagogy, (2) science/knowledge, (3) policy analysis, (4) policy solutions, and (5) emancipation. In this brief array, single purposes can overlap. Most diagnoses contain explicit or implicit "solutions" to problems. Pedagogy and knowledge, teaching and research, often are almost inseparable activities. And policy solutions may take the form of emancipatory programs. But sometimes theoretical enterprises in international relations take on one coloration to the virtual exclusion of others, only to be criticized for failing to make a significant contribution in another domain. Take pedagogy as an example. Presumably our function as teachers is to help make a complex world more intelligible to our students and to provide them with the theoretical and methodological tools they can use to develop their own approaches, conclusions, and generalizations. But for some critics, teachers only perpetuate their orthodoxies and create young duplicates of themselves (cf. Ashley, 1984: 230). Yet others see pedagogy in a broader light; its role is not just to carry on intellectual traditions and generate new perspectives but also to inspire good citizenship and to develop professional competence among those who someday may make policy decisions (cf. Wright, 1955: ch. 7).

The failure to recognize the plurality of motivations in pedagogy may give rise to serious misunderstandings. Teachers of future policy makers may be impatient with the metatheoretical musings of various authors because the latter do not address the problems and issues of the "real world." In contrast, theorists may dismiss as politically tainted the policy-oriented curricula of those concerned primarily with professional competence. Those whose agenda is primarily emancipatory—whether philosophically, epistemologically, or politically—may have little respect for "scientists" who emphasize, above all, such values as reliability and reproducibility of evidence. Some adepts of postmodernism prefer to reject positivism not only on epistemological grounds but essentially because they seek to get on with a new political agenda. They tend to dismiss work driven primarily by the search for knowledge, deeming it conservative, protective of the status quo, and conspiratorial in its "silencing" or "marginalization" of other voices (Ashley and Walker, 1990; cf. Krippendorff's chapter, this volume). For their part, scientists condemn those with an emancipatory agenda for playing footloose with facts, for ignoring bodies of authoritative information, for lacking an organized research agenda, and for valuing partisan aspirations above sound methodological canons. In such debates, the issue of establishing a truth for the emancipatory theorist seems less urgent, since what is more strongly desired here is to change the world rather than to understand it. Many feminists, for example, denounce Realists as purveyors of patriarchy, whereas researchers of significant anomalies in the international system counter that feminists are driven by a myopic political agenda rather than by the desiderata of reliable knowledge. Policy specialists in turn are impatient with the games metatheorists play, whereas the latter criticize technocratic "problem solvers" for their atheoretical, and above all politically inspired, work.

SOLUTIONS?

There are no easy "solutions" to these intricate "problems." Resource hindrances can be overcome, although there is hardly any evidence that by itself increased fundings can correct parochial language and reading habits. Many scholars remain nationally "captured," barely deigning to read foreign publications (cf. Strange, 1995: 290). A cursory review of citations in American journals such as *International Organization* or *International Security* suggests the existence of a fairly restricted circle of authors who apparently read little else than each other's works. On the other hand, the working conditions of scholars in most of the developing countries does not seem to improve. Of course, there are important exceptions in all countries, but the habits and problems that I outlined in *The Dividing Discipline* (Holsti, 1985) do not seem to have changed yet, over more than a decade.[5]

What, then, can we do to reduce problems of misunderstanding for the many who place precedence on the theoretical enterprise? No authoritative prescription follows neatly from the diagnosis above. No one person can play the role of a Martha Stewart in international relations: appear to fix everything neatly, and easily, within the budgetary limits of a modest household. The best one can hope for is that scholars in international relations (1) openly recognize and state their motivations, be they a dose of healthy curiosity aroused by significant trends and anomalies or loftier moral/political concerns; (2) willingly acknowledge that, consequently, there cannot be an objective "grand" theory of international relations; (3) readily admit that scholarship is endowed with different social functions; and (4) concede that what we choose to emphasize, and how we go about doing our work, will inevitably be colored by whichever of the functions is at play. A more explicit acknowledgment of our priorities and preferences in these regards may help reduce the exclusionary, denunciatory, and eliminatory efforts that characterize so many of the debates in the field today.

Is this a plea for intellectual pluralism? To the extent that we recognize the inherent power of many different types of intellectual activity and roles to shape the nature of theory, without failing to acknowledge the rigorous standards that govern scholarly obligations, it is. There are, after all, limits to abusive scholarship. The point of no return in such matters lies precisely where roles and purposes become blurred in the mind and hidden in the heart of the scholar. Policy prescription parading as science ultimately never succeeds. And scientific pursuits embedded in national biases and motivated by parochial priorities cannot attain universal recognition or acceptance. Some forms of partisanship are simply incompatible with scholarship. The best solution for such ills is an honesty of purpose and an acquired taste for straightforwardness regarding the why and the how of each of our undertakings. To acquiesce frankly that we theorize because we are morally and/ or politically concerned with a social problem can only enhance the science of our understanding and the understanding of our science. The canons of science refer not to problem selection but to problem analysis.[6] Those who place priority on emancipation should specify clearly what emancipation means and if and in what ways a redesigned field of international politics or international relations would help solve such social problems, the majority of which take root in the family, region, or national community. Requisite clarity in the explicitation of roles, purposes, and moral choices should make it all the easier to face up to the fact that international relations always has been, and will continue to be, at once an art, a science, and a philosophy. Such awareness is not cause for angst, let alone for denunciation. It is when we forget our own history that we create the greatest of all hindrances to a clear understanding.

NOTES

1. It is perhaps one of the curiosities of contemporary debates in international theory that the relevant literatures happen to be predominantly in the English language. The same comment applies to feminist perspectives on international relations. Most North American scholars typically do not read works in languages other than English and do not even know if there are important analyses written in, for example, Urdu, Korean, or Burmese. The sustained monolingualism of North American scholars remains a main blot on their pretensions of scientific or metatheoretical universalism.

2. A less generous interpretation, and one that is open to serious criticism, is the notion that all theory advances an identifiable class or political interest. This view

underlies the thinking of some postmodernist and poststructuralist critics who argue that theories of international relations are precious little more than apologias for vested interests, in particular those of the American capitalist Cold War state (cf. George, 1994). This rendering displays little familiarity with the development of international theory over the centuries. Rousseau's highly critical stance against monarchism, Woodrow Wilson's theoretical subversion of the principles of Realpolitik, and Karl Deutsch's antistatism may be *for* something, including knowledge, but they certainly did not promote conservative interests, no matter how those might be defined.

3. This discussion of what theorists do is by no means exhaustive. In addition to the activities mentioned, there are others such as definitional and taxonomic work, the empirical identification of trends, and speculation about their consequences as well as formal explanations of limited phenomena such as alliances, regional integration, and the like. As for methodological work, V. Spike Peterson (1992: 6–9) mentions deconstruction of error, such as in eliminating "falsehoods" generated by sex-biased inquiry (but why not by nation- or class-biased inquiry?); reconstruction of fact (as when incorporating women's activities and perspectives); and the reconstruction of theory, which involves a rethinking of fundamental relations among knowledge, power, and community.

4. There are some exceptions to the discussion. Rousseau, for example, viewed all forms of interaction between states and societies as mere instruments of state stratagems to deal with conflicts. Hence, trade and international law were parts of the state's armory for waging campaigns against adversaries, rather than aspects of international cooperation and collaboration. Some textbooks of the 1950s continued the tradition of failing to distinguish international politics from international relations.

5. Scholarship continues to harbor implicit and explicit national biases. A comprehensive review of the comparative foreign policy literature (Hudson, 1995) demonstrates that a vast majority of studies use the United States as their data or case study source. Of 228 bibliography items, I have found only 24 (or 10.5 percent) to be genuinely comparative or focused explicitly on a country other than the United States. Those lacking in theoretically inspired foreign policy studies include France, Germany, and England, to say nothing of Nigeria, India, and Brazil. The lack of citation by way of inclusion in a comprehensive bibliography does not, of course, indicate that no such studies exist. Seemingly, however, comparative foreign policy, a subfield of international relations that aspires to universal and comparative status, utilizes only a single country out of more than a possible 185 as the predominant empirical basis for its "comparative" generalizations.

6. A succinct analysis of the science/value debate can be found in Michael Nicholson (1996), esp. ch. 9.

REFERENCES

Ashley, R. K. (1984). The Poverty of Neorealism. *International Organization* 38: 226–87.

Ashley, R. K., and R.B.J. Walker (1990). Reading Dissidence/Writing the Discipline: Crisis and the Question of Sovereignty in International Relations. *International Studies Quarterly* 34: 367–416.

Bajpai, K. (1995). Introduction: International Theory, International Society, Regional Politics, and Foreign Policy. Pp. 11–42 in K. Bajpai and H. Shukul (eds.), *Interpreting World Politics: Essays for A. P. Rana*. New Delhi: Sage Publications.

Brecher, M. (1995). Reflections on a Life in Academe. *International Studies Notes* 20: 1–8.

Buzan, Barry, Charles Jones, and Richard Little (1993). *The Logic of Anarchy: Neorealism to Structural Realism*. New York: Columbia University Press.

Cox, R. (1986) Social Forces, States and World Orders: Beyond International Relations Theory. Pp. 204–54 in Robert Keohane (ed.), *Neorealism and Its Critics*. New York: Columbia University Press.

Crawford, R. (1996). *Regime Theory in the Post–Cold War World: Rethinking Neoliberal Approaches to International Relations*. Aldershot, U.K.: Dartmouth.

Ferguson, Y., and R. W. Mansbach (1988). *The Elusive Quest*. Columbia: University of South Carolina Press.

George, J. (1994). *Discourses of Global Politics: A Critical (Re)Introduction to International Relations*. Boulder, CO: Lynne Rienner.

Groom, A.J.R. (1995). International Relations: Anglo-American Aspects—A Study in Parochialism. Pp. 45–89 in K. Bajpai and H. Shukul (eds.), *Interpreting World Politics: Essays for A. P. Rana*. New Delhi: Sage Publications.

Halliday, F. (1994). *Rethinking International Relations*. Vancouver: University of British Columbia Press.

Hollis, M., and S. Smith (1991). *Explaining and Understanding International Relations*. Oxford: Clarendon Press.

Holsti, K. (1970). Retreat from Utopia: International Relations Theory, 1945–1970. *Canadian Journal of Political Science* 4: 165–77.

Holsti, K. (1985). *The Dividing Discipline: Hegemony and Diversity in International Theory*. London: Allen & Unwin.

Holsti, K. (1989). Mirror, Mirror on the Wall, Which Are the Fairest Theories of All? *International Studies Quarterly* 33: 255–63.

Holsti, K. (1994). The Post–Cold War "Settlement" in Comparative Perspective. Pp. 37–70 in D. Stuart and S. Szabo (eds.), *Discord and Collaboration in a New Europe: Essays in Honor of Arnold Wolfers*. Washington, D.C: Paul H. Nitze School of Advanced International Studies, Johns Hopkins University.

Hudson, V., with C. Vore (1995). Foreign Policy Analysis Yesterday, Today and Tomorrow. *Mershon International Studies Review* 39 (supp. 2):209–38.

Kaplan, M. (1957). *System and Process in International Politics*. New York: Wiley.

Lapid, J. (1989). The Third Debate: On the Prospects of International Theory in a Post-Positivist Era. *International Studies Quarterly* 33: 235–54.

Mearsheimer, J. (1990). Back to the Future: Instability in Europe after the Cold War. *International Security* 15: 5–56.

Neufeld, M. (1993). Reflexivity and International Relations Theory. *Millennium: Journal of International Studies* 22: 53–76.

Nicholson, M. (1996). *Causes and Consequences in International Relations: A Conceptual Study*. London: Pinter.

Peterson, V. (1992). *Gendered States: Feminist (Re)Visions of International Relations Theory*. Boulder, CO: Lynne Rienner.

Rosenau, J. N. (1990). *Turbulence in World Politics: A Theory of Change and Continuity*. Princeton, NJ: Princeton University Press.

Russell, F. M. (1936). *Theories of International Relations*. New York: Appleton-Century.

Strange, S. (1995). ISA as a Microcosm. *International Studies Quarterly* 39: 289–95.

Waltz, K. (1959). *Man, the State, and War*. New York: Columbia University Press.

Waltz, K. (1979). *Theory of International Politics*. Reading, MA: Addison-Wesley.

Wendt, A. E. (1992). Anarchy Is What States Make of It: The Social Construction of Power Politics. *International Organization* 46: 351–425.

Wright, Q. (1955). *The Study of International Relations*. New York: Appleton-Century-Crofts.

CHAPTER 3

The Theory and Practice of Power in International Relations: Past and Future

BARRY BUZAN

INTRODUCTION

In 1989, Stoll and Ward argued: "[W]e believe that the majority of the field would support the assertion that power is the most central concept in world politics" (p. 1). Their choice of the term "world politics" is unfortunate, because for those who understand power as that which identifies the political, their statement becomes circular. More interesting is whether the statement was, and is, true for the multidisciplinary field of international relations (IR). To put the question in this form may simply be to ask whether international relations is dominated generally by politics and specifically by the "power politics" school of thought known as Realism. But it may also contain a wider question that crosses disciplinary boundaries. Not everyone thinks that power is confined to the political, and it is by no means impossible that a truly multidisciplinary international relations could still be dominated by the concept of power (Guzzini, 1994: ch. 2).

There is little question that power has dominated thinking about international relations for much of the period since World War II. Most of the academic study of international relations is still located within departments of political science, and Realism's status as the orthodoxy of the field has been confirmed by the numerous attempts to challenge it. But since the 1970s, economic factors have played an increasing role in thinking about international relations and the world system. In this development, theoretical thinking within the field is simply following the agenda set by current events. Arguably, this has always been the case. After World War I, IR was concerned with peace; after World War II, it was concerned with security; and after World War III (the Cold War), it is responding to the increasing role of international economic structures and actors. If this is seen as down-grading the state—traditional repository of power in IR thinking—then it opens up the possibility that the concept of power will decline in importance in thinking about IR. If the real world is moving away from a Westphalian system of power-balancing states toward an international political economy of interdependence, then hard questions about core concepts will have to be asked. Either power will decline in relevance along with its main carrier, the state, or it will have to take on a reformulated meaning in order to keep up with the changing character of the real world. It is obvious from the contemporary literature that many people in the field think that some such transformation is under way. There are of course some diehard Realists who still believe that, as Gray (1994: 2) puts it, "[i]f there is a golden rule in world politics it is to the effect that bad times return," and for them the centrality of power in its traditional meaning has not changed.

At this point the astute reader will already be asking what is meant by "power," for even these opening remarks begin to hinge on the issue of definition. Here we are at the nub of why I have been asked (and have agreed) to write this chapter. The concept of power is notorious for com-bining two qualities: (1) a sustained centrality in nearly all discussions about human relations, whether they be relations between genders, classes, gangs, firms, nations, or states; and (2) a conceptual slipperyness and multidimen-sionality that makes agreed definitions difficult and that has largely defeated attempts at measurement. If the centrality of the concept of power to so much discourse makes it stimulating and attractive, the slipperyness makes it frustrating and annoying. Whether these two qualities are distinct, or somehow mutually reinforcing, is difficult to say. What can be observed is that the term *power* is used indiscriminately, not only in everyday prose and conversation but also in much academic analysis. Sometimes it expresses cause, sometimes effect. Sometimes it is associated narrowly with relation-ships of coercion, and sometimes it is used more broadly as a synonym for influence and authority. We speak easily of many different types of power—military, political, economic, ideological, physical, sexual, social—without pausing to consider what, if anything, connects all of these into a meaningful single concept.

For those academics of a positivist scientific disposition, the centrality of power stands as a challenge to clean up and harden its usage. The Holy Grail of this quest is to find a way of measuring power. To cage power in this way offers the prospect of following economics in applying the huge (and powerful) arsenal of quantitative methods to a large swath of human relations. If power could be treated like money, as a measurable and fungible quality, then social science would be transformed. Among other things, it would enable various theories about power to be put to the test—and per-haps rejected (Vasquez, 1983; de Mesquita and Lalman, 1989).

I do not propose to tackle the problem of measurement, and I should confess that I am among the skeptics as to whether it can be solved. In the next section I will review the problems in defining power. The third section focuses on the relationship between debates about power and developments in the real world of international relations, arguing that power is substantially shaped by social context. And section four uses this approach to think ahead about the future(s) of power in IR.

AMBIGUITIES IN THE DEFINITION OF POWER

Attempts to think systematically about power in a social context seem inevitably to lead down several distinct channels. It is hardly possible to read anything on the subject without encountering this fragmenting typology, although it does not yet come with an accepted set of labels. We will look first at four different ways of conceptualizing what power is and where it is located (attributive, relational, control, structural), then at the debate as to whether power should be treated as a single, aggregated phenomenon or as a multiple, disaggregated one.

The simplest meaning of power derives from the natural sciences and refers to the capability of units to perform specified tasks as a result of the attributes they possess. I call this type of power *attributive*. Given their attributes, states or other units either can or cannot do certain things, like building nuclear weapons or establishing a stable currency. This is the same type of power as one refers to when talking about the horsepower of engines or the lifting power of rockets. It can come in many forms: military, ideological, economic, technological, organizational, informational. The relevance of these forms depends on the nature of relations and rivalries in the international system. Nye (1996), for example, argues that control over information is now the key to world power. For most of this century, the key to power has been industrial capability and its military offshoots. In the international political system, as in engineering, attributive power is non-zero-sum. It is open-ended, in that all units can increase (or decrease) their levels of it through such capability-expanding activities as technological development, industrialization, administrative efficiency, and collective identity. In theory, attributive power should be objectively measurable. The fact that it has many forms and can and does change markedly and rapidly in both quantity and quality means that power, and its implications for international relations, is continuously subject to significant change. Think, for example, of the way in which the absolute power of states both to inflict damage on each other and to absorb each other's exports has increased over the last 150 years regardless of their relative power. Because it is both diverse and changeable, the real significance of attributive power is always under debate.

But neither classical nor neo-Realists see power as primarily attributive. Instead, they prefer to see it in relative terms as wholly positional and zero-sum, referring only to the pattern of distribution of power among the units in the system. This understanding of power is often referred to as *relational*. Relational power takes no cognizance of the open-ended character of attributive power except inasmuch as this affects the zero-sum distribution of power among units. If all units increased their attributive power in the same proportion, there would be no change in the relational power ranking among them even though their absolute capabilities might have increased enormously. The bipolar distributional structure after World War II would have existed regardless of nuclear weapons but the existence of those weapons, made a huge difference to the absolute capabilities of the two superpowers to inflict damage on each other and the rest of the world. Relational power is the idea that underlies most thinking about balance of power and hegemony in international relations. Relational power is what classifies states as superpowers, great powers, middle powers, or small powers. It is also what identifies hegemons. Some count seventeenth-century Holland as a hegemonic power even though its level of attributive power was tiny compared with a contemporary hegemon such as the United States.

But both attributive and relational power are very difficult to measure or evaluate. One problem is that they are highly subject to perceptual variables. Declining powers may be living on their reputations or, conversely, may have declined less than pessimists say. Consequently, social "facts" may be more important than real ones in determining outcomes: The perceived power of a state, therefore its ability to determine outcomes, may exceed (or understate) its real capabilities. Another problem is posed by the difference between (1) latent or potential power and (2) actual power. How is one to compare the power of a highly mobilized state (like, say, Japan or Germany circa 1940) with one that is not mobilized but clearly has great potential to do so (such as the United States in 1940)? Similar to this are problems posed by distance and will. Does power diminish, and therefore become less effective, over distance? Is will part of power, and how does one deal with actors that possess strong capabilities but are hesitant about using them as policy instruments? The true weight of the various elements of power is also continuously contested. Has military power declined in significance as global markets and interdependence have spread? Is Nye correct to say that information is now the key to world power? At the end of the day, only war can give a final answer to many of these questions about power.

But war presupposes hostility, which raises another type of difficulty than mere assessment in thinking about power as a cause. Clearly not all international relations are hostile. Does power theory only explain relationships of competition or hostility? It seems clear that the amity/enmity factor has a significant effect on the logic of power (Guzzini, 1994: ch. 4). Friendly states do not fear each other's military capability, and therefore a power analysis based purely on capability will miss out on a crucial element. Security interdependence can as easily be based on amity, as it is in Western Europe and ASEAN (Association of Southeast Asian Nations), as it can on enmity, as during the Cold War (Buzan, 1991: 189–90, 218–19). There is also the more philosophical question of whether the exercise of power has to be intentional or whether the logic of power works abstractly, and thus apart from the motives of actors (Guzzini, 1994: ch. 6).

In principle, attributive and relational power could be used as the basis for causal hypotheses about how units within the international system do and will relate to each other. Power is interesting because it is expected to determine outcomes. There would be little theoretical reason to have the concept if it did not work in this way. Possession of power, whether attributive or relative, is supposed to give a unit the ability to determine, or at least to shape, the behavior of others and the ability to prevent others from determining or shaping its behavior against its will.

Belief in the causal role of power, merged with frustration at the difficulty of measuring attributive and relational power, has led some analysts to adopt a third understanding, often called *control power* (or sometimes "decisional"; see Caporaso and Haggard, 1989: 103). Control power focuses on the ability of one actor to get another to do something that it would not otherwise do. It approaches the problem retrospectively, in terms of outcomes. In other words, if actor A determined actor B's behavior, then A must have had more power than B. Using control power has its attractions in specific case studies. It does get around the problem of the apparently multifarious nature of power as a lever on behavior ranging from forceful coercion, through the power of economic and status incentives, to the power of ideas. Each case can be looked at in terms of the particular configuration of power(s) that determined behavior. But as an understanding of the concept, control power creates the widely recognized difficulty of a circular definition (where the cause is defined in terms of its effect). Power can only be known when its effects have been seen and only identified by working backward from outcome to causes. Having no discernable reality other than its effects, control power cannot be used as a basis for positivist scientific theory, which requires that causes be identified in advance of effects (Keohane, 1984: 18–22).

Attributive, relational, and control power are all directly focused on the ability of one actor to change the behavior of another. But if power is seen as the ability to shape or change the behavior of actors, then there is an alternative approach available: *structural* power. Structural power locates the ability to influence behavior not in the capabilities of other actors but in the nature of the systems in which actors are embedded. Waltz (1979), for example, has famously argued that political structures (which he sees in terms of the organizing principles of the system and the distribution of capabilities, i.e., anarchy and polarity) shape and shove the behavior of the states within them. The rather social Darwinist logic goes that if states in an international anarchy fail to pursue self-help and balance-of-power strategies, they risk elimination from the system. Socialization and competition within system structure encourage states to copy the features of the most successful among them and to react against any attempt by one power to dominate the whole system. Marxists, themselves no strangers to arguments about power, offer a structural approach focusing on one's location in the class system generated by the prevailing mode of finance and production. For them, the structure is capitalism. For liberals, the market is the essential structure that shapes and constrains the behavior of the units operating within it. Contemporary debates about the "power of the markets" in relation to exchange rates capture nicely the sense that a lot of power is located above the state, in structures that are not obviously under anyone's conscious control. Indeed, all of these theories share the idea that very significant amounts of power can be located above the unit level, in the arrangements of the system that contains the units and structures the ways in which they relate to each other. By definition, structural power can work apart from the motives or intentions of actors. It is not usually thought of in attributive terms, but Waltz counts the pattern of distribution in relational power (polarity) as a level of system structure. Anarchy, capitalism, market, and class are ordering principles of the system whose power lies in their ability to shape the behavior of the units in the system. And some postmodernists are beginning to argue (Waever, 1994) that discourse can also be seen as a behavior shaping structure (cf. the notion of "languaging" in Krippendorff, this volume).

Unfortunately, within the discourse of international relations the word *structure* is used almost as loosely as is *power*. One consequence of this abuse is to blur the distinction between structural power in the meaning just defined and power analysis at the unit level. Susan Strange (1988, 1994) is an exemplar of this muddying, with her idea of "structural power." By "structural power" she means the ability of some actors to manipulate and constrain the behavior of other actors in the system by determining what is and is not on the political agenda and by what rules (or in what forums) decisions get made. In the present scheme, this would be a version of control power. She sees "structural power" to be operating in four main system "structures": security, production, finance, and knowledge (which are not structures but sectors of activity). "Structural power" in this sense is not about the power of structures; it is about the power of actors within structures. What Strange and her followers are trying to do is to identify different ways, or levels, in which power can be exercised by actors. The most superficial is when one actor changes the behavior of another within a defined set of rules (e.g., A chases B out of the slave trade). More subtle, and deeper, is the "structural power" act of setting the agenda and the rules (i.e., A gets the slave trade declared illegal). Deepest of all is the ability to determine the basic epistemological frameworks and belief systems that shape how issues are conceived and what is and is not conceived of as problematic (A founds an equalitarian view of human rights that makes slavery seem morally wrong) (Strange, 1994: 8–10).

This type of approach raises an entirely different agenda, not about where power is located but about how to categorize and classify the many qualities that power seems to possess: the capacity to coerce, the capacity to manipulate, the capacity to persuade, and so forth. These are important issues, perhaps most obviously because coercive power is likely to be seen in a quite different normative light from the power to persuade and because some of the more subtle forms of power may not be noticed by those on whom they operate.

By highlighting the many faces of power, this approach points toward the underlying question as to whether power is a single, aggregated phenomenon, applicable across all sectors of behavior, or a multiple, disaggregated one, in which each sector has its own distinctive forms of power (i.e., political, military, economic, etc.). The aggregated view holds out the possibility of relatively simple power theory and is advocated most strongly by those Realists who want to emulate in the political sector the positivist theory achievements of economics (Morgenthau, 1978: 5; Waltz, 1979; Guzzini, 1994: ch. 4). In order to sustain the utility of power, those who opt for the aggregated view have to assume that power, like money, is broadly fungible.

Strange's approach suggests strongly that power can and should be disaggregated into separate spheres. This threatens to create a much more complex theoretical world, breaking the debate into potentially numberless subsets: oil power, production power, financial power, knowledge power, water power, food power, football power, and so forth. But it does solve a lot of problems if power turns out to have only limited fungibility—for example, if classical military power turns out to have little impact on economic or environmental issues. As I have argued elsewhere, there is no theoretically convincing case for aggregating power—and several good reasons for disaggregating it (Buzan, Jones, and Little, 1993: 51–65). Capabilities do not cluster evenly across sectors, and there is no clearer illustration of the limitations of aggregating power than the paralysis that it produces in contemporary discussions about ranking powers. Is Japan a great power? Well, yes and no. A strictly aggregating approach would force one to say no, therefore, to miss out a player that has huge capability and clout in some area(s) of international relations.

However much one might disapprove of her choice of terms, Strange is by no means alone in her move to disaggregate power. E. H. Carr (1946: ch. 8) divided it into military power, economic power, and power over opinion. Even Waltz (1979: 131) goes part way down the path of disaggregation when he says that powers rank "according to how they score on *all* of the following items: size of population and territory, resource endowment, economic capability, military strength, political stability and competence." But he insists on aggregating all of these into a single package, an approach followed by many of those who have tried to construct objective measures for power (Stoll and Ward, 1989: chs. 2–5). Michael Mann (1986: ch. 1) is perhaps the most systematic and elaborate of the disaggregators; his scheme shares many of the points made by Strange, as well as incorporating the traditional views. Mann notes four distinct "sources" of social power: ideological, economic, military, and political (covering some of the same ground as attributive power but overlapping with Strange's system "structures," and my own approach, in looking at power in terms of sectors). He divides social power into "distributive" (encompassing what I have here called relational and control power, i.e., zero-sum) and "collective" (the power of cooperation against third parties or nature—an aspect not so far discussed and notably absent from realist thinking about power; but more on this later). To this, Mann adds two contrasting pairs of forms of power:

- "intensive" (in the form of tight command and high commitment such as found in military organizations) versus "extensive" (in the form of a loose set of rules prevailing over a wide area, as in trading systems); and
- "authoritative" (meaning, willed by groups or institutions) versus "diffused" (covering much of the meaning of what I have here called structural power but also including some of what Strange is getting at with the idea that power can be exercised at different social depths, i.e., embodied, institutionalized, unquestioned, and uncommanded).

Mann's scheme is intended for a large-scale analysis in the mode of historical sociology and is appropriately nuanced and subtle. It pays for this with a complexity that would probably render it inoperable for the purposes of those trying to found a positivist science of power similar to that in economics.

To sum up, the academic debates about power seem to fall into two pairs of debates. The first of these can be seen as part of the levels of analysis debate that permeates much other thinking in international relations (Buzan, 1995; Onuf, 1995). Here the question is whether one focuses on power at the unit level (whether attribute, relational, or control) or at the system level (structural power, *not* in Strange's sense). These two positions are not, for the most part, mutually exclusive. One can use both.

The second debate is not so easy to characterize, but in some ways it is about academic disciplines (or in my language, sectors of analysis). It also tends to be more zero-sum in demanding that one choose between the alternative positions. Aggregators, for the most part, want to operate within the single discipline/sector of politics: Waltz (1979: 79) and Morgenthau (1978: 5) make it very clear that they are constructing single-sector political theories. Whether they do so for the sake of simplicity or because they conceive of politics as some kind of master sector is less clear. Aggregators are often associated with positivist-leaning theoretical projects that are attempting to marry the methodologies of the natural sciences with the insights of Realist theory. Disaggregators tend to see the study of IR in more multidisciplinary, multisectoral terms. Because they prefer to look at a wider range of dynamics (political, military, economic, societal, environmental), they see more forms and types of power and have much greater difficulty aggregating what they see into meaningful clusters. Perforce, they are less likely to be seeking overarching theories. They may focus more on historicist or constructivist types of explanation, or if they are in the positivist tradition, they will be seeking more narrowly based measures and theories of power.

As far as I can see, there is no significant interaction between these two pairs of debates. Both aggregators and disaggregators operate at both the unit and the system levels. Since our focus here is on the past and future of power in IR, the key question is whether and how these different approaches to power can be seen as responses to developments in the international system. If, like so much else in IR theory, they are responses to developments in the real world, then that connection might give us some handles on how the debate about power will unfold in the future.

THE DEBATE ABOUT POWER AND THE NATURE OF PREVAILING INTERNATIONAL RELATIONS: A LINK?

Is there a connection between the general character of relations prevalent within the international system and the understanding of power that runs in parallel with it? Hans Morgenthau (1978: 9) clearly thought that there was:

[T]he kind of interest determining political action in a particular period of history depends upon the political and cultural context within which foreign policy is formulated. . . . The same observations apply to the concept of power. Its content and the manner of its use are determined by the political and cultural environment.

Others, including de Wilde (1994: 166), have made similar arguments:

Means of power are culture-bound and situation-bound; they change. The nature of power may have an absolute value at a high level of abstraction (in philosophy), but as soon as one descends to lower levels it becomes a variable. In practice power coincides with the possession or the presence of concrete means needed to dominate within a specific culture or to handle a specific situation. Phrased differently: power is a derivative of specific human skills, of resources that are instrumental to these skills, and of their cultural appreciation by a given population.

If the content of power is determined by its social context, then a number of consequences follow. First is that the attempt to define or pin down power can only succeed, if at all, at some very high level of philosophical generalization. The closer one gets to practical affairs, the more fluid and slippery the concept will become. Second, and following on from this, the project to make a positivist political science out of power would seem to be doomed to failure or at least able to succeed only within specific sets of rather tightly defined, and presumably short-term, social conditions. Third, it would seem to place the disaggregators, with their inherent flexibility of view, in a stronger position than the aggregators. The pursuit of aggregated power rather presupposes that there is substantial continuity in the content of power. Fourth, if social context determines power, and social context is itself a variable, then we should expect debates about power to be a permanent feature of human society. Some might want to see this as a constructivist view of power—that in some senses the debate is not just about power but itself contributes to the construction of power. In an extreme constructivist view, the discourse itself becomes what power is.

This line of thinking raises the rather immense question of whether the relationship between the conceptualization of power, on the one hand, and the nature of the social context, on the other, is systematic. Do given types of social context generate distinctive conceptualizations of power? Merely to pose such a question raises the theoretical stakes considerably. As if understanding power was not difficult enough in itself, we now have to have a systematic taxonomy of social systems against which to compare it! No such thing (or at least no consensus on it) is on offer, and yet the idea that social context provides much of the content of power remains alluring. One can seek some refuge on this front in a historicist account.

It is perhaps no accident that extreme forms of power politics, virtually marrying the state and power (as in the German *Machtschule*) rose up during the nineteenth century at a time when the making of the modern national state was the defining political event of the time. It is of course also true that economic liberalism emerged during this period and made great strides toward the construction of a global market. These two developments might have been at odds—but they were not, because both political and economic elites were committed to building up the state (Polanyi, 1957; Helleiner, 1995). And as Ole Waever (1997) points out, it is also no accident that this phase of "power politics" thinking is generally left out when Realists invoke the long historical pedigree of their theory—whereby one leaps back from Morgenthau to Machiavelli, somehow passing over the contributions of von Treitschke and Hegel.

Similarly, it is perhaps no accident that, in the aftermath of the catastrophe of World War I, *Machtschule* thinking was rejected in favor of a version of Mann's *collective* power. We remember this (or in some cases, forget this) as the foundational idealism, which gave rise to international relations as a distinctive subject during the interwar years. Since the naked pursuit of individual state power had proved so costly and destructive to the European powers, it was entirely logical that they should attempt an exercise in collective power—the League of Nations and collective security—in a bid to block a recurrence of state power rivalries leading to all-out war. An attempt to restore the global market during the 1920s was part of this process. That this bid failed doesn't matter for the point being made here, which is that the social context coming out of World War I did shape the discourse about power during the following two decades. For a time, most academics and some practitioners were more focused on how to tame power through collective security than they were on the game of power competition among the leading states.

This story now moves onto ground familiar to everyone who has studied international relations. The failure of collective power during the 1930s led to World War II, which generated a new social context. This failure might have turned the focus toward structural power in the international economy, but the political effects of the economic collapse were so overwhelming that this did not happen. Instead, the failure of collective power pushed the pendulum right back toward *Machtpolitik*, but not all the way back. Thus was born what we think of as "classical" Realism: Carr, Morgenthau, Herz, Wight, Kissinger, Bull, and others. This was "power politics" to be sure, and that tendency was reinforced by the onset of the Cold War, which within a couple of years of the 1945 ceasefire had reconstructed international politics around a fierce new ideological and power rivalry. But it was not pure Realpolitik. Classical realism retained the lessons learned from World War I about the dangers of an unrestrained pursuit of power. It was deeply conscious of the security dilemma and of the need to treat the struggle for power as an adaptive, not just as a conflictual, process. Despite its use of the language of power, classical realism was in many ways more centered around the pursuit of security than that of power (Buzan, 1996).

The social context of power during the Cold War was marked by two increasingly strongly contrasting lines of development. On the one hand was the superpower rivalry. This constructed power along the lines of traditional Westphalian anarchy. The focus was firmly on zero-sum power rivalries between the major states. Although the Cold War started with a broad-spectrum sense of security—a sense that the confrontation was not just political and military but also social and economic—the growing arms competition quite quickly narrowed the focus to the military sector. And the brief postwar attempt to construct a global collective power framework in the United Nation was pushed to the margins. Collective power appeared only in the rival alliance systems that the two superpowers built up around themselves. The Cold War emphasized attributive power—in the narrow form of evolving nuclear weapons, the long-range delivery systems for them, and through the possible means of intercepting them. It emphasized relational power—in the specific form of who might win a war in Europe, and in the general form of which camp's system of political economy and society would determine the future of industrial society (provided that the rivalry between them did not destroy it for both). Relational power was the key to this struggle at the unit level, in the balance between the two sides; and that enabled it to acquire system structural standing in Waltz's (1979) neo-Realist theory, expressed as the degree of system polarity. In this starkly simple context of highly focused all-out rivalry, with two competing systems stacked up against each other head-to-head, it made reasonable sense to view power in aggregated terms.

But the Cold War was not the only "social context" in play during this period. From quite early on, there was the rapid growth of a liberal international economic order (LIEO) centered on the Western bloc but penetrating into much of the Third World. In its early—Bretton Woods—form, this LIEO was, like its interwar and nineteenth-century predecessors, closely wedded to the state. Although the state project was a different one (see Lipschutz, this volume), reflecting the advance of social democracy, it still meant that the economic project was not fundamentally out of line with the political one. Bretton Woods was based on what Ruggie (1982) has called "embedded liberalism." It involved a package of freeing up trade and stabilizing exchange rates, building a welfare state to deal with the effects of trade deregulation, and mounting tight regulation of finance in order to protect the welfare state and exchange rates against the interest of finance capital.

But from the early 1970s onward, the Bretton Woods package began to break down, and along with it the link between state power and the economic liberalization project. Financial liberalization, led by the United Kingdom and the United States, steadily undermined both the welfare state and exchange rate stability. By the 1990s, the welfare state was under full-scale assault in most countries, and unstable floating exchange rates were the norm. Before the end of the Cold War, this process was well advanced toward a social context in which the nature of power in Cold War terms was becoming increasingly divorced from the nature of power in the LIEO. The post–Bretton Woods liberalization project was not linked to the state in any strong way, although financial deregulation empowered banks and transnational corporations (TNCs) against the state and empowered markets (especially financial markets) against both. This move opened up a new angle on power that had increasingly little to do with the perspective and pursuit generated by the Cold War.

In the brave new LIEO, the economic sector was substantially liberated from the political one, becoming free to generate its own logic of power. This logic was neither state based nor Westphalian. It was not (necessarily) zero-sum. States still played in this game, but so did banks, firms, and global markets (see Teune and Mlinar, also Mansbach, in this volume). Collective power became extremely important in maintaining the rules on which the functioning of the LIEO depended. Relative power was by no means dead. Interdependence put great constraints on what actors could and couldn't do. But as even the leading neoliberals of the day clearly acknowledged, asymmetries of interdependence were a source of power (Keohane and Nye, 1977). Yet relative power was not, as in the Cold War, the main focus. Instead, the LIEO raised structural power—and also, attributive power—to a new central importance. Attributive power was focused on the role of the hegemonic leader(s) in the LIEO. The question was whether any state, or group of states, had the capability to underpin the LIEO by way of providing a core currency, a security framework, support for the rules and institutions, and acting as lender of last resort. Some thought that without such a leader, the LIEO would be unstable. Structural power became important because of the increased independence of the markets in relation to states. With all states embedded in a hugely complex system of global markets, structural power had two qualities. First was the power of markets against states (most visible in assaults on currencies and through rising unemployment in the old industrial states). Second was the risk that crises within the market system would inflict a general catastrophe on the whole LIEO. With states and firms having adapted themselves to operate in a global economy, the prospect of a major collapse of credit, or shutdown of trade, left all the players exposed. In this situation, Strange's questions about the different depths of power, and who exercised them, became extremely relevant.

Even before the end of the Cold War, the growing divorce between these two social contexts of power was causing confusion. Neorealism continued to project a Westphalian conception, in which power was state centered and aggregated. But neoliberalism, and even more so various forms of globalization (see Zartman, also Pirages, in this volume), were busily disaggregating power into many different types wielded by many different sorts of actors in many different situations. In the world of international political economy, it simply was not possible to deal with power other than in disaggregated form. Nowhere was this confusion more apparent than in attempts to think about system structure. The collapse of the Soviet Union forced a reassessment of the bipolar structure model. Strict neo-Realists, still locked into aggregated power, could at most conclude that the system had become unipolar, with at best a distant prospect that a burgeoning China might constitute another pole of power in the middle-term future. But from an international political economy (IPE) perspective, such a conclusion seemed to confuse matters rather more than it clarified them. In military terms (though not in nuclear ones) and up to a point in terms of political leadership, the post–Cold War international system was unipolar. But in economic terms, it was at least tripolar. Hard questions had to be asked about the political weight of peculiar actors such as Japan and the European Union (EU) in a world in which military power no longer seemed so important in the overall game of international relations. And even harder questions had to be asked about the relevance of polarity in a system where structural power was rising in importance compared with the power of units of whatever type. Given the huge downgrading in the salience of military power triggered by Mikhail Gorbachev's transformation of the Soviet Union, the IPE approach to power seemed to be in the driving seat for the foreseeable future.

THE FUTURE(S) OF POWER

If, as argued above, it is true that the theory and practice of power depend on the prevailing social context, then to think ahead about them one needs to think about the nature of that social context and how it relates to those that have come before. The account just given suggests, if not anything so fully blown as a learning process, at least a discernible pattern of action-outcome-reaction. The snag here is, of course, that we cannot predict the character of the new social context with any accuracy. What the post–Cold War world is like and how it will unfold are themselves contested. As Ayoob (1995: 116) notes with characteristic pithiness: "There is no firm consensus among scholars, analysts and statesmen on what the post–Cold War world will ultimately look like in terms of the distribution of the various dimensions of power—political, military and economic—among the major claimants to the status of great power. . . . Neither is there a consensus on the interaction among these various dimensions of power and their fungibility." Broadly speaking, the images of this present and future world fall into three general schemes: on one extreme, the "hard Realist"; on the other, the "liberal transformational"; and lying between them, the "two-worlds" view.

The hard Realist view, in line with Gray's dictum cited above that "bad times return," supposes that nothing fundamental has changed in the international system and that the future will be business as usual on much the same (Realist) terms as the past. This means that power struggles, and the willingness to deploy, and possibly to use, force in pursuit of them, are a constant feature of the human condition, even if fear of consequences makes all-out war among the great powers highly unlikely. In this view, the downgrading of the state and of military power must be seen as reflecting temporary conditions of the post–Cold War transition. Soon the post–Cold War euphoria will be overwhelmed by bad times (some think that Somalia and Bosnia have already accomplished this), as was the case not long after both world wars. If this view is correct, then one would expect a return to aggregated relational modes as the dominant way of thinking about power wherein cooperative power would feature only in the form of alliances. But for such a shift to take place, this would require both a major breakdown, or winding down, of the LIEO and the rise of a new great power rivalry. Those who follow Huntington's (1993) idea of a "clash of civilizations" might be able to imagine as plausible such a scenario even if, to me, that likelihood seems remote.

At the other extreme, the liberal transformational view supposes that the foundations of the international system are shifting (or have shifted) away from the territorial state toward a global transnational division of labor. The supposition is that the Westphalian system is being downgraded, or overtaken, by a more complex and more ordered form of international society. The elements of this view are mostly found in international political economy (Stopford and Strange, 1991; Zacher, 1992; Ruggie, 1993; Strange, 1994; Cerny, 1995). This picture displays an international system with many different sorts of actors in play (states, firms, nations, intergovernmental organizations [IGOs], international nongovernmental organizations [INGOs], criminal mafias) and entertaining many different types of relationship. This scenario, in effect, sees the end of the Cold War as largely removing the Westphalian aspect of power from the scene and replacing it with the LIEO agenda of power. The implication of such a view is that the world would be much more dominated by a complex web of networks, regimes, institutions, and structures and much less by units of any sort than it is now. Units would be diverse, and their relations complex and multilayered. Power would continue to explain some, possibly many, relations among them, with cooperative power being at least as prominent as the various forms of rival power. In Carr's terms, economic power and power over opinion would play larger roles than military power. However, structural power arising from networks of complex social systems would probably dominate all. Nobody thinks that this world is with us yet, but many see it as lying not too far over the horizon.

Perhaps the least clear thing about this scenario is its level of stability/ instability. Those eager to escape from the centuries-old tyrannies of sovereignty, territoriality, and war might hope for some kind of liberal-democratic peace to follow. There is a powerful logic in market-dominated relations that pushes toward cooperative power (de Wilde, 1991: 23–25). But those sensitive to the fragility of order note that in liberalized systems authority per se tends to evaporate (Strange, 1994: 15), with the markets hollowing out the ability of the state to maintain political and social order but not replacing the state with anything else. As has been argued elsewhere (Buzan and Segal, 1996), liberalization makes even great powers go "lite," thereby undermining both their ability and their interest in maintaining global order. Not all of the actors in this scenario are even potentially benign, for the dark side of liberal pluralism is that it makes room for criminal organizations as major players in the international political economy. Among other things, this points to the possibility that a highly liberalized international system would not be any sort of peaceful utopia. One of the few authors to try to think this through (Cerny, 1995: 50–53) suggests that the disaggregation, diffusion, and complexity of power in a "plurilateral" world would tend to constrain system-wide conflicts but might well exacerbate a whole range of more localized disputes (see Teune and Mlinar, this volume).

In between the extremes of the hard Realist and transformational views of the future lies the two-worlds view (Goldgeier and McFaul, 1992; Singer and Wildavsky, 1993; or, in an earlier and more implicit version, Keohane and Nye, 1977). This view supposes that a partial transformation of the international system has taken place. Rather than being a single politico-strategic space, with a single set of rules of the game, the international system has divided into two worlds. One world (call it the "zone of peace") is defined by a postmodern security community of powerful advanced industrial democracies among which international relations no longer operate according to old Realist rules. War between the major powers in this world is ruled out, economies and societies are highly open and interdependent, transnational players are numerous and strong, and international relations are heavily institutionalized. The other world (call it the "zone of conflict") is composed of a mixture of modern and premodern states. In relations among (and within) these states, classical Realist rules still obtain, and war is a usable and utilized instrument of policy. The problem in this scenario lies in the large unanswered question of how these two zones are going to relate to each other. Will the zone of conflict begin to penetrate and impinge upon the zone of peace, or will the zone of peace penetrate and influence the zone of conflict?

In my view, this is the most plausible general representation of where we are now. Unfortunately it is also the most complicated and therefore does not offer easy guidelines on how its social context will shape the content of power. One very simple way of looking at this scenario is to take its two-worlds idea rather literally and to assume two *separate* worlds. This approach gives us both the hard Realist and transformation scenarios, the former applying to the zone of conflict and the latter to the zone of peace. But this would mean two separate discourses on power. One would put an emphasis on the shift away from units and toward structures; from military to economic and "power over opinion"; and from rival to cooperative power. The other would still be dominated by considerations of absolute (nuclear) and relative power among rival states, with the military dimension remaining mainstream and in some places dominant. This dualism would have some resemblance to that during the Cold War, except that the two discourses would be separate, rather than—as if this were still the Cold War—inter-linked.

But strict separation of the two worlds does not itself seem very plausible. That leaves three possibilities. First, if the zone of peace were to penetrate and dominate the zone of conflict, then the whole scenario would shift toward the transformational one sketched above. Given the unwillingness of the "lite" powers in the zone of peace to get entangled in the zone of conflict unless events there threaten their core interests directly, such a development would seem unlikely. Liberalized states have become too postmodern and all too hollowed out to play such imperial or hegemonic roles. Second, given the imbalance of power against the zone of peace, and its own myriad internal divisions against itself, the zone of conflict as well should not find it easy to penetrate the zone of peace to a sufficient extent that could generalize the hard Realist scenario on a global scale.

If both the extremes are implausible, then the third possibility remains alive: a long-term game of edgy interpenetration between the two worlds, sometimes along porous boundary zones and sometimes owing to the ensnaring of many parts of the zone of conflict into the global economy. Many current developments point in this direction. There is already a strong tendency toward constructing boundary areas between the zone of peace and the zone of conflict. Thus, NAFTA's (North American Free Trade Agreement) inclusion of Mexico can be seen in this light, as can the EU's relations with Turkey and many Central European and North African states. Where the issue is not physical adjacency but economic interest, as in the Gulf, it also seems abundantly clear that the zone of peace is going to remain quite selectively engaged in the zone of conflict. But perhaps the biggest factor of all is the unresolved question of how China, Russia, and, to a rather lesser extent, India are going to fit into the new world order. Because of its limited power, its local rivalries, and its relative geographical removal from the zone of peace, India can probably be treated as a regional power and consigned to the zone of conflict. But Russia and China cannot be so easily marginalized. As both are revisionist powers, neither seems a likely candidate for membership in the zone of peace in the short or medium term. And as both are also substantial powers, whose stage and pace of development suggest a real possibility of traditional power-political behavior, their spheres of influence affect the zone of peace. Europe cannot simply ignore Russia (unless Russia remains mired in its own internal and local turmoil), just as Japan and Southeast Asia cannot afford to ignore China. The United States can, up to a point, afford to ignore both, though only at the cost of giving up its position as leader of the West. Given the relative economic success of China, and its apparent willingness to threaten and use military instruments, China probably poses the biggest challenge to any attempt to keep the two zones separate.

If the two zones cannot be kept separate, but do not merge into a single global social context, then the two discourses on power will inevitably become mixed and confused. Structural power might well have considerable global standing, although it will be more concentrated in the zone of peace. Questions of absolute and relative power will have fairly low salience with the zone of peace but high salience within the zone of conflict. And if substantial powers arise outside the zone of peace, then these traditional aspects of power will also play an increasing role in thinking about relations between the two zones. This development is already evident in discussions about China as a coming challenger for world power status within the next few decades.

On this basis, one can predict with some degree of certainty that a mainstream feature of debates about power during the coming decades will be the liberal-Realist dilemma. This dilemma is already faced by Asian and Western traders and investors in China. By engaging with the Chinese economy, they enrich themselves and China, entangling Beijing in the liberal incentive scheme of joint gains, which require peaceful relations. But by enriching a still authoritarian China, and upgrading its technological capacity and economic weight, they also make it more powerful, increasing its means to make trouble, should its leaders want to go in that direction. There is no easy escape from this dilemma. Traders and investors are competing with each other, making coordinated action difficult. If Japan, for example, began to fear Chinese power, it could not easily switch from liberal to Realist behavior. For doing so would simply turn the profits from the Chinese market over to other players, weaken Japan, and antagonize China. Taiwan already faces this dilemma in acute form. So long as the liberal logic remains strong, as it seems certain to do in the zone of peace, China will be able to feed on the resources of those it may later wish to confront. Only if its behavior managed to frighten all of its neighbors, as well as the West, would there be any possibility of coordinated economic action to restrain China's power. The light at the end of the tunnel is that China will eventually become so entangled in the world economy that structural power will kick in, and the ensuing gains and restraints of interdependence will begin to moderate its behavior. Depending on how one understands the arguments about democracy and peace, however, that may take a very long time, indeed.

It would seem, then, that the two-worlds future will, like the Cold War, generate a social context that promotes different and crosscutting conceptions of power at the same time. To the extent that the two zones remain separate, these conceptions of power can be kept relatively distinct. But if, as seems likely, there is substantial blurring between the two, then—as in the Cold War—some contradictory conceptions of power will be operating at the same time. Structural and positive-sum cooperative understandings of power will be awkwardly entangled with unit-based, relational, and zero-sum understandings. These two languages of power will service different sets of policy interests. And the contradictions between them will continue to make life awkward for analysts.

CONCLUSION

One can conclude that power will definitely remain central to both the theory and practice of international relations in the future. Given the nature of power, the positivist project to make it into the basis of a formalized discipline is highly unlikely to succeed and will remain on the fringes of the field. At the end of the day, power will remain central because it is an attractive way of discussing the political and one that has crossed all cultural boundaries to become effectively universal. As such, it is endlessly mutable in form, and its dependence on social context suggests that the debates about it are not likely to become simpler or more homogenous. The probable scenario is one in which at least two social contexts are shaping the discourse of power at the same time. As during the Cold War, and still at the time of writing, this makes the terms of the debate easily subject to confusion. That, however, is nothing new and has not so far discouraged people from putting power at the center of political discussion and analysis.

REFERENCES

Ayoob, Mohammed (1995). *The Third World Security Predicament*. Boulder, CO: Lynne Rienner.

Buzan, Barry (1991). *People, States and Fear*. London: Harvester Wheatsheaf.

Buzan, Barry (1995). The Level of Analysis Problem in International Relations Reconsidered. In Ken Booth and Steve Smith (eds.), *International Political Theory Today*. London: Polity Press.

Buzan, Barry (1996). The Timeless Wisdom of Realism? Ch. 2 in Steve Smith, Ken Booth, and Marysia Zalewski (eds.), *Theorising International Relations: Positivism and After*. Cambridge: Cambridge University Press.

Buzan, Barry, Charles Jones, and Richard Little (1993). *The Logic of Anarchy: Neorealism to Structural Realism*. New York: Columbia University Press.

Buzan, Barry, and Gerald Segal (1996). Lite Powers. Unpublished manuscript.

Caporaso, James A., and Stephan Haggard (1989). Power in the International Political Economy. In Richard Stoll and Michael Ward (eds.), *Power in World Politics*. Boulder, CO: Lynne Rienner.

Carr, E. H. (1946). *The Twenty Years' Crisis, 1919–1939: An Introduction to the Study of International Relations*. London: Macmillan.

Cerny, Philip (1995). Globalization and Structural Differentiation. Paper presented to the ECPR-SGIR Conference, Paris, September.

Goldgeier, James M., and Michael McFaul (1992). A Tale of Two Worlds: Core and Periphery in the Post–Cold War Era. *International Organization* 46: 467–91.

Gray, Colin (1994). Villains, Victims and Sheriffs: Strategic Studies and Security for an Inter-War Period. Inaugural Lecture, University of Hull Press.

Guzzini, Stefano (1993). Structural Power: The Limits of Neorealist Power Analysis. *International Organization* 47: 443–78.

Guzzini, Stefano (1994). Power Analysis as a Critique of Power Politics: Understanding Power and Governance in the Second Gulf War. Ph.D. diss., European University Institute, Florence.

Helleiner, Eric (1995). Great Transformations: A Polanyian Perspective on the Contemporary Global Financial Order. *Studies in Political Economy* 48: 149–64.

Huntington, Samuel P. (1993). The Clash of Civilizations? *Foreign Affairs* 72: 22–49.

Keohane, Robert O. (1984). *After Hegemony: Cooperation and Discord in the World Political Economy.* Princeton, NJ: Princeton University Press.

Keohane, Robert O., and Joseph Nye (1977). *Power and Interdependence.* Boston: Little, Brown.

Mann, Michael (1986). *The Sources of Social Power.* Cambridge: Cambridge University Press.

Mesquita, Bruce Bueno de, and David Lalman (1989). Dyadic Power, Expectations and War. In Richard Stoll and Michael Ward (eds.), *Power in World Politics.* Boulder, CO: Lynne Rienner.

Morgenthau, Hans (1978). *Politics among Nations.* 5th ed. New York: Knopf.

Nye, Joseph S. (1996). America's Information Edge. *Foreign Affairs* (March–April).

Onuf, Nicholas (1995). Levels. *European Journal of International Relations* 1: 35–58.

Polanyi, Karl (1957). *The Great Transformation.* Boston: Beacon Press.

Ruggie, John (1982). International Regimes, Transactions and Change: Embedded Liberalism in the Postwar Economic Order. *International Organization* 36: 379–415.

Ruggie, John (1993). Territoriality and Beyond: Problematizing Modernity in International Relations. *International Organization* 47: 139–74.

Singer, Max, and Aaron Wildavsky (1993). *The Real World Order: Zones of Peace, Zones of Turmoil.* Chatham, NJ: Chatham House Publishers.

Stoll, Richard, and Michael Ward (eds.) (1989). *Power in World Politics.* Boulder, CO: Lynne Rienner.

Stopford, John, and Susan Strange, with John S. Henley (1991). *Rival States, Rival Firms.* Cambridge: Cambridge University Press.

Strange, Susan (1988). *States and Markets: An Introduction to International Political Economy.* London: Pinter.

Strange, Susan (1994). Who Governs? Networks of Power in World Society. *Hitotsubashi Journal of Law and Politics*, Special Issue (June): 5–17.

Vasquez, John A. (1983). *The Power of Power Politics: A Critique.* London: Pinter.

Waever, Ole (1994). Resisting the Temptation of Post-Foreign Policy Analysis. Pp. 238–73 in Walter Carlsnaes and Steve Smith (eds.), *European Foreign Policy: The EC and Changing Perspectives in Europe.* London: ECPR/Sage.

Waever, Ole (1997). Introduction. In Iver Neumann and Ole Waever (eds.), *Twelve International Relations Theorists Re-assessed: Masters in the Making.* London: Routledge.

Waltz, Kenneth N. (1979). *Theory of International Politics.* Reading, MA: Addison-Wesley.

Wilde, Jaap de (1991). *Saved from Oblivion.* Aldershot: Dartmouth.

Wilde, Jaap de (1994). The Power Politics of Sustainability, Equity and Liveability. In P. B. Smith, S. E. Okoye, J. H. de Wilde, and P. Deshingkar (eds.), *The World at the Crossroads: Towards a Sustainable, Liveable and Equitable World.* London: Earthscan.

Zacher, Mark (1992). The Decaying Pillars of the Westphalian Temple: Implications for International Order and Governance. In James N. Rosenau and Ernst-Otto Czempiel (eds.), *Governance without Government: Order and Change in World Politics.* Cambridge: Cambridge University Press.

CHAPTER 4

The State as Moral Authority in an Evolving Global Political Economy

RONNIE D. LIPSCHUTZ

INTRODUCTION

On March 3, 1983, President Ronald Reagan appeared on national television to announce a new program designed to protect the United States against the threat of a first-strike attack by Soviet nuclear-tipped intercontinental ballistic missiles. The Strategic Defense Initiative (SDI), or "Star Wars" as it was almost immediately tagged by its detractors, was proffered by supporters as a means of overcoming the moral dilemma inherent in Mutually Assured Destruction (MAD): the holding hostage of one's people to potential nuclear annihilation as a means of preventing the enemy from even contemplating such an attack. This dilemma had already created political disorder throughout American and European politics, manifested most clearly in the Nuclear Freeze movement, the Catholic Bishops' statement on nuclear weapons, and massive antinuclear protests throughout Western Europe (Meyer, 1990; Wirls, 1992). Seizing on citizens' fears of nuclear holocaust, Reagan offered SDI as an alternative means of protection, in an attempt to render the arguments of Freezniks, bishops, and other dissenters ineffective and impotent.

Most critics, however, chose not to contest SDI on moral grounds but, rather, to launch a technological critique. This, they hoped, would blast to bits what they saw as a dangerous and destabilizing U.S. attempt to gain viable first-strike capacity against the USSR. But here was an insoluble dilemma: Inasmuch as one could never prove conclusively that an effective shield could never be built, how could one justify halting the project? Ultimately, the defense sectors of the United States and a number of its allies managed to absorb tens of billions of dollars in a largely fruitless attempt to develop the required technologies, although this has not deterred various parties from continuing to argue that a strategic defense system is both feasible and desirable (Rowny, 1997).

What was largely ignored in the exchange over SDI was its essentially *moral* purpose and the role of the American state in providing an impenetrable shield—not so much against nuclear missiles, rogues, and accidental wars as against propensities to détente, disarmament, and other signs of political weakness. In offering SDI, Ronald Reagan was promising to build a barrier that would redraw the potentially unstable dividers between the Free World and its Unfree *Doppelgänger*, namely, between democracy and totalitarianism, between the "City on the Hill" and the "Evil Empire." Indeed, SDI was a moral statement, but more than that, it was also a re-imagining and reinforcing of the borders between nations, between nationalisms, between what was permitted and what was forbidden.

The collapse of the Soviet Union in 1991 destroyed utterly the conceptual (albeit invisible) barrier between the good of the Free World and the evil of the bloc, hence exposing the American people to all sorts of pernicious forces, malevolent beliefs, immoral tendencies, and attending social decay; no wonder then that the domestic politics of morality have become so pronounced in the United States, full as they may be of contradictions and inconsistencies (e.g., "Get the government off of our backs but into the bedrooms of teenage mothers") and ever more strongly extended, as they are, into the international arena (e.g., the Helms-Burton Act, aimed at third-party exchanges with Cuba).

Paradoxically, perhaps, the fundamental causal explanations for these oddities and contradictions are to be found not in domestic politics, as is conventionally thought, but in a kind of "second-image reversed" phenomenon (Gourevitch, 1978) involving the very nature of the nation-state itself, in its somewhat more uncertain place within a changing global political economy and in the spread of the norms and practices of political and economic liberalism (see Teune and Mlinar, also Pirages, this volume). Far from being amoral, as is so often claimed, state behavior—as encoded in the language (see Krippendorff, this volume) and the practice (see Buzan, this volume) of realism, nationalism, state-centricity, and anarchy—exemplifies morality in the extreme, with each unit representing a self-contained, exclusionary *moralstaat*.

Moral is a term with multiple meanings. In this chapter, I use the term to refer to a set of internally consistent norms and principles to which followers must adhere without question or challenge. I distinguish *morality*, as a system of absolutes, from *ethics*, which I see as much more relativistic and forgiving. To be ethical is to judge others not on the basis of their violation of fixed principles but as human beings embedded in evolving sets of social relations that are contextual and contingent. In this view, consequently, realism can be understood as a moral system from the perspective of individual states, whereas idealism can be understood as an ethical system that does not seek to discipline the behavior of others.

In this chapter, I explore these matters as they relate to the state. I begin by describing the features of the "moral state," as I call it, and review briefly the antecedents to this phenomenon. I begin with the nation-state prior to 1648 and a specific focus on the ways in which states, as constituted after the Thirty Years War, also functioned as moral authorities. I then turn to the emergence of nationalism—the "civil religion" of the state—as a new source of moral authority. In the third part of the chapter, I examine the emerging contradiction between the moralities of nationalism and that of the liberal, economic individual, especially as it developed after 1945. Next, I address the collapse of state-centered moral authority in the New World Order of global liberalization. I conclude with a brief discussion of efforts to restore (b)orders and speculate on the implications of such an impossible task for twenty-first-century global politics.

REALSTATE OR MORALSTATE?

In contemporary international relations theory, the nation-state is seen largely in realist, functionalist terms. The state serves toward protecting itself and its citizens against external enemies and defending the sanctity of contracts and of property rights from internal foes. Morality, as George Kennan and others have never tired of telling us, should play no role in the life of the *realstaat*; for it to do so is to risk both safety and credibility (Kennan, 1985–1986). But *can* the state stand simply for the protection of material things and nothing else? After all, the essential constitutive element of the nation-state—the *nation*—stands for the eternal continuity of specific values. Conversely, the defeat of these values, whether in war *or* peace, represents a mortal wound both to the nation and to the authority and legitimacy of the state that protects it.

This aspect of the state is largely ignored by conventional wisdoms, whether realist or liberal. Advocates of both fail to historicize the state, for perceiving it as having no genealogy. They thereby omit from their stories of international politics one critical fact: The European state, as heir to the authority of the Catholic Church, was originally constituted as a *moral* order, defining a prescriptive standard of legitimate authority through containment of its citizens within well-defined physical *and* moral (b)orders. The legitimacy of authority does not grow simply out of material power; it also rests on the presumption that its holder is both *good* and *right* (Brown, 1992: chs. 2–3). And although legitimacy is normally addressed only within the context of domestic politics, history—from the Thirty Years War on—illustrates that domestic legitimacy does matter considerably also in international politics.

One might argue, of course, that "that was then, and this is now." The contemporary state no longer fulfills this moral role and has not done so for many decades. Contemporary threats to state and polity are almost wholly material: Terrorists throw bombs, illegal immigrants take our resources, diseases make us sick. I argue here to the contrary: The modern nation-state acts not only to protect its inhabitants from threatening material forces; it also acts to limit their exposure to noxious schemes by establishing boundaries that discipline domestic behavior and beliefs (after all, what is a "terrorist" but someone with bad ideas? In what is an "illegal" immigrant better than someone who knowingly violates public norms?). A state that cannot maintain such (b)orders becomes a prime candidate for disorder. And, as I shall argue below, it is the collapse of these moral (b)orders and the misguided efforts to restore them that are responsible for much of the political disorder throughout the world today.[1]

More specifically, the so-called culture wars within and between countries constitute a struggle over where, and on whom, the powers-that-be would like to reinscribe such moral borders (Huntington, 1996). This is hardly an interrogation of what is moral and what is immoral (or amoral) within the confines of 50 American states or 190 countries. Rather, the asking about is a question of whether the borders of a contemporary moral community are to be national or global (Brown, 1992). If pernicious forces have free reign across formerly impermeable borders, how can the struggle stop at the water's edge? And, if these foes threaten to permeate the body politic by their black schemes, how can one not carry one's own culture wars into the international realm?

Consequently, on the one side of this struggle are those who would reinscribe the national—by excluding or expelling those who do not live up to the moral standards of the nation's parents and also by extending the borders of that morality abroad through example and discipline. And on the other side are those who, for better or worse, by virtue of choice or as an accidental outcome of the chances for change, find themselves swept up or away by the disintegration of national *and* moral (b)orders. Valiant efforts to fortify the dikes that protect insides from outsides continue, but the forces of moral erosion are vast and mighty.

WHAT WAS WESTPHALIA?

For most international relations scholars and for mainstream international relations (IR) theory, the defining moment of contemporary world politics was 1648, when the Treaty of Westphalia brought an end to the Thirty Years War; critically observed, accounts of this history "offer nothing less than an edifying tale of modernization in which we witness the overcoming of chaos and the establishment of order through the rise of sovereign states" (Campbell, 1992: 47). This teleological story of the origins of the modern state offers two central signifiers: *anarchy* and *sovereignty*. Through anarchy, we are told, the princes who put their names to the document agreed that there would no longer stand a universal authority—the Roman Catholic Church—over them. Through sovereignty, each prince would come to constitute the highest authority within each state and, enjoined from interfering in the affairs of any other, would have no authority anywhere outside of his state's borders. This state of affairs, with its distinction between domestic "order" and the interstate "nonorder," was later reified through realist Hobbesianism—by hard interpretations of the writings of Thomas Hobbes and others (Walker, 1993).

The princes were probably not very concerned about this particular inside/outside distinction; if one looks at the map of sixteenth- and seventeenth-century Europe, relations between polities were clearly more intra- and interfamilial than international. More than this, relations within domestic orders had as much to do with *which* branch and member of a certain family would rule over what territory as with each branch and individual's religion (a point best illustrated by the intrafamily wars among British royalty and nobility). While Westphalia did not put an end to these intrafamily squabbles, it did replace the old hierarchy of Church over sovereign with a new one that placed prince or king above duke and lord. Whether Protestant or Catholic, the princes nevertheless remained very sensitive to religion, invoking the moral authority of God to sanctify and to legitimate this new arrangement throughout Western Europe.

Westphalia, in other words, was nothing short of a social contract for European society. It lacked many of the elements of domestic orders, to be sure—including a sovereign—although it did substitute specific moral principles for a ruler. True, its new principles were frequently violated (although probably more often observed than not), but they did form the basis for a continent-wide society. Not altogether accidentally, contemporary IR theory has been little concerned with the *domestic* implications of anarchy and sovereignty, addressing instead their functional significance for relations among states. But both trends can be regarded as expressions of a state-centric *morality* that presumes a legitimate order within and an illegitimate disorder without.

A shortcoming is best found in Kenneth Waltz's (1979) well-known (and flawed) invocation of the market as a structurally-anarchic parallel to international politics. In invoking the headless market, Waltz draws on Adam Smith's metaphor of the "invisible hand" to explain outcomes of relations between states but fails to recognize that the "invisible foot" of international politics may well produce results very different from the orderly outcome posited by Smith. The error committed by both Smith and Waltz is to regard markets and international politics as self-regulating, driven by nothing more than self-interest or power (to be entirely fair, Smith did hope that religious belief would constrain people's appetites and passions). Markets, as social institutions, are subject to implicit and explicit regulations, instilled either by society or by state. So, too, between states; the two precepts, anarchy and sovereignty, are both constitutive of the international system and regulative of it. They constitute also moral boundaries for the state by preserving the fiction of *international* (dis)order and *domestic* order (Brown, 1992: ch. 5).

It follows from this that sovereignty and anarchy have *moral* and, in consequence, *legal* implications for domestic as well as for international politics. As Hobbes put it,

[T]he multitude so united in one person, is called a COMMONWEALTH, in Latin CIVITAS. This is the generation of that great LEVIATHAN, or rather, to speak more reverently, of that *mortal god*, to which we owe under the *immortal God*, our peace and defense. (1962: ch. 17, p. 132)

In establishing borders between states and permitting rulers to be sovereign within them, Westphalia also granted to princes the right to establish within their jursidictions autonomous systems of law, with both functional *and* moral content. These systems enjoined certain activities in order to prevent consequences that would be disruptive of the order of the state—that is, order as the way things should be, according to the prince's vision. Or, as Hobbes argued, "But when a [covenant] is made, then to break it is *unjust*: and the definition of INJUSTICE, is no other than *the not performance of covenant*" (1962: ch. 15, p. 113). Thus, a violation of the covenant is not simply the breaking of the law; it is a repudiation of the underlying moral code of the society.

Hobbes argued that coercive power, entrusted to Leviathan, was necessary to ensure "performance of covenant" and the safety and security of each man who subscribed to that covenant. But even though the seventeenth century was quite violent, overt coercion was nevertheless relatively uncommon. It was the possibility of discipline and ostracism by the state (as well as by the other subscribers to the covenant) as a result of a violation of order, not simply the dread of day-to-day punishment, that kept subjects from violating the prince's laws or the social contract.[2] Most, if not all, of the legal systems of the time, moreover, acknowledged the hegemony of Christianity—as later manifested in the "divine right of kings"—even when they disagreed on how the religion was to be practiced.[3] Hence, although princes opposed a universal morality or empire that could impose sanctions on them against their wills, they sought to foster such an order within their own jurisdictions, based on their right to do so under God.

The fact that war and interstate violence among princes did not cease after Westphalia does not mean, moreover, that morality was absent or that combatants in war were motivated by merely functional needs or appetites. The moral basis of a political entity—its ontology—provides a justification for the existence of that entity along with the implication that any entities that reject it as their ontology are morally illicit. By defining who had the "right to act as a power" (Ruggie, 1989: 28), it has been argued that the Westphalian Treaty succeeded in including within its purview the numerous small and weak German territories; the treaty acknowledged both a moral right of existence for these units and the right of each prince to impose his morality on his subjects, no matter how small and weak he and his state were.

Westphalia did not require that each prince recognize the morality of other princes or of their rule. War and interstate violence can thus be understood as moral as well as material events. To be conquered was punishment for immoral domestic beliefs and practices; to conquer was reward for moral domestic beliefs and practices.[4] Although, by agreement, Westphalia did take for granted domestic morality and international amorality (the latter, a rule rather than a condition), this tenet did not prevent princes from trying to extend the boundaries of their domestic morality, to engulf the domains of "immoral" princes, especially if such was needed to sustain one's own moral order.

The original Westphalian system lasted only about 150 years, if that long. Although the royal sovereign was invested with authority via a mysterious God, Enlightenment efforts to usher in rationalism into political rule succeeded all too well in Western Europe. Whereas some empirical scientists, such as Isaac Newton, saw their work as illuminating the workings of a universe created by God, others took a more physicalist view and searched for answers elsewhere. Gradually, religious morality succumbed to scientific experimentation and explanation. Philosophers and theorists next sought to justify political order by reference to Nature (which some still equated with God, albeit a distant one). From this tendency there emerged what came to be called "nationalism."

FROM *CORPUS CHRISTI* TO *CORPUS POLITICUM*

The first true nation-states, it is usually agreed, were Britain and France. In Britain, the nation emerged out of the Civil War of the seventeenth century, as Parliament went to war with the king over the right of rule and the power of the purse. The Puritan Revolution represented an effort to impose on the state a moral order that was both Christian and a harbinger of capitalist individualism, but even then it used no external temporal sources or referents. Thus, Puritans portrayed Rome and its adherents (including, putatively, the deposed English sovereign) as mortal enemies of Cromwell's Commonwealth and England. This effort to purify the body politic of religious heresy could not succeed, however, so long as heretics could not be expelled from national territory or eliminated through extermination (a familiar problem even today).[5] The Restoration, which placed Charles II on the British throne, was as much a recognition of the intractability of the moral exclusion of a portion of the body politic as a reaction against the harshness of the Commonwealth. The rise of the British "nation" during the following century—the renewal of war with France during the 1700s—redrew the moral boundaries of society at the edges of the sovereign's state and established loyalty to God, King and Country as a value above all others.

In France, the Revolution launched a process whereby the source of state legitimacy was transferred from a discredited sovereign to the "people." Initially, the French nation did not attempt to establish a new moral order; that arrived a few years later. But the French Revolution did mark a major change in the *ontology* of the moral state. Whereas the princely state derived authority directly from God, the new French state relied for its authority on a "natural" entity called the "nation."

Enlightenment rationalism sought in science explanations for the workings of the universe; even Hobbes looked to Nature to explain politics and provide a model for the Commonwealth. What could be more logical than to look for the origins of the nation in Nature? By the end of the nineteenth century, even though the very concept of nation was less than a century old, nations had been transmogrified into constructs whose origins were lost in the dim mists of antiquity but whose continuity was attributed to their connections to specific natural territories, on the one hand, and to the natural result of the "survival of the fittest," on the other.

This new age of moral imperialism was rooted in Darwin's ideas about natural selection even as it extended from individual organisms as members of species to states (Darwin, himself, had no truck with these ideas; see Agnew and Corbridge, 1995). Leaders and elites of "nations" that 50 years earlier had not even been imagined (Anderson, 1991) now competed to see whose history was more ancient and which had survived greater travails for longer periods of time—as a means of establishing greater legitimacy and authority (a process that continues, even today, in places such as Serbia and Croatia). In time, this provided nations with the moral right to occupy particular spaces and delegitimated the rights of all others to possess or populate these domains.

Inherent in such national organicism was also a notion of "purity," not only of origins but also of motives. Long-term survival could not be attributed simply to chance; it had, as well, to be the result of a nation's inherent superiority in protecting its cultural distinctiveness from those who were not of the nation. Maintenance of this distinction through culture was not sufficient for this purpose; there also had to be dangers to the nation associated with difference. These dangers, often imagined into being as "real" and sometimes lacking objectivity, helped harden the borders now separating one nation or state from another.[6] Those living in borderlands were compelled to choose one side or the other; those on the "wrong" side of the border were, often as not, made to migrate across them, as Greeks and Turks were forced to move after World War I, Germans after World War II, and Serbs, Croats, and Muslims after the Cold War. Once again, a form of moral order was invoked to claim moral purity.

The apotheosis of this politics of danger took place during World War II in those areas of Europe that fell under Nazi rule. To the National Socialist regime, guardian of the moral and biological purity of Germans, races of a lower order were threats to both. The Nazi moral hierarchy could live with Slavs contained; it could not tolerate Jews, Gypsies, and homosexuals, all of whom tended toward high mobility across social, geographical, and sexual borders. Inasmuch as containment in ghettos and in camps was insufficient to protect the German nation from these impurities, extermination came to be seen as a necessity. Ethnic cleansing thus serves a double purpose. Whereas forced transfer leaves alive aggrieved populations, genocide does not. Not only does it remove contenders for title to property; it also eliminates all witnesses to the acts of the "moral community"—and, at times, as in some Bosnian towns and cities, all physical traces, too. Left behind are those of the Nation who will always testify to the evil intentions of all the Others, who happen to be mysteriously absent, if all too conveniently removed from the scene.

EVERY WO/MAN A STATE!

The state possessed by the siren song of its own moral efficacy is not yet an artifact of history. As illustrated by international indignation over Rwanda and Bosnia, the acts of purification demanded by extreme nationalism are not so willingly accepted in today's world as they once might have been, although involvement still tends to eschew ethical principles.

Interventions, when they do take place, are explained by the old statist morality—the "balance of power" or national security or some such. But a new phenomenon has emerged to challenge the moral logic of realism, indeed, to destroy it: The morality of the market is filtering in to replace the morality of the state. We are usually told that the market has no morality. Driven by an ethic of self-interest, the individual is only motivated to consume as much as possible, within the constraints of the utter cumulative limit on one's credit cards (Drainville, 1995; Gill, 1995). And yet, there *is* an implicit morality embedded in the rhetoric of market liberalism and economic growth.

According to traditional liberal principles, the behaviors of individuals in free exchange, taken together, conduce to the betterment of their society as a whole, without the intervention of politics or power. Indeed, "free exchange" among individuals is portrayed as a "natural" institution, whose organic expansion is not unlike that of the Darwinian states of yore.[7] Hence, the unfettered market generates an unequivocal *good*, which ought to be morally desirable. Conversely, the intervention of politics or power obstructs the generation of good and must therefore be immoral.

The idea of the market as an institution that reflects both individual and collective morality originated with the Calvinist notion of the elect. The idea has been repeated again and again in academic, economic, and ideological tracts, as also in American presidential inaugural addresses, of which Bill Clinton's was only the latest expression.[8] Not long ago, individual material production was taken to reflect one's moral superiority; today, one's material consumption is indicative of one's contribution to the moral uplifting of the world. In the nascent global economy, consumption is becoming both a material individual good and a moral collective "good," no less. Consumption spawns prosperity, which in turn improves people's well-being and their contentment with the status quo. The resultant stability of social relations becomes a morally desirable outcome. In Deng Xiaoping's slightly modified dictum for the occasion, today "it is good to consume."

The intentional dissemination of liberal market principles throughout the world, including liberalization, privatization, and structural adjustment, thus begins to acquire the character of a teleological moral crusade, not just a pursuit of self-interest, as we are promised a better world for all. Much public ownership and welfare spending is inefficient and wasteful. Resources are expended on projects that contribute to corruption and indolence and undermine individuals' efforts to improve their own position and status by dint of moral reasoning and good works. Whether state, corporation, or individual, the discipline of the market rewards those who hew to its principles. And those who cannot or will not do so must be left to suffer the consequences of their economic apostasy. Of course, things are never quite this easy or simple.

NOTHING SUCCEEDS LIKE SUCCESS

In the United States, attacks on "liberals," right-wing violence against both the federal government and the "New World Order," and support for "family values" can be understood as an attempt to reimpose a nationalistic moral frame on what appears to be turning into a socially anarchic society. The Kulturkampf at home is precisely parallel to the recent transformation of state practice from military-based to discipline-based behavior, especially where U.S. foreign policy is concerned. A closer investigation suggests that the two are of a piece as, for example, in the convergence of a draconian welfare policy with an increasingly vocal movement against immigrants, whatever their legal status. Welfare is deemed to sap the moral vitality of the poor, to foster promiscuity and illegitimacy, and more generally, to be a form of "theft" from righteous citizens. With no regard for statistics, which show that most welfare recipients are U.S. citizens, much of the political fire is directed at immigrants, whose moral claim to be here is deemed to be weak or nonexistent. The film *Independence Day*, in which a disciplinary environmental sensibility (*RECYCLE!*) is set against "aliens stealing our resources," nicely illustrates how domestic and foreign policy have come together around the extension of morality from the private (domestic) to the public (international) sphere (and even farther, into interstellar space).[9]

How might we explain such behaviors? While the demise of social (and moral) discipline has been instrumental in the erosion of the citizen–state relationship (Drainville, 1995), this is a proximate rather than a primary cause. To explain the sources of social disorder—in this instance, the decline of the state's moral authority—we must look back to the immediate post–World War II period and to the establishment of the Bretton Woods regime that put in place the basis for the current social crisis. The fundamental contradiction in the American and British goal of liberalizing the world economy was that the interests of citizen and state would continue to coincide only so long as there loomed a threat against which the state alone could protect the citizen. By extending the American economic system abroad, throughout the "Free World," but pointedly drawing lines around the threatening Soviet bloc, the arrangement elicited broad support among Western publics, largely eliminating the security rationale inside of the Free World's borders[10] (cf. Buzan, also Mansbach, this volume).

Originally, of course, this space was not called the Free World, inasmuch as the Soviets had not yet been definitively tagged as the new enemy (it was called the "Grand Area"; see Shoup and Minter, 1977). Harry Truman's felicitous doctrinal phrasing concerning "free peoples everywhere" provided the label; the imperialism of the dollar and the fear of Reds did the rest. Within the borders of the Free World, all states were united in pursuit of common goals based on the human propensity to "truck and barter"; outside of those borders were those whose behavior was "unnatural"—those referred to as "rotten apples" threatening the Free World's barrel. As films such as *Invasion of the Body Snatchers* suggested, communism was a pathology of nature, not an ideology of men; it would take you over; you could not take it on (Lipschutz, 1997: ch. 3).

Keeping the enemy out and contained meant, therefore, not only imposing secure boundaries around the world but also setting limits on one's self. The domino theory was not only about the fall of states; any rupture of containment would breach the self, too. The success of the Free World thus depended on extending boundaries around a natural community (Stone, 1988) that had not heretofore existed. But in order to maintain its sovereignty and autonomy, this natural community had to be juxtaposed against another. Thus, on one side of the boundary of containment was to be found a unit (the Free World) whose sovereignty depended upon keeping out the influences of a unit situated on the other side (the bloc) of the coin. The Free World could never have existed without its corresponding "Unfree World."

But within the borders of the Free World, there remained a problem: The protection of state sovereignty and autonomy—until then viewed to be part of the natural order of things (Lipschutz, 1998)—threatened to undermine the integrity of the whole. This was especially difficult from the American point of view, as well illustrated in the famous confrontation between "isolationists" and "internationalists."[11] The solution to this dilemma was what John Ruggie called "embedded liberalism" (1983, 1991), a form of multilateral economic nationalism. Inside the boundaries of the Free World, states were granted the right to manage their national economies but only so long as they agreed to move toward and eventually adopt the tenets of internationalized liberalism. With respect to the area outside the boundaries, however, the Free World would to the extent possible remain neomercantilistic (Lipschutz, 1989: ch. 5; Crawford, 1993).

Already in the late 1950s, the morality of this arrangement was being challenged by movements opposed to the threat-based logic of East–West relations (Deudney, 1995). By the early 1980s, the Free World's social contract was becoming fragile as a result of détente, the growing international emphasis on human rights, and the economic troubles of the 1970s. The first two threatened to undermine moral order within the Free World by turning friends into enemies, and vice versa, whereas the third threatened to thwart moral order within the United States. Clearly, this required the renewal of Cold War that would reestablish the moral polarities of East and West and help excuse the vile behaviors of American allies in the name of meeting the greater moral threats of Soviet adventurism and a loss of faith in America. Alas, to no avail! The subsequent collapse of communism and the apparent triumph of liberalism and democracy foiled the moral authority of the West, inasmuch as there was no longer a global "evil" against which to pose a global "good." The efforts of some to reinstate a moral divide—as by Huntington and his clashing civilizations (1996)—have not, so far, been conspicuously successful.

To restore its moral authority, the nation-state must redraw the boundaries of good and evil; it has to replace disorder with (b)orders. The clearest illustration of this practice can be seen in the behavior of the United States, whose government is attempting to restore order at home and abroad in two ways: First is the official foreign policy of "democratization and enlargement," a successor to "containment," representing an attempt to expand the boundaries of the "Good World." Those who follow democracy and free markets subscribe to a moral order that makes the world safe for Goodness. This underlies the now-conventional wisdom that democracies never go to war with each other (Mansfield and Snyder, 1995). Second is a sustained policy of "disciplinary deterrence," directed against so-called rogue states, terrorists, and others of the "Bad bloc," who are said to pose mortal threats to the Good World, even though they possess only a fraction of the authority, influence, and destructive power of the latter.[12] Ordinary deterrence aims against any state with the capabilities to threaten or attack; disciplinary deterrence, rather, is an act of national morality.

WAR, BONDAGE, DOMINATION

Disciplinary deterrence is warfare by other means: through demonstration, through publicity, through punishment. Deterrence of this form has the trappings of an effort to discipline wayward parties, those who fall out of line and violate the principles of a world moral order whose form and rules are not always so clear. It is deterrence in the media age. It relies on rapid widespread communication, the receipt of the message by those who may think of resisting but who are forced to think twice before yielding in their own best interests. The major difficulty with disciplinary deterrence is that there is no "there," there. It is conducted against imagined enemies, with imaginary capabilities and the worst of imagined intentions (Lipschutz, 1995: 12). Where these enemies might choose to issue a challenge, or why they would do so, is not at all evident. But that these enemies represent the worst of all possible moral actors is hardly questioned. One only needs to recall the fate of that "mother of all bad foes," Iraq.

Ever since it was defeated by the UN coalition in 1991, Iraq has existed in a state of limited sovereignty, as a zone that the United States holds in semi-legal bondage and domination. Iraq also serves a disciplinary function as a reminder to other rogues and adventurers of their fate, should they violate the moral code of the new global Dominatrix. Herein lies an explanation of the odd events of September 1996 when, though fighting took place in the Kurdish region, in the north, the United States, for reasons left floating, loosed cruise missiles on Iraqi radar stations in the south. Such actions can be viewed not only as a retaliation but also as the international equivalent of corporal punishment for a recalcitrant adolescent. This episode also illustrates an emerging paradox associated with disciplinary deterrence and warfare: Whereas countries once tried to keep their military capabilities a secret, so as not to alert real or potential foes, it is now common practice to reveal—rather than to use—them in an attempt to frighten wayward actors back into the straight and narrow.[13] Typically, such insinuations can be found in the many advertisements placed by Northrop Grumman and by other defense contractors in world magazines such as *The Economist*, presumably read by political and economic elites around the globe.[14]

Disciplinary deterrence as a moral exercise is not, however, limited to those outside of the country; it is also applied at home. Routinely issued warnings from on high, that the "world is a dangerous place," serve to replace the disciplining threat of communism with new menaces whose location is left vague (Kugler, 1995). Such warnings are, however, unduly unclear. We are told that weapons of mass destruction—nuclear, biological, chemical—could turn up in a truck or suitcase. We are warned that unnamed terrorists—usually Muslim, although sometimes the "boy or girl next door" (Kifner, 1995)—might infiltrate our borders. We are alerted that computer hackers, at home and abroad, could bring the country to its knees. The Clinton administration seeks to create a "special computer tracking system to flag, or 'profile,' passengers and to identify those with suspicious travel patterns or criminal histories" (Broder, 1996: A10). In a dozen major U.S. cities, the Federal Bureau of Investigation (FBI) now houses "'counter terrorism task forces,'" "dedicated full time to the investigation of acts of domestic and international terrorism and the gathering of intelligence and [*sic*] international terrorism" (Rosenfeld, 1997: A1). Very clearly, disorder knows of no borders. We must therefore have faith and trust in the authorities' ability to prevent such eventualities, even though the damage done by a weapon, terrorist, or hacker would never approach the destructive potential that still rests in the arsenals of those states with nuclear weapon capabilities.

IT'S THE ECONOMY, STUPID!

Stephen Gill has written perceptively about the ways in which the "global panopticon" of liberal markets acts to impose their peculiar morality on both, the credit-worthy and the credit-risky (1995). As the nation-state and nationalism have lost the moral authority they once commanded, such authority has shifted increasingly to the market and its disciplines. Gill points out that access to credit is a prerequisite for citizenship in any contemporary liberal democracy:

[T]he substantive conception of citizenship involves not only a political-legal conception, but also an economic idea. Full citizenship requires not only a claim of political rights and obligations, but access to and participation in a system of production and consumption. (1995: 22)

Beginning in adolescence, this, he argues, acts to discipline and socialize consumers. Failure to meet the terms of economic citizenship—a good credit record—means social marginalization. The threat of such exclusion keeps consumers in line. The result, Gill says, is the replacement of "traditional forms of discipline associated with the family and the school with market discipline" (p. 26; see also Drainville, 1995). In this way, the workers of the world-of-the-future are bound into the new global economy.

But there is more religion to the market than meets the eye. Those who do not adhere to the standards of the credit-givers (and-takers!)—whether individual or state—are cast out of the blessed innermost circle of the global economy. To be readmitted requires a strict regimen of self-discipline, denial, and ultimate redemption. But even those who have good credit ratings are not free of this moral regime; inundated by banks with additional credit offers and below-market interest rates, they are kept to the straight and narrow by fear of punishment, should they violate the code of the credit-rating agencies. The proper response to such offers is, of course, "Get thee from me, Satan!" although not everyone can rise above such temptation.

But it is here that we see the true genius of the globalized credit system. Whereas Church authority was akin to regulation—the same rules for everybody, with damnation conferred by the community—market-based morality relies on *self-regulation*, keyed to individual capacity to carry maximum bearable credit loads—different strokes for different folks and self-damnation. As we know from experience, self-regulation is a weak reed on which to base a social system. And the desire to consume to the limit of one's individual credit limit does carry a larger consequence: the domestic social anarchy that arises from self-interest as the sole moral standard to which each individual consumer hews.

Faced with this new world morality, can the nation-state recapture its moral authority and reimpose the borders of order? In some places like the former Yugoslavia the agents of virulent ethnonationalisms have tried, but only with limited success. More recently, in places like Guatemala and El Salvador, the lure of riches in the market have come to outweigh the shaky certainty of accumulation through forced appropriation. In other places, such as the United States and Europe, culture wars have been launched against those who would deviate from "traditional" social norms, in a forced effort to bring the heretics back in by invoking the religious principles relied on by Adam Smith. But hedonism, cultural innovation, and social reorganization are hallmarks of the market so loved by conservatives who have launched these domestic offensives in a fruitless effort (Elliot, 1997; Gabriel, 1997).

Short of reimposing autarchy on their societies—which, in any case, would be vigorously opposed by cosmopolitan economic elites, traders, and financiers who benefit from globalization and would also lead to domestic economic disruption and upheaval on a massive scale—the nation-states have almost no recourse in facing this new world. National borders might be guarded by armies, navies, and police armed to the teeth, but the borders of nationalist moralities, drawn in the minds of the "nation," have always been fluid and difficult to demarcate. Imagination knows no boundaries. Carried to extreme, the market will turn each of us into a nation of one, every man and woman a state, a world of 10 billion atomized countries. Then, indeed, will we enter into the "borderless world," but at what price, and at what cost.

NOTES

1. Note that in making this argument I do not propose the restoration of theocracy or of absolutist patriotism; I do, however, believe that norms are important to social cohesion.

2. This point is evident, as well, in "traditional" societies and common pool resource systems, where violation of the mutual bonds of obligation and responsibility can result in eviction from the community.

3. Does this mean that we now subscribe to a secular order? See Bragg (1997).

4. The notion of "just war," which represented an effort to impose morality on the conduct of war, does not contradict this argument, I think. Civilians were the subjects of the prince and of his morality, not necessarily of the source of that morality.

5. The Jews, who had earlier been expelled from England, were sufficiently powerless and few in number to make this practical; but there were altogether too many Catholics for either expulsion or extermination to be considered practical.

6. Thereby creating an inversion of Benedict Anderson's "imagined communities," which we might call "unimaginable communities."

7. The mantra of economic competitiveness fuses the Social Darwinism of geopolitics with the Social Darwinism of the market; as always, only "the fittest" will survive. Those old welfare state ideas of community are not only *passé*; they are the sure path to failure. See, for example, Cohen (1997).

8. It has also been explored in great detail for the American context by Sacvan Bercovitch (1978).

9. One is left to wonder what might happen should we make contact with nonterrestrial life, whether intelligent or not. See Leary (1997).

10. That is not to say that domestic security was not a concern; the ever-vigilant search for ideological threats was pursued by a transnational network of intelligence and surveillance agencies, whose capacity was often far in excess of any demonstrated need.

11. The distinction was never as great as claimed. Isolationists wanted to keep pernicious influences out; internationalists, to keep them contained. Both endeavored to avoid "contamination."

12. The defection of Yassir Arafat from the Bad bloc to the Good bloc clearly demonstrates how membership in both has more to do with morality than power.

13. This is James Der Derian's argument: "Eyeing the Other: Technical Oversight, Simulated Foresight and Theoretical Blindspots in the Infosphere," talk given November 11, 1996, University of California at Santa Cruz.

14. One such ad I remember having seen in a major newspaper some time ago tells the reader about "information warfare": "The ability to exploit, deceive and disrupt adversary information systems while simultaneously protecting our own. Example: EA-6B Prowler. . . . In the future, conflicts will be resolved with information as well as hardware. Northrop Grumman has the capability to create and integrate advanced Information Warfare technologies, such as electronic countermeasures and sensors. Northrop Grumann. Systems integration, defense electronics, military aircraft, precision weapons, commercial and military aerostructures. The right technologies. Right now." Accompanying the text is a shadow of an "EA-6B Prowler" superimposed over an unidentified landscape of land and water, with a clearly marked target point on the water's surface.

REFERENCES

Agnew, John, and Stuart Corbridge (1995). *Mastering Space—Hegemony, Territory and International Political Economy*. London: Routledge.

Anderson, Benedict (1991). *Imagined Communities*. Rev. ed. London: Verso.

Bercovitch, Sacvan (1978). *The American Jeremiad*. Madison: University of Wisconsin Press.

Bragg, Rick (1997). Judge Lets God's Law Mix with Alabama's. *New York Times*, February 15 (national edition), p. A11.

Broder, John P. (1996). Clinton Seeks $1.1 Billion to Fight Terror. *Los Angeles Times*, September 10, p. A10.

Brown, Chris (1992). *International Relations Theory—New Normative Approaches*. New York: Columbia University Press.

Campbell, David (1992). *Writing Security: United States Foreign Policy and the Politics of Identity*. Minneapolis: University of Minnesota Press.

Cohen, Roger (1997). For France, Sagging Self-Image and Esprit. *New York Times*, February 11 (national edition), p. A1.

Crawford, Beverly (1993). *Economic Vulnerability in International Relations*. New York: Columbia University Press.

Deudney, Daniel (1995). Political Fission: State Structure, Civil Society, and Nuclear Weapons in the United States. Pp. 87–123 in Ronnie D. Lipschutz (ed.), *On Security*. New York: Columbia University Press.

Drainville, André C. (1995). Of Social Spaces, Citizenship, and the Nature of Power in the World Economy. *Alternatives* 20, 1 (January–March): 51–79.

Elliot, Stuart (1997). The New Campaign for 3 Musketeers Adds Diversity to Portray Contemporary America. *New York Times*, February 12 (national edition), p. C6.

Gabriel, Trip (1997). Six Figures of Fun: Bonus Season on Wall Street. *New York Times*, February 12 (national edition), p. A19.

Gill, Stephen (1995). The Global Panopticon? The Neoliberal State, Economic Life, and Democratic Surveillance. *Alternatives* 2: 1–49.

Gourevitch, Peter A. (1978). The Second Image Reversed: The International Sources of Domestic Politics. *International Organization* 32: 881–913.

Hobbes, Thomas (1962). *Leviathan*. Oakeshott ed. New York: Collier.

Huntington, Samuel P. (1996). *The Clash of Civilizations and the Remaking of World Order*. New York: Simon & Schuster.

Kennan, George F. (1985–1986). Morality and Foreign Policy. *Foreign Affairs* (Winter): 205–18.

Kifner, John (1995). Bombing Suspect: Portrait of a Man's Frayed Life. *San Francisco Examiner* (*New York Times* wire service); December 31, p. A4.

Kugler, Richard (1995). *Toward a Dangerous World*. Santa Monica, CA: RAND.

Leary, Warren E. (1997). Science Fiction's Microbe Peril from Mars Is Unlikely But Possible, Panel Warns. *New York Times*, March 7 (national edition), p. A10.

Lipschutz, Ronnie D. (1989). *When Nations Clash: Raw Materials, Ideology & Foreign Policy*. New York: Ballinger/Harper & Row.

Lipschutz, Ronnie D. (1995). On Security. Pp. 1–23 in Ronnie D. Lipschutz (ed.), *On Security*. New York: Columbia University Press.

Lipschutz, Ronnie D. (1997). What Did You Do in the Cold War, Daddy? Reading U.S. Foreign Policy in Contemporary Film and Fiction. Draft manuscript.

Lipschutz, Ronnie D. (1998). The Nature of Sovereignty and the Sovereignty of Nature: Problematizing the Boundaries between Self, Society, State and System. Ch. 6 in Karen T. Litfin (ed.), *The Greening of Sovereignty in World Politics*. Cambridge, MA: MIT Press.

Mansfield, Edward, and Jack Snyder (1995). Democratization and War. *Foreign Affairs* 74, 4 (May–June): 79–97.

Meyer, David S. (1990). *A Winter of Discontent: The Nuclear Freeze and American Politics*. New York: Praeger.

Rosenfeld, Seth (1997). FBI Wants S.F. Cops to Join Spy Squad. *San Francisco Examiner*, January 12, p. A1.

Rowny, Edward L. (1997). What Will Prevent a Missile Attack? *New York Times*, January 24 (national edition), p. A17.

Ruggie, John G. (1983). International Regimes, Transactions, and Change: Embedded Liberalism in the Postwar Economic Order. Pp. 195–232 in Stephen D. Krasner (ed.), *International Regimes*. Ithaca, NY: Cornell University Press.

Ruggie, John G. (1989). International Structure and International Transformation: Space, Time, and Method. Pp. 21–35 in Ernst-Otto Czempiel and James N. Rosenau (eds.), *Global Changes and Theoretical Challenges*. Lexington, MA: Lexington Books.

Ruggie, John G. (1991). Embedded Liberalism Revisited: Institutions and Progress in International Economic Relations. Pp. 210–34 in Emanuel Adler and Beverly Crawford (eds.), *Progress in International Relations*. New York: Columbia University Press.

Shoup, Laurence H., and William Minter (1977). *Imperial Brain Trust: The Council on Foreign Relations and United States Foreign Policy*. New York: Monthly Review Press.

Stone, Deborah A. (1988). *Policy Paradox and Political Reason*. New York: HarperCollins.

Walker, R.B.J. (1993). *Inside/Outside: International Relations as Political Theory*. Cambridge: Cambridge University Press.

Waltz, Kenneth N. (1979). *Theory of International Politics*. Reading, MA: Addison-Wesley.

Wirls, Daniel (1992). *Buildup: The Politics of Defense in the Reagan Era*. Ithaca, NY: Cornell University Press.

CHAPTER 5

Self and Space: Negotiating a Future from the Past

I. WILLIAM ZARTMAN

INTRODUCTION

Identity and territory are inseparably linked. Indeed, in a topologist's puzzle, they can be said to underlie each other. We are where we came from, recently or originally, and we were there in the first place because of who we are. Who and where we are in turn determine our place in the world and our ability to maintain or to challenge that place. Space and self are thus the basic ingredients of international (and many other) relations, with ideological relations providing the fourth dimension to the standard three geographic dimensions, both types of relations subsuming the time dimension through which they derive and project their meaning.

Both space and self are fixed and essentialist entities: We are something and somewhere. Even if we may be a little vague sometimes about what and where that is, that vagueness is (or can be seen as) not a characteristic of the thing and place itself but of our awareness of it. As bounded attributes, territory and identity are the building blocks of relations, with clear edges and sharp corners. But they can also be the vectors of expanding universes, so that being gives way to becoming, and locating is turned into transporting. If there is a certain meaning to modernization, applicable in any era to the process of change, it lies in the transformation of building blocks into motor blocks.

ZERO-SUM AND POSITIVE-SUM WORLDS

Both space and self are concepts, relating to the fixed and tangible element of territory in one case; the somewhat more precise, even if not tangible, traits or characteristics in the other. Fixed and essentialist though these concepts are, our awareness of self and space can be more or less precise and unbending, more or less hard or soft. Hard identities and territories are well defined and coherent; soft ones loose and accommodating. Types can harden on contact; previously soft notions of space and self can become exclusivist and unforgiving when they run up against a neighbor or new neighbor, or what the French term "the Other." There are two types of relations within each of the concepts. One is *zero-sum* and *distributive*: My space and my identity stop at yours, expanding and contracting only in relation to yours.

In regard to territory, this is a classical notion of bounded ownership: Lines separate possessions, both holding their contents and hindering their contest. When the meeting of two possessed spaces at one line would be too explosive, boundaries-in-depth, such as marches, buffers, no-man's-lands, neutral zones, and demilitarized zones, attenuate the confrontation (Kratochwil, 1986). Territorial disputes are archetypically zero-sum in nature. Although space need not be disputed, it tends to be, from within and from without, particularly under pressures from exploring individuals and expanding populations (see Lipschutz, Teune and Mlinar, also Pirages, in this volume).

Identity, like territory, is often an exclusive possession, differentiated from others and bounded by the differences. It is frequently a quality quite independent of neighboring identities since there is no finite quantity of identity and no sum within it. In some cases one identity is a function of another. This can be true in a positive sense or in such a way that the realization of one depends on the abasement of the other. The identifying characteristics of one become not only different but superior to those of the other, and the zero-sum relationship is clear. Even where qualities are shared by neighboring identities, a zero-sum relationship can emerge when one of them claims to be the most or the best. Conflicts can also arise, in a most zero-sum sense, when one identity denies another ("Who are the Palestinians?" asked Golda Meir, in response to the Palestinians' denial of Israel's right to exist).

There are a limited number of ways in which zero-sum conflicts can be handled. They can be won by one side, in court or in combat, when one party's claim to space or identity is sustained at the expense of the other's. They can be negotiated, by exchange or by division, either traded off against another claim or split according to some principle of justice or according to some salient feature (Schelling, 1960; Zartman et al., 1996). All of these measures for solution sustain the zero-sum nature of the conflict. Parties in international relations have long settled such matters by combat, and it is seen as a sign of progress that they have occasionally been submitted to judicial determination. But adjudication is still an adversarial process because it generally creates a winner and a loser. Negotiation is also considered a more civilized way of handling the conflict, preferable in comparison to the costs of war; it may be either a zero- or positive-sum exercise (Walton and McKersie, 1965).

The other model of spatial and identity relations is *positive-sum* and *integrative*, whereby possessions can expand, penetrate, and overlap without doing so at the expense of each other. Identities are the easiest to conceive of in these terms. Nested identities allow people to be several things at the same time, even contradictory things, without fear of conflict or incoherence. Furthermore, the nests themselves are not fully self-contained; they may spill over and overlap. Conflicts are resolved by establishing priorities, but these priorities are only rarely a matter of crisis. Multiple identities allow for broader relations and larger empowerment, a truly positive-sum situation. Thus, a Frenchman can also identify as a European and, in addition (for example) as a Catholic, a Parisian, a Frenchspeaker, a businessman in electronics, and so on, and can think and act along each of these parameters. When such thought or action is inconsistent with the dictates of a competing identity, a choice is made without destroying either identification (see Krippendorff, also Holsti, this volume.)

In regard to space, the same image allows for a similar positive-sum conception. Thus, while there can be only one territory at a given place, there can be nested senses of territorial ownership as well as permeable boundaries, unbundling of territoriality (Kratochwil, 1986; Ruggie, 1993). While one cannot be in several places at the same time, one can be in several spaces or in a severally-owned space, provided that, as in the case of identity, the notion of space-possession, like self-possession, is soft enough to permit nonexclusive ownership. In that case, conflicts are resolved by establishing priorities, and exclusive jurisdictions are merely the means of avoiding conflict in a situation of overlapping and penetrated possession (see Buzan, also Mansbach, this volume.)

Like the idea of nested identities, the notion of layered (or *mille feuille*) space makes room for comparative advantage, economies of scale, cross fertilization, and multiple use, all of which are positive-sum concepts (Lefebvre, 1991; Niemann, 1996). Many people live and operate within the nested jurisdictions of a city, county, province (state), and country (state) at the same time, and also within a parish, diocese, commercial "territory," customs zone, telephone exchange, delivery area, currency zone, and so on. While these spheres are of varying importance and they cover varying amounts of activity, they share two main characteristics: They nest or overlap, and not least, they involve constraining regulations that coexist (except where prohibited by law). These regulations can be seen by either face: They restrain or they allow, enabling what happens within their boundaries and/ or excluding it from happening outside.

Extended to their limits, positive-sum relationships exclude conflict (Axelrod, 1970). However, such maximum extensions are rare, and conflicts within relationships of a less-than-infinitely positive-sum character need to be resolved. This can be done by asserting preeminent jurisdiction, such as prohibition by law, or by a more flexible arrangement also decided by adjudication. In both cases, though the outcome may be either zero- or positive-sum, the process remains hierarchical and judicative. The typical conflict management mechanism in the case of overlapping or even nested jurisdictions is one of negotiation. Here the parties are held equal in standing even when unequal in power, each party retains a veto over the outcome, and there is no institutionalized mechanism for the authoritative establishment of terms of trade and no set price for items traded (Zartman and Berman, 1982). Where conflicts are over incompatible claims, they can be turned into a positive-sum conflict for easier resolution, through differential values (for division), through side payments (for exchange), or through reframing (Pruitt and Olczak, 1995).

Initially, there is at least a conceptual difference between cooperation and integration. Cooperation occurs between units and can take place between hard notions of self and space, creating positive-sum outcomes. Integration entails the breakdown of units, the creation of softer selves and spaces until a new larger unit is created (which can itself be either hard or soft). It is true that cooperation can erode the hardness of the cooperating units and come to demonstrate that only integration preserves the mutually beneficial nature of the outcome. The clash between these two concepts will be noted further down, using the construction of Europe as an example.

REMEMBRANCE OF SUMS PAST

It is meaningful caricature to attribute the zero-sum image to the Cold War era and to assign the positive-sum image to its future evolution. The world is emerging from a system of global order governed by a single overarching conflict of self and space. It was deeply concerned about the lines that separated one side from the other in identity and on territory. Where the two sides' "territories" met, "boundaries" were fought over and readjusted so as to be more defensible—in Korea, in Berlin, in Vietnam, on the quarantine perimeter around Cuba, to name the most notable crises, but also over Ethiopia, Angola, Nicaragua, and Afghanistan, where the Soviet Union appeared to be breaking out of its assigned space. Indeed, it was the death-rattle triumph of the Soviet Union that it finally got its territorial conquests in Europe recognized at the Helsinki Conference as the price for including eventually intrusive baskets in the Convention of Security and Confidence in Europe (Ghebali, 1988; Leatherman, 1996). There is no doubt that the Cold War was a conflict over fixed and defined territories.

Notions of identity, on the other hand, were less well established, although the rhetoric on either side sounded as if they were. In their most Manichean moments, representatives of each side accused their own deviants of thinking like the opponent. But more deeply, each side knew who it was—the West was pluralist, the East unitarian; the unitarians had a more standard vocabulary to express their identity than the pluralists.

The best test of the separate space and selves under the Cold War was the way in which intermediate territories and identities were conceived. Countries of the Non-Aligned Movement rejected not only alignment on either of the two blocs but also identification with capitalism and communism, across a wide spectrum of policy stances. Given the pluralism that was characteristic of Western philosophy and identity, it is more accurate to think of these countries as a nonaligned part of the Free World, a notion that only reinforces the territorial and identificatory boundary of Eastern self and space. This is a generous interpretation in some notable cases like Ethiopia, Angola, Syria, and Cambodia (Kampuchea), but even these children were not acknowledged as legitimate by Moscow and Beijing, despite enormous debates on the subject.

Among themselves, new nations of the Third World also had very strict notions of their own identity and territory. Arabs and Israelis, Indians and Pakistanis, Greeks and Turks (between themselves but also on Cyprus, where they cohabited), and Somalis and Ethiopians lived out historic myths about their separate and antagonistic existence (despite the fact that they actually lived quite peacefully together for long periods), and they also proved that historic mythology by their present-day practice. Beyond these exemplary cases, many other neighbors also invented past history and present ideology to justify separateness and hostility and to overcome these traits' absence in objective reality. Such inventions are highly functional in that they buttress separate state existences where, in their absence, nothing else would justify an interstate border. Thus, to take one example, Moroccans and Algerians attributed their different political systems to a long history of antagonisms and a deep current of ideological incompatibilities, marked by two wars over long-undelimited boundaries. Similar stories could be told of Argentina and Chile, China and India, Zaire and Angola, and even Italy and Austria. Border conflicts are both a harmful by-product and a functional adjunct of nation building.

Conflicts of self and space in this context were handled in a number of ways. As expected, they were often decided in battle, both in the crises of the Cold War and in the more frequent contests of the Third World, some of which were both abetted and restrained by Cold War attentions. For the most part, such territorial conflicts accomplished little except to turn a status quo ante into a hardened stalemate. After 1949, the only significant inter-bloc boundary move was in Vietnam, a live testimony to the effectiveness of "containment"—just another word for the zero-sum relationship. Similarly, throughout the Third World, large investments were made in interstate wars, not to achieve permanent gains of territory but to maintain the status quo. In some cases, it took a long period to prove that point, as in the up to thirty years of occupation of the Israeli border lands. The only major change in the shape of states was the separation of East and West Pakistan in sovereignty as well as in geography, but of course East Pakistan was true to its recast identity and did not become part of India.

Identity conflicts are a more subtle matter. As noted, identity has often been an artificial construction, to give meaning to territory. This was particularly important during the Cold War, itself a structural conflict justified by ideology (Gaddis, 1993). This does not mean, as some have suggested, that identity differences were false claims: The distinction between a pluralist, open society and a unitarian, closed society is enormous and fundamental. Yet the conflict between the two societies' spokescountries in international relations was structural. It was a contest of rank and rivalry rather than simply a clash of ideology and identity. Once that structural confrontation between the superpowers was won, the Cold War was over, even though the contending ideas and identities remain.

In such circumstances, resolution of identity conflicts was typically a military exercise. Mechanisms like conquest, conversion, displacement, and subordination were used rather than, say, cohabitation, submergence, and reframing, among others. The forced population movements of the Ostländer as Poland was moved westward; the rigorous nonintegration of Palestinians in the United Nations Relief & Works Agency (UNRWA) refugee camps; the governments-in-exile of first the Poles and then the Baltics; the identity as well as territorial splits of Germans, Koreans, Vietnamese, and Chinese—all were distributive responses to identity conflicts around the Cold War world.

In the rest of the world, the postwar era was predominantly the age of insurgent nationalisms and anticolonial liberation. Colonial leaders rejected the notion that they were fellow-moderns along the image of their colonizers, and turning their backs on achievemental identity, they made common cause with fellow nationals in search of ascriptive identity as the colonized (Cary, 1948; Fanon, 1952; Brown, 1964; Memmi, 1967; Zartman, 1980). And yes, initially, if often also lastingly, such identity was only negative, with a positive content perhaps still open to definition; Abd al-Hamid ben Badis's formulation—"Algeria is not France, cannot be France, does not want to be France"—was the negative clarification of the original declaration, "Islam is my religion, Arabic my language, and Algeria my fatherland" (Gordon, 1966: 32–33). Thereafter, it took Algeria a number of decades and also a series of charters (Soummam in 1956, Tripoli in 1962, Algiers in 1977, revised in 1986) to define what it really was, and the country is still searching. It would be erroneous to imply that such identity dialectics remained forever in the confrontational stage and did not move on to a synthesis between national form and modern (Western) content, but at this point, it is important to stress the initial and prolonged confrontational stage (Zartman, 1985, 1992). The dominant effort of the period was to assert sovereignty over self and space.

To be sure, there is a certain déjà vu in portraying past and future in such Manichean terms; it has been done before, and the new is often only relatively newer, not essentially different (Laidi, in Badie and Smouts, 1995). The difference of the future will be dealt with below, but it can easily be noted that the past was not as uniformly compartmentalized as suggested. Yet since the focus of this discussion is rather on future evolutions, it is not necessary to debate the details of the past. It is only necessary to note in passing, however, that eras (already a loose and overlapping concept) are marked by characteristics, not uniformities, and that the fixed, bounded, and rectified nature of what passes for the past era is characteristic enough to permit some comparisons with the likely characteristics of the future as an anticipated era.

MAKING SOFT AND OPEN SPACE

In comparison, it is an integrative world that the 1990s open up to the ensuing millennium. If the distributive characteristics of the Cold War period were sharply evident, even if not exclusive, the positive-sum manifestations of the new era, too, have been already identified. The permeability of the territorial state, clearly noted at the height of the Cold War as an emerging phenomenon (Herz, 1957, 1968), has been taken up in many forms to indicate a conceptual change in the "billiard ball" model of international politics. Today, quite frequently, permeability appears as the economic face of international relations and boundedness as their political face, although neither of these characteristics is exclusive. In environmental as well as in economic matters, international regimes do impinge on territorial sovereignty. Nonstate actors do penetrate state space, adding new layers to citizens' identity. These days, it would seem that "[n]onterritorial functional space is the place wherein international society is anchored" (Ruggie, 1993: 165).

Much has been written and discussed about the reach of economic activities across boundaries and about the imperviousness of ecology—and more broadly, of nature—to man-made lines on a map. But less attention has been given to the overflow of political space. Despite the passing of the Communist International and of the extensive regional links of various nationalist and anticolonialist movements, many a country's political space—the territory on which its politics is played—still by far extends its state boundaries (Zartman, 1989: ch. 4). A number of democratic parties—Christian Democrats and Socialists in Europe, Republicans and Democrats in the United States—help like-minded parties in other parts of the world; leaders in the United States and elsewhere endorse candidate leaders in other lands; not only do French leaders support African leaders, but African leaders fund

French parties; exiled and refugee populations contain opposition parties and leaders that are often more politically active than official organizations operating on home soil. While examples of each of these types of extended political space could be found in the Cold War era and even before, their continuation and multiplication constitute a salient trait of the contemporary period (Teune and Mlinar, also Lipschutz, this volume).

Territorially, the post–Cold War era has seen the rise of a new breed of "entities," semisovereign units that have not (yet?) attained state status. The Palestinian Autonomous Self-Governing Authority has a solid existence if a disputed future outcome. It is also a noncontiguous unit, intracommunicating across hitherto hostile territory. The northern East Prussia of Russia is also accessible to the mainland across sovereign Lithuania and Belarus. The Kurdish entity is governed autonomously within Iraq. Somaliland is unrecognizedly independent from an imperceptible state of Somalia. A sovereign but "unrecognizable" entity, the Republican China, on Taiwan is castigated for wanting to "declare its independence" from the People's Republican China on the mainland, against the agreement of both sovereign units that they are part of a single (but which?) China. Bosnia, a new state, for the moment contains two entities—one of them a federation of two more entities. Two sovereign states, Russia and Belarus, have united into one yet-to-be-identified sovereign union. Proponents both of an Afrikaner Volksstaat and of kwaZulu want their identity-based territories to become sovereign entities inside the sovereign state of South Africa. All of these anomalies may well be only transitional, but most have lasted for a number of years, somewhat comfortable in their protracted transition.

In regard to an increasing number of territorial entities that are recognized as states, the concept of sovereignty to which somehow they have acceded is eroding and evolving. Where sovereignty formerly meant protection from interference, permission for internal autonomy, and formal standing among sovereign equals, it has now come to connote only putative jurisdiction, neither exclusive nor unaccountable. Boutros Boutros-Ghali, ex-secretary general of a worldwide organization for which sovereignty is a qualification for membership, has indicated that "absolute and exclusive sovereignty" is a thing of the past (Boutros-Ghali, 1995: 44). And yes, in the past, sovereignty was claimed to be indivisible, that is, absolute and exclusive (James, 1986). Although not zero-sum, the indivisibility of sovereignty is a hard concept as, by definition, it cannot be shared.

Far from license, sovereignty is increasingly seen as responsibility, in two directions (Elkins, 1995; Lyons and Mastanduno, 1995; Deng et al., 1996). First, states are primarily accountable for the domestic welfare of their citizens, not just for their protection against other states. If they are overwhelmed by the task, they can call on outside help from other states, from international agencies, from nongovernmental organizations. Second, in the pursuit of their accountabilities, states are responsible also for aiding other states, for responding to other states' invitations for assistance or to the populations of the latter, calling for help. In this view, sovereignty is neither absolute nor exclusive and specifically not unaccountable.

This notion is fraught with enormous difficulties, and it returns the concept of sovereignty to pre-Westphalian days where the strong had the right, in the name of responsibility, to help the weak even against its will (see Lipschutz, this volume). There is as yet no standard to govern the exercise of responsible interference in an other's internal affairs; and the restraining organization of higher responsibility, the United Nations, is merely the agent of its strongest members. Yet it is also imbued with more creative potentialities. The threat of justified intervention removes the possibility of a state's neglect or repression toward a part of its population with impunity. Such a threat can well return the state's attention to its responsibilities, knowing it cannot ignore them so lightly anymore. In theory, like any good threat, this one may never have to be used, once its seriousness is demonstrated. The very threat of a standby force ready to intervene in Burundi in March 1996 caused the Burundian government to deal more constructively with internal tensions; and the decision to intervene in Zaire in November 1996 in order to provide relief and repatriation for 2 million refugees did lead various agencies in Zaire and Rwanda to do the job themselves. Similarly, the justification of responsible intervention can create a larger community of nations, pooling resources and helping each other in emergency, as is already done. Both military and mediatory North Atlantic Treaty Organization (NATO) intervention in Bosnia in 1995 brought a multilateral sense of responsibility toward a country that both the United States and the European Union had earlier considered to be outside their area of concern. This is the theory; the practice will surely be a mixed picture. Currently, it is not so much the intrusiveness of the strong as their neglect that plagues the question of responsibility.

In addition to permeability and responsibility, there are other characteristics of space in the emerging era. Over large surfaces of the world, boundaries have ceased to be a problem. Within the security communities of North America and Europe, boundaries are only loosely tended, and their location is uncontested. Even within Africa, there have been remarkably few boundary wars and even fewer negotiated boundary changes; the most common source of dispute in recent years has been the extension of boundaries offshore across submarine oilfields (as between Tunisia–Libya, Senegal–Guinea Bissau, Nigeria–Cameroon). Indeed, African boundaries tend to be extremely permeable, outside of the main roads, and ordinary activity and large population movements alike sweep back and forth across them. Boundaries are also rendered less important for most of the world by subregional free trade zones (FTZs), even if these FTZs are not always fully respected (Lancaster, 1995). Some Third World boundaries do matter, however—such as the borders that keep boat people in and out.

The boundaries that are important and carefully controlled are those between the North and the South. Even Westerners with "Third World looks" are now scrutinized at European passport controls, whatever their citizenship. The southern internal boundary in the North Atlantic Free Trade Area, between the United States and Mexico, is more tightly controlled than the northern internal boundary, between the United States and Canada.

All of these features of the emerging era indicate that political and economic self-sufficiency is inadequate for an expanding world. Unlike the Western Hemisphere after the half century of independence (1775–1825), the newly independent countries of the post–Cold War world cannot throw a doctrine around themselves and temporarily withdraw from the world so as to consolidate their polities and economies. As the northern protections against immigration suggest, southern populations are determined to join the developed world on their own, if their countries do not do it for them first and fast enough. For their part, the industrialized countries of the North, which have long penetrated the South, find themselves in turn penetrated. Those southerners who manage to penetrate the North impose identity crises on their new country of welcome; they remain in close contact with their countries of origin and with their own families left behind, whereas, as new citizens of the host country, they seek to be both what they would like to remain and what they would like to become. They bring Arabic, Turkish, and Islam to French- and German-speaking Christian Europe; Spanish to English-speaking America; and Singhalese and Buddhism, Filipino and Catholicism, to Arab Muslim Saudi Arabia, for example. And because these multiple locutions and locations enjoy different degrees of nestedness, some immigrants remain *Gastarbeitern*, even as others become new citizens and social pluralizers, with multiple overlapping identities.

BUILDING INTEGRATIVE IDENTITIES

The integrative features of such multiple selves are mixed. The sense of identity as a "Free Worlder" or anticommunist that the common external enemy used to provide during the Cold War has receded, leaving its various components to stand out on their own. In the absence of a sharply differentiated Free World to lead, Americans fall back on their own identity. For the East, too, the unifying effect of identification as communists, whatever its operational shortcomings, has dissolved. There remain other cases of nested identities in the political sphere, however, beyond those involving professional and social identifications. Whereas the European movement of the immediate postwar period sought to overcome separate nationalities with pan-Europeanism (Boisdeffre, 1952), now—half a century later—European identity recognizes component national identities. Similarly, although the death of a pan-Arab identity has been announced (Ajami, 1986), popular reactions to the second Gulf War show the sense of the Arab self to be quite alive, containing component national identities, just as Islamic identity also cuts across national allegiances.

Yet undeniably, in many places, strong indivisible identity claims have risen in salience to counter the integrative effects of transactions across territory. In some areas, there are no overarching identities. Both nationalisms and identities formerly described as subnationalisms are on the rise. A newspaper headline on China claimed: "Maoism, Confucianism Blur into Nationalism" (*Washington Post*, March, 19 1996), even as analysts were and continue to be concerned whether an entity as large as China can hold together, not so much because of its territorial expanse as owing to the strains on the unity of its single identity. In large parts of the world, the move is toward demanding smaller identity units; although this trend is not yet marked by success, it is strong enough to be considered worth dying for by many and worth making many others die for it as well.

But reverse effects are also produced, wherein clashes of specific identities produce a flight to broader, often ideological, identities and sometimes even to fanatical extremes: Turks fighting Kurds to the point of elimination, and Kurds reacting in kind, turn to Islam as a newfound identity and ideology. French, Britons, and Germans confronted with a foreign national and religious presence (ironically, in the first two cases, from their own former colonies; and in the third, from their former ally) turn xenophobic, even fascistic; as do Americans, fresh out of the melting pot, when faced with new and unfamiliar ingredients in the stew. Students of internal conflict have aptly taken over the term *security dilemma* from international relations, to indicate internal situations where one identity group's attempts to self-realize and to be secure only makes others (who formerly had no security problems) more insecure—such a process conducing those who formerly lived together in harmony now to sort themselves out in hostility (Posen, 1993; Lake and Rothchild, 1996). Examples abound:

The southern Sudanese have long aspired to a regional autonomy that would allow them to be themselves yet permit them to identify also as Sudanese. When they began to sense that the northern Sudanese could be themselves only by repressing others and by eliminating alien identity groups, they felt threatened. Thus, the southerners (who have no collective name) opted for self-determination (Deng, 1995). And although Tamils once occupied a favored position in Sri Lanka and benefited strongly from its education system, radicalized Tamil leaders and their followers—deeming that they can simply not be both Tamils and Sri Lankans—elected to fight murderously for their independence (Kapferer, 1994). When northern Somalis, who were once integral to an irredentist movement seeking more territory for their own identity group, began to see that years of neglect had made it impossible for them to live with other Somalis in the same state, they chose to proclaim an unrecognized independence (Adam, 1995). When they gained their independence from a South Slav (Yugo-slav) state, Croa-

tians aspired to a maximized territory, including land inhabited by eastern
Slavonian Serbs and by Bosnian Muslims. But Serbs rather preferred a single
state comprising the places where they live (but not necessarily predominate), including Kosovo, eastern Slavonia, and the Serb Republic of Bosnia,
as well as Serbia itself. Russian leaders fear the Chechen independence movement, not because it would cast off a rebellious minority, but because
Chechnya's success would serve as a bellwether for other similar movements
(Lebedeva, 1996). These examples are illustrative and by no means exhaustive.

The idea of an overlapping, integrative notion of identity in spaces such
as Bosnia, Sri Lanka, Western Sahara, Ogoniland, and even Ulster seems
still far away. Yet the same ideal is being realized in Euskadi, Alto Adige
(Südtirol), Bavaria, Wales, South Carolina, Lancaster County, and Hok-
kaido. The location of these examples in the developed North of the world
suggests that in the South a phenomenon of breakaway identities is tending
to rip the state apart into small nationalist pieces, in deep contradiction to
the breakdown of territorial autarky and the spread of penetrating communications and overlapping jurisdictions in the modern, northern world.
Yet there are many times more nested identities within Third World states
than in the North—potential cases of mininationalism that have not risen
up and broken away. It is those very nation-building efforts by new state-
nations that, in specific cases, have triggered a reaction among parts of the
population, thereby spurring mini-identities. The glass is indeed more than
half full: And it is remarkable that there are not even more breakaway reactions to Third World endeavors to create state-nations and to the collapse
of the once-unifying communist ideology.

NEGOTIATING SPACE AND SELF

Yet except for establishing a baseline for normalcy, it is not the filled part
of the glass that is interesting. What is more compelling is rather the unfilled
part and the challenge it places to the resolution of future conflicts over
space and self—and to theory building in the field. Integrative conflict resolution can reach out to combine competing values or to create new ones,
if the parties can be brought to see the situation in positive-sum terms.
Conversely, in a zero-sum situation, one or more sides must abandon their
initial resistance in order to fit into a single outcome (Nicolson, 1964; Zartman and Berman, 1982; Ury, 1991). Note that the hardening of a conflict
into zero-sum positions not only escalates the conflict; it also eliminates
potential integrative solutions. For example, while federation or regional
autonomy is a likely meeting point between demands for national unity and
for self-determination in Sudan, a solution of the kind has been used up and
even voided by President Jaafar al-Nimeiry's reneging on federation in the
early 1980s. That devaluation of potential solutions now makes even local

autonomy unacceptable to southerners, who insist on being part of the national regime and not merely recipients of a local dispensation. By far more important than the potential solutions, the minimal requisite trust for contingent agreements to obtain is absent.

A dynamic era in an expanding universe requires soft space and soft identities to overcome the necessarily conflictual and distributive nature of hardbounded territories and self-senses with an awareness of self and place that is present but flexible and permeable. A positive-sum solution among intransigent parties depends on the establishment of complementary trade-offs through cooperation or on the elimination, the total softening, of the sides through integration. The former calls for a reinforcement of identities so that they can exchange preferred roles and outcomes with one another; the latter requires the (sub)mergence of the conflicting selves in a higher, superordinate identity or goal. The former is far easier to inaugurate, since the identities come first, the negotiation of trade-offs follows, and the integrative payoffs come later. If it fails, the parties can always fall back on their zerosum notions of themselves, now hardened by the failure of integration. The latter takes longer to achieve because separate identities have to be put on hold, so as to give the overarching process a chance to prove itself. If it fails, it will do so early rather than late, succumbing to the offputting inability of the parties to adjust or suspend their conflicting identities.

The option based on reinforced identities and complementary trade-offs was the essence of the independence of Eritrea and its continued economic union with Ethiopia: Distributional identity needs were met by separating the two countries (neither of which, a nation) and by territorial integration through a free trade zone and a common currency. It is still too early to evaluate the ultimate success of the experiment, begun as late as in 1993.

The option based on a superordinate identity is the story of America, of the Western alliance, or of Tito's Yugoslavia—not the theme of any of the more recent experiments known. Here, the openness of the identity was embodied in its achievemental nature, designed to melt any ascriptive hard edges. In the successful and continuing experiments, hard notions of the former selves were overcome, in virtue of an openly integrating ideal that made room for many. In the first two cases, moreover, soft identity was reinforced by soft space—an expanding territory in search of a frontier, which in fact was no frontier at all but an open space. But even here, we have at least two problems to consider.

The first problem resides not in the fact that there are two possible types of solutions at which to aim but that the conditions of these two options are antithetical. Working toward one solution reduces the chances of working toward the other if the first one fails. Where soft territory and soft identity can be combined, however, intermediate examples become possible. For example, the reorganization of Spain into 17 autonomous regions after the early 1980s did accommodate both regional and national identities, while also preserving a national economy capable of fostering regional specializations (Gunther, 1993). Over the first half of the 1990s, 40 to 50 percent of the population identified as equally regional and Spanish, whereas only 30 percent identified themselves as predominantly or solely Spanish (Moreno, 1994). The five autonomous provinces of Italy, too, enhance the regional identities to flourish within a national economy, whereas a different mix of solutions, involving both cooperation and integration, is seen to take shape in the construction of Europe. In the latter case, it is not clear as yet whether extant and reinforced national selves are engaged in a rather selfish trade-off aiming at diminishing the chances of war, at increasing the economic payoffs, although limited by preserved component identities (in a manner true to de Gaulle's idea of *Europe des patries*), or whether the palpable drag imposed by separate selves can be overcome only by their dissolution in a new European identity—built on the realities of a shared security and a common economy, in addition to a single currency.

The second problem with the two options involves the deeper notion of solutions and outcomes that each entails. The world still tends to search for fixed or definite resolutions, pacts that must be servanda, referenda that determine the self, solutions that are final, and treaties that are measured by compliance (Jacobsen and Weiss, 1995)—in sum, through a conclusive hardness of space and of self. The contrasting view is one of continual process, dynamic solutions, periodically revisable agreements, mechanisms for handling disputes (Spector, 1995)—in sum, resilience and softness of territory and of identity. The second view lies beyond the current world levels of tolerance for ambiguity and revisability, even with the attitudinal dynamism that comes with modernism. In many cases, the most successful solutions are often provided by a combination of the two—setting a firm standard with room for trimming change that precludes the need for total revisions. Examples in some areas of activity would include a broadly worded constitution with room for amendment; and legal or religious principles that evolve through interpretation. It is more difficult to see the middle ground that would provide for periodic review of identity and of territory, let alone to generalize such theoretically.

Another alternative that may see its day again is the end of the modern territorial state and the reappearance of the premodern social state (cf. Teune and Mlinar, Pirages, Lipshutz, and Mansbach, this volume). In many parts of the world during precolonial times, land was governed by usufruct codes, not by ownership laws; and the state was a polity based on an identifiable population, wherever it be located (Flory, 1957; Lattimore, 1962; Kopytoff, 1987). Members of several states, each with their own jurisdiction, could inhabit the same land. The most formalized version of this structure in recent times was the Ottoman *millet* system, the ultimate soft self in the soft space, where nested and overlapping identities would cohabit across loosely sovereign spaces (Davidson, 1963). In the modern era, political control over dispersed populations is made even easier by communications technology, but the territorial state still stakes its claims. The increased intensity of such interactions and the absence of an overarching authority, no matter how loose, offer a nonterritorial social state a much greater conceptual and operational challenge than that once faced by the Sublime Porte.

Other courses are less promising. Current calls for hardened space and self, through autarky, nationalist secessions, economic protectionism, and enhanced identity groups, simply run counter to the current reality of increased territorial integration, to which they are usually a reaction. One school, focusing on "basic needs," maintains that it is better for all the determined selves to be allowed their own self-determination, so that the vast energy now spent toward making separatist voices to be heard is freed to more constructive ends of allowing hard identity to condone soft territory (Burton, 1990). This is poor advice, drawn from a misreading of current conflicts. It portrays identity as the highest need and purports that it can be delineated as a distinguishable absolute. In reality, it encourages additional entities to turn wasteful energies into asserting the need and claiming the right. Creating a positive-sum outcome by resolving zero-sum conflicts is a circuitous and ultimately inefficient path to integration, if and when it works at all.

Identity is a more fragile entity than territory, since it only exists in the mind. The reaffirmation of identities, and even their reinvention, frequently is a compensation for the persisting softening of space. Overcorrections can lead to overhardenings over time. Ways of preserving meaningful senses of the self are needed, so that selves are not lost in space and integration does not overwhelm identity. And this requires a delicate balance, for which there is no cut-and-dried formula.

Space and self, identity and territory, hard and soft, zero- and positive-sum, distributive and integrative—is this all merely an intriguing interplay of concepts of no practical significance to a world condemned to be populated by selfish identity-territories, that is, states cooperating only at the margin and reverting to conflict (even while cooperating) whenever they run up against another's notions of self and space?

In the absence of the idealism, however illusory, that underlay the Manichean world of the Cold War, is there anything in the successor epoch that can generate a comparable commitment toward easing entities into some soft, positive, integrative interaction—indeed, toward any form of common existence other than the need or compellance to operate under constraints of technological penetration, threats of economic vulnerability, and fears of environmental interdependence? Nothing in recent state conduct would tend to suggest so, except for the hope for vision in leadership, the aspirations of supporters, the opportunity of dynamic rather than static constructs—as motors, not bricks—and the urgency to expand productivity and capability faster than the rate of growth of the population. But the concepts of international relations can only offer a choice, depending on their applicability; an elucidation of consequences, subject to a model's validity in a particular situation; and after the fact, an evaluation of the intelligence in adopting a path or of the wisdom in eschewing a direction.

REFERENCES

Adam, Hussein (1995). Somalia: A Terrible Beauty Being Born? In I. William Zartman (ed.), *Collapsed States: The Disintegration and Restoration of Legitimate Authority*. Boulder, CO: Lynne Rienner.

Ajami, Fouad (1986). *The Vanished Imam: Musa al Sadr and the Shia of Lebanon*. Ithaca, NY: Cornell University Press.

Axelrod, Robert (1970). *Conflict of Interest*. Chicago: Markham.

Badie, Bertrand, and Marie-Claude Smouts (eds.) (1995). *L'international sans territoire*. Colloquium in Paris, at the Institut d'Etudes Politiques de Paris.

Boisdeffre, Pierre (1952). La jeunesse européenne veut-elle faire l'Europe? *Hommes et Mondes* 67 (February): 268; 68 (March): 431; 69 (April): 574.

Boutros-Ghali, Boutros (1995). *An Agenda for Peace*. 2nd ed. New York: United Nations.

Brown, L. Carl (1964). Stages in the Process of Change. In L. Carl Brown, Clement Moore, and Charles Micaud (eds.), *Tunisia: The Politics of Modernization*. New York: Praeger.

Burton, John W. (ed.) (1990). *Conflict: Human Needs Theory*. New York: St. Martin's Press.

Cary, Joyce (1948). *Mister Johnson*. New York: Harper & Brothers.

Davidson, Roderick (1963). *Reform in the Ottoman Empire*. Princeton, NJ: Princeton University Press.

Deng, Francis (1995). *War of Visions: Conflict of Identities in the Sudan*. Washington, DC: Brookings Institution.

Deng, Francis, Sadikiel Kimaro, Terrence Lyons, Donald Rothchild, and I. William Zartman (1996). *Sovereignty as Responsibility: Conflict Management in Africa*. Washington, DC: Brookings Institution.

Elkins, David (1995). *Beyond Sovereignty: Territory and Political Economy in the Twenty-first Century*. Toronto: University of Toronto Press.

Fanon, Frantz (1952). *Black Skin, White Masks* [Peau noire, masques blancs]. Paris: Seuil, 1952] Transl. Ch. L. Markmann. New York: Grove Press, 1967.

Flory, Maurice (1957). La notion du territoire arabe et son application au problème du Sahara. *Annuaire français du droit international* 3: 73–91.

Gaddis, John Lewis (1993). The Cold War, the Long Peace, and the Future. In Geir Lundstad and Odd Arne Westad (eds.), *Beyond the Cold War*. N.p.: Scandinavia University Press.

Ghebali, Victor (1988). *La diplomatie de la détente*. Brussels: Bruylant.

Gordon, David (1966). *The Passing of French Algeria*. London and New York: Oxford University Press.

Gottlieb, Gidon (1993). *Nation against State*. Council on Foreign Relations. Washington, DC: Brookings Institution.

Gunther, Richard (ed.) (1993). *Politics, Society, and Democracy: The Case of Spain.* In *Essays in Honor of Juan J. Linz* series. Boulder, CO: Westview Press.

Herbst, Jeffrey (1992). The Challenges to Africa's Boundaries. *Journal of International Affairs* 1 (Summer): 17–31.

Herz, John (1957). Rise and Demise of the Territorial States. *World Politics* 9 (July): 473–93. Reprinted in Herz, John (1967). *The Nation-State and the Crisis of World Politics.* New York: McKay.

Herz, John (1968). The Territorial State Revisited. *Polity* 1(Fall): 11–34.

Jackson, Robert (1990). *Quasi-States: Sovereignty, International Relations and the Third World.* New York: Cambridge University Press.

Jacobson, Harold K., and Edith Brown Weiss (1995). Strengthening Compliance with International Environmental Accords: Preliminary Observations from a Collaborative Project. *Global Governance*, 1, 2 (May–June), 119–48.

James, Alan (1986). *Sovereign Statehood: The Basis of International Society.* London: Allen & Unwin.

Kapferer, Bruce (1994). Remythologizations of Power and Identity: Nationalism and Violence in Sri Lanka. In Kumar Rupesinghe and Marcial Rubio Correa (eds.), *The Culture of Violence.* New York: United Nations University Press.

Kopytoff, Igor (ed.) (1987). *The African Frontier.* Bloomington: Indiana University Press.

Kratochwil, Friedrich (1986). Of Systems, Boundaries, and Territoriality. *World Politics* 34, 1 (October): 27–52.

Lake, David, and Donald Rothchild (eds.) (1996). *Ethnic Fears and Global Engagement.* Princeton, NJ: Princeton University Press.

Lancaster, Carol (1995). The Lagos Three: Economic Regionalism in Sub-Saharan Africa. In John Harbeson and Donald Rothchild (eds.), *Africa in World Politics.* Boulder, CO: Westview Press.

Lattimore, Owen (1962). *Studies in Frontier History.* London and New York: Oxford University Press.

Leatherman, Janie (1996). *Principles and Paradoxes of Peaceful Change.* Syracuse, NY: Syracuse University Press.

Lebedeva, Marina (1996). Why Conflicts in the Former Soviet Union Are So Difficult to Negotiate and Mediate. *International Negotiation* 1: 3.

Lefebvre, H. (1991). *The Production of Space.* London: Basil Blackwell.

Lustig, Ian (1994). *Unsettled States, Disputed Lands.* Ithaca, NY: Cornell University Press.

Lyons, Gene M., and Michael Mastanduno (eds.) (1995). *Beyond Westphalia? State Sovereignty and International Intervention.* Baltimore, MD: Johns Hopkins University Press.

McCreary, Scott, and Francisco Szekely (1987). Applying the Principles on Environmental Dispute Resolution to International Transboundary Conflicts: The Case of a US-Mexico Border Environmental Issue. Working Paper 5. Cambridge, MA: The American Academy of Arts & Sciences, Program on Processes of International Negotiation.

Memmi, Albert (1967). *The Colonizer and the Colonized.* Boston: Beacon Press.

Moreno, Luis (1994). Ethnoterritorial Accommodation and Democratic Development in Spain. Paper presented to the XVI Congress of IPSA, Berlin.

Nicolson, Harold George, Sir (1963). *Diplomacy*. New York: Oxford University Press.

Niemann, Michael (1996). Space and IR Theory. Paper presented to the International Studies Association, San Diego.

Posen, Barry (1993). The Security Dilemma in Ethnic Conflict. In Michael Brown (ed.), *Ethnic Conflict and International Security*. Princeton, NJ: Princeton University Press.

Pruitt, Dean, and Paul Olczak (1995). Beyond Hope: Approaches to Resolving Seemingly Intractable Conflict. In Barbara Bunker and Jeffrey Z. Rubin (eds.), *Conflict, Cooperation and Justice*. San Francisco: Jossey-Bass.

Ravenhill, John (1988). Redrawing the Map of Africa. In Naomi Chazan and Donald Rothchild (eds.), *The Precarious Balance: State and Society in Africa*. Boulder, CO: Westview Press.

Ruggie, John G. (1993). Territoriality and Beyond. *International Organization* 1 (Winter): 139–74.

Rupesinghe, Kumar, and Marcial Rubio Correa (eds.) (1994). *The Culture of Violence*. New York: United Nations University Press.

Schelling, Thomas (1960). *The Strategy of Conflict*. Cambridge, MA: Harvard University Press.

Sowell, Thomas (1995). *Migrations and Cultures*. New York: Basic Books.

Spector, Bertram (ed.) (1995). *The Evolution of Regimes*. Washington, DC: U.S. Institute of Peace.

Spruyt, Henrik (1994). *The Sovereign State and Its Competitors*. Princeton, NJ: Princeton University Press.

Stares, Paul (1996). *Global Habit: The Drug Problem in a Borderless World*. Washington, DC: Brookings Institution.

Ury, William (1991). *Getting Past No*. New York: Bantam Books.

Walton, Richard, and Robert McKersie. (1965). *A Behavioral Theory of Labor Negotiations*. New York: McGraw-Hill.

Weiner, Myron (ed.) (1993). *International Migration and Security*. Boulder, CO: Westview Press.

Young, Crawford (1991). Self-Determination, Territorial Integrity, and the African State System. In Francis Deng and I. William Zartman (eds.), *Conflict Resolution in Africa*. Washington, DC: Brookings Institution.

Zartman, I. William (ed.) (1980). *Elites in the Middle East*. New York: Praeger.

Zartman, I. William (1985). The Political Dynamics of the Maghrib: The Cultural Dialectic. In Halim Barakat (ed.), *Contemporary North Africa*. London: Croom Helm.

Zartman, I. William (1989). *Ripe for Revolution: Conflict and Intervention in Africa* (updated edition). New York: Oxford University Press.

Zartman, I. William (1992). Democracy and Islam: The Cultural Dialectic. *Annals of the American Academy of Political and Social Sciences* 524 (November): 181–91.

Zartman, I. William (ed.) (1995a). *Collapsed States: The Disintegration and Restoration of Legitimate Authority*. Boulder, CO: Lynne Rienner.

Zartman, I. William (ed.) (1995b). *Elusive Peace: Negotiating an End to Civil Wars*. Washington, DC: Brookings Institution.

Zartman, I. William, and Maureen Berman. (1982). *The Practical Negotiator*. New Haven, CT: Yale University Press.

Zartman, I. William, and associates (1994). *International Multilateral Negotiation: Approaches to the Management of Complexity*. San Francisco: Jossey-Bass.

CHAPTER 6

The Developmental Logic of Globalization

HENRY TEUNE AND ZDRAVKO MLINAR

INTRODUCTION

Globalization is integral to social development. It refers to processes that both integrate diversity and produce even more diversity. It is explained by theories of developmental change. Its driving, self-conflicting logic permeates differentiation and integration within the practical limits of the individual at the lowest level, on the one end, and the world as a whole at the highest, most encompassing level, on the other.

Globalization as development is a concept distinguishable from constructs utilized toward explaining theoretically other processes of international integration, both willful and dynamic. First, it is a concept different from those that explain an intensification and expansion of international relations among states through diplomacy, organization and law, or subversion, threat, and war—the very processes that encapsulated the whole world as a system of states. Second, the concept differs also from transnational activities that, although conducted from within countries, traverse the boundaries of states through communication, commerce, and the circulation of people and ideas. Though often perceived to be global, structures of transnational activities are bi- or multilateral at best, usually between and among entities across countries—be they universities, volunteer doctors' associations, or corporations. Third, it further differs from the institutionalization of supranational entities, their organizations, and the norms held therein—be they the European Union (EU), the North American Free Trade Agreement (NAFTA), or the World Trade Organization (WTO). All of the latter comprise states that agree to subordinate their sovereignty to a common decision-making body of more or less federal nature. And although most supranational organizations are regional, the WTO provides an example of a supranational organization that happens to cover most of the world even if unable to be global in its fundamental organizational principles. States can join and withdraw; also, they might, but need not, be integrated into a global trade and exchange system attributable to the WTO or, for that matter, to any other trading association or organization.

Globalization and universalism are also different. The first is a concept with temporal and spatial parameters; the second, a characteristic of principles that can be applied without regard to time and space. Universal principles are observably manifest only in a particular place or period. Globalization, in contrast, extends the applications of universal principles everywhere. Modern scientific knowledge started in a small Western European niche from which it spread globally. The growth of this type of knowledge, if not merely that, is a mainspring of contemporary global social development.

The spread of universal principles does not necessarily imply homogenization, everything becoming the same everywhere. Rather, these appear locally in practically limitless, distinct, unique combinations and recombinations. For instance, as the science of materials advances, and as architectural variations improve and multiply, they even help preserve and recreate older designs.

As a concept, globalization must be defined in a theoretical context. But since it is very often theoretically not clearly embedded, it is signified as characterizing two separate domains: (1) one in which territorial diffusion of things, people, and ideas occurs and (2) another, in which different parts of the world gradually become interdependent. Which is why globalization contradictorily indicates the world becoming concomitantly bigger and smaller. This is connoted in references to "McDonaldization," "Cocacolization," "world football," indeed, "Americanization" (Featherstone, 1990). As powerful persuaders, these loaded exemplifications convey both positively and negatively charged images that distort the underlying reality of contemporary change and also warp the explanatory power of development as a general dynamic of global change.

The facile explanations of globalization are technologies of satellite communications, air transport, computer internets, and worldwide television programming, all of which very substantially reduce the physical and social constraints of space and time, in some cases to nearly nothing at all. Yet, what are the social forces that explain these technologies and their use? Each has more expensive and difficult alternatives; all are improvable and substitutable. The fax machine was around for years, providing wire photos for newspapers, long before that same technology became a recognized element of the bundle of technologies that are these days reputed to be "causing" globalization. Although technologies may be engaged to facilitate development, and thus at certain critical periods may even become the "necessity" that compels one invention or another, they remain subordinate to the developmental processes themselves.

Globalization must be understood theoretically as a general social developmental process. Or else it will be seen politically as a willy-nilly product of technologies, which themselves can be manipulated to control any unwanted consequences of change. The popular perception of globalization at this moment in history is as an altogether benign force amply capable of accounting for our everyday observations of change and explaining the spread of the familiar everywhere with good and bad consequences. In order to deal with the politics of globalization, one needs to recognize and understand the winners, the losers, and also their likely responses. It is not enough to anticipate globalization as the bearer of the next golden age, to abhor its casualties, or to fear the reactions of its enemies. Yes, a different kind of society is likely to take shape; yes, factories may well close; and yes, fundamentalists will challenge. But globalization will proceed. And the political issues of journalistic relevance will continue to be about the consequences of the pretentious premise that governments can continue to deal with the problems emanating from globalization—even though these are matters that have long escaped the purview, let alone the reach, of their authority.

Surrogate references to globalization as telecommunications, computer networks, electronic shopping, and high-speed transport are pseudoexplanations that invite familiar Luddite reactions of astonishment and resistance. Fundamentalist responses, aggressive assertions of ethnic and national character are all but mere perturbations on these processes. They are typical of sectors and regions of the world that are socially the least diversified and differentiated—and that, by definition, constitute the world's new backward areas now impacted by ever-expanding globalization.

NATIONAL DEVELOPMENT

Since the late eighteenth century, beginning with Adam Smith, both economic growth and development have been perceived as led by the formation of the nation-state. The reasons for this are at once as transparent as obscure. First, compelled by reasons of defense or survival, the state built infrastructures that integrated territory, and it brought together those within a territory, so as to encourage general exchange and production. Second, the spread of norms through the extension of law made exchanges predictable. Finally, technologies—those great inputs of growth that boosted production—helped to modernize transportation and to accelerate communications, under the protection of "the state." These are among the most evident general forces that—by creating roads, canals, railroads, shipping services, patent offices, currencies, markets, reliable banking services, but also legally enforceable contracts—marked the momentous productive transformations: from animate to inanimate power, from coal-generated steam outlets to electricity, from compound new industrial materials to fission and fusion in chemistry, among others.

The less obvious of these factors in the historic shift from sustainable survival to strategic surplus and to fast growth are discussed today in the context of the still too poorly identified ingredients of innovation and of the yet to be understood basic constituents of success, all of which are so necessary in organizing production for all of tomorrow's markets waiting to be created.

Why some states came together, and embarked on a path of autonomous growth, thereby achieving "economic takeoff," whereas other starters became targets of opportunity to the appetites of ascendant states, constitutes questions that rank high among the most important historical-theoretical puzzles still awaiting an answer. Argentina and Canada, both vast spans of land with sparse European populations implanted on top of scattered indigenous populations, shared similar prospects for growth and development in the early twentieth century, at the end of which a big economic gap now separates them. And although "economically comparable" at the starting gate, in the early nineteenth century, Mexico and the United States followed widely divergent paths in their economic growth and as to their national integration, only a few decades later.

The reasons advanced by evolving theoretical interpretations of the wealth of nations range from the imperatives of war to the very happenstance of good government and the opportune choices of political leaders. Such explanations aside, autonomous national economic growth is known to have proceeded even without the all-too-obvious benefits of resource-rich territory, the blessings of an invigorating climate, or the coincidence of cultural splendor. Comparisons of China and Japan, of England and France, of Prussia and Russia, have opened paths of explanation touching on religion, on politics, and—not least—on the diffusion of innovations.

By the end of the 1970s it should have become apparent, and by the mid-1990s certainly obvious, that development was more than the simple economic growth of nations. That, in reality, it was a feat embedded in the social advancements that had managed to slip through the cage bars and the traditional constraints imposed by the states. Once, only those countries successful in harnessing their resources grew to lead the world. Wars among the growth-driven states were of such a large magnitude that they were seen as "world wars." Today, even in countries unable to achieve much national economic success, populations can benefit from processes of social development and thereby experience the positive effects of economic growth. Such, too, is the outcome of global social development—itself the fruit of generalized social development, which, after nearly three centuries of very gradual internationalization, now touches almost all parts of the planet with worldwide impact.

GLOBALIZATION AS SOCIAL DEVELOPMENT

Our theoretical perspective places globalization centrally, as a core element indispensable to the explanation of the general processes of social development at a time when the world needs to come to terms with its ecological margins (see chapter by Pirages but also those by Krippendorff, Holsti, Lipschutz, Zartman, and Mansbach, this volume). First, so as to situate our theory of developmental change in context, we shall examine why sociology did not until recently recognize globalization as the historical watershed it is; why so little progress has been made in grasping the concept; and what manifold consequences have thus ensued. Second, we shall propose a theory of development that is capable of conceptualizing the process of globalization. Intended to be general and comprehensive, our theory must be compatible with the traditions of the macrosociological theories of the nineteenth century that serve to explain the unquestionably profound transformation, to which commonly we refer as "modernity" today. Third, we shall discuss some of the consequences of globalization in an outline of a different kind of world order.

SOCIOLOGY AND TWENTIETH-CENTURY WORLD SYSTEMS

The role of social science in the development of the world during the twentieth century is a complicated story, yet to be told (Albrow and King, 1990). The general understanding is that the rise of the social sciences coincided with the emergence and expansion of a world of states. Scholars ascribed meaning to the concept of nation-state, more out of idealistic aspiration (see chapter by Holsti) than on grounds of justifiable evidence (see Krippendorff, also Lipschutz, this volume). The study of human development then quickly retreated from its nineteenth-century origins in Marx, Spencer, and Weber, distancing itself from their macrotheoretical interpretations of both massive change and future directions. A world of peoples, empires, great religions, mores, and cultures became compressed into a planet of political cages—most of which were very confining; many among them, often also packed with mutually hostile occupants.

The end of World War I transformed the nation-state into a moral force for justice (see chapter by Lipschutz)—an entity wholly capable of reconfiguring liberated human beings into organizations geared to production but also one likely to use its newly demonstrated deadly capacities for war on an unprecedented scale. The main query for professional economists became the why of economic prosperity and the wherefore of inequality among nations. Soon their quests would discover new paths in the orthodoxies of Keynesian national economic policies promising economic growth and justice. States erected barriers along their boundaries and prepared not only to

defend but possibly also to expand them. And the main questions for political scientists became those of war and peace, including the calculation of
national interests and the materialization of vast state bureaucracies for collective action. Sociology lost its way in these intellectual quests. Submitting
to the dogma of the nation-state (that the nation-state was the principal
agent of change for social justice), sociology dutifully searched for social
order, addressing social problems in a variety of national societies within
specific countries. As a result, comparative research contrasted countries,
their political systems, their societies, and their economies, at the expense
of scholarly work on self and space (see Zartman, this volume).

The emancipation of individuals inside liberal democratic states—through
private ownership, citizens' rights, and public welfare—dissolved in the
1920s into the many communalisms of that period. Nationalism, fascism,
and "national" communism gave way to violent conflicts and government-
ally induced deaths. And already by the 1950s, their casualties would make
of the twentieth century the bloodiest yet in human history (Rummel,
1997). During that period of ascendant communalisms and well into the
end of the current century, sociologists became apologists, exiles, or marginalized critics, most of them abandoning their nineteenth-century
traditions of global theories of change.

Political scientists and economists embraced the new world order of competitive and conflicting states. An internationally dominant theoretical paradigm for political scientists became the "zero-sum" game. For economists,
the name of that deadly rivalry was "competition," zero-sum with all the
theoretical corollaries. The former developed a major field of study and research in both international relations and world politics; the latter excelled
in international and world economics. A few studies of "cultural" and social
influences among nations aside, sociologists remained mostly commentators
on the side. A somewhat late exception was *The Modern World-System* (Wallerstein, 1974). But even that work was primarily an analysis of economic
relations between core states, semiperipheral states, and peripheral ones. It
was a quest to bridge Marxist and capitalist interpretations of global change
with ideas derived from mercantilism, imperialism, and the history of the
West. And although a field of international sociology did not thereby
emerge, a comparative cross-national sociology did somehow come into focus.

Nonetheless, the second half of the twentieth century witnessed much
more than high-profile trade and power politics or the mere construction
of institutions to bring nations together in a world of prosperity without
wars. Although less visible, deep changes in values, in relations among
groups engaged in economic production and distribution, did create the
conditions for two of the most important institutional and structural changes
of the end of the century. The first secured the institutions for the European
Union; the second managed the transformation of nationalist communist

states from closed to open, if not wholly democratic, systems. Each of these major changes appeared to have taken place independently: the first, by virtue of the special relationships established between the political leaders of Germany and France; the second, owing to the leadership qualities of Gorbachev. Yet both were part of the developmental processes of globalization, as were the North American Free Trade Agreement (NAFTA), the WTO, the fast rise of international derivative markets, and the growth of certain Asian economies. The historic occasion of the Maastricht Treaty, the dissolution of the Soviet Union, the opening up of countries all over the world, and even the responses to the wars in the Balkans and inside Russia are integral to the processes of world development on a global scale.

Only a development theory of change, capable of articulating the transformation of an international system made of states and nations, yet still able to explain the processes of an emerging world system of individuals, can provide the sound theoretical foundation for a global sociology whose deep grasp and broad reach neither comparative sociology nor, indeed, international sociology could ever hope or purport to achieve.

A SOCIOLOGICAL THEORY OF GLOBALIZATION

For sociology to make a theoretical contribution to the study of global processes of change, it has to acquire the likes of a theory of comparative advantage in economics or iterative game theory in political science. What sociology can draw upon is a tradition of theories of social development, once instrumental in explaining the massive changes that led to the modern era. But those were the days of large nation-states, emerging cities and markets, and nascent science. What can sociology do to rid itself from the limitations of that earlier historical period, in order more aptly to assume the challenges set by the century ahead?

Our book *The Developmental Logic of Social Systems* (Teune and Mlinar, 1978) defined "development" as integrated diversity. Our general theory was presented as characteristic of certain societies, indeed, of the human race as a single system. In our view, the Roman Empire was developmental. It integrated diversity, as have also smaller societies—early Athens being an example—that were not dominated by the expansionist imperatives of empires, yet left many lasting legacies for human development.

For a variety of reasons, certain nation-state systems found themselves linked to developmental processes sometime in mid-seventeenth century. They used the benefits of their scale to swallow up some societies still stuck in the rudiments of reproducing themselves through adaptations to their environments—including their own neighbors. And much of it involved warfare. Those ecological human systems depended heavily on production, trade, and war for their sustenance and defense. Developmental systems, in contrast, generate change autonomously; they integrate it and create even more change. A few of these dynamics and processes of development need to be discussed to show why the world's human system is becoming globally developmental in character and in tenor.

Integration has three dimensions: *strength, inclusiveness,* and *extensiveness.* Strength depends on the interdependence of the components, whereby a change in one element leads to a change in others as well as in the first, owing to feedback with variable probability. The average of these probabilities across components is the overall strength of integration. Thus, maximum integration obtains where a change in one component *determines* a change in all others; dissolution, where change becomes a random process. Inclusiveness, on the other hand, refers to the *equiprobability* that a change in one component will lead to change(s) in the others. Notwithstanding the strength of the relationships among the components of a system, the components' overall deviation from the average constitutes a measure of the inclusiveness of the system's integration. And extensiveness is the *proportion* of each component's properties affected by the system, regardless of the total number of properties that these components may possess. Thus, a component is said to be partially, or fully, integrated into the system, depending on how much of what it has is engaged in system-related behavior.

Diversity is the other essential part of development. It is the sum total of differences in the properties of all components of a system, all combinations of such properties included. Every single component has similarities with, and differences from, any other single component. The important dynamic of diversity is that as each component acquires more properties, the probability of its having properties that are both similar to and different from those of the other components increases—this probability growing exponentially when *combinations* of component properties are at play. Thus everybody can have shoes, but some will have shoes and automobiles; others, shoes, automobiles, and houses, and so on, as basics are diffused and novelties trickle down.

The questions here are why development and why the scale of system increases? Beyond economic growth and modernity—the very preoccupation of macrosocial science—what does a system's scale imply? There are three basic types of systems: *co-action* systems, interaction systems, and transaction systems. *Co-action* refers to variety *among* "traditional" societies and to similarities *within* them. Here, integration is based on shared characteristics within the society and common differences from outsiders. *Interaction* relies on similarities and differences within and among societies altogether giving rise to exchange and conflicts. *Transaction* is composed primarily of differences in a system where integration is based on flows of activities and ideas.

The great transformation in the nineteenth century, explained via processes of differentiation and integration by Marx and others, was from co-action (small-scale and self-reproductive) systems to interaction (exchange/

conflict) systems wherein competition and discontent constitute the core dynamics of change. Developing systems create differences, cleavages, between urban and rural, between central and peripheral, wealthy and poor. They intensify conflicts not solely among themselves but also among groups with different cultures and religions by bringing them into contact with each other. The days of great transformations in production and exchange were also those in which differences were suppressed through state ideology, force, expulsion, imprisonment, and death. The twentieth-century state communalisms can be interpreted to have been short-term successful reactions mounted against change that threatened disintegration. The concepts of winners and losers and zero-sum games quite aptly seized the dynamics of change from co-action communities to exchange-oriented, capitalistic societies armed to have their way (see Buzan, this volume) by all means.

The transformation from exchange/conflict systems (especially those organized as states) to transaction systems constitutes the main processes of globalization: Differences are encompassed in networks; territorial boundaries become fuzzy; goods and services flow instead of being pushed or dragged across conflict-intensive exchange organizations; and unlike a variety of communalisms that would rather embrace group uniformities, democratic ideologies do very much respect individuals, celebrating their differences.

Our developmental theory is not one of nation-states nor one of corporations, let alone one of communities to be explained by a variety of ecological theories of growth and human settlements. Rather, it is an articulation of the significance of the evolving levels of territorial social organizations—from villages, towns, cities, regions, to the supranational. Here, conflicts among the entities, be they over the emergence of newer levels or about the weakening and the restructuring of older ones, are tantamount to manifestations of those processes of deep transformation, which ultimately succeed in converting the world from a territorially organized system into a globally reconfigured entity, for which new maps are needed (see Mansbach's chapter, this volume).

TOWARD A WORLD SYSTEM

The weakening of states by new claimants of autonomy, on the one hand, and the birth of supranational regions and the emergence of transnational networks, on the other, are both integral to the developmental process. What we are witnessing today is a turning away of sorts from the nation-state as the coordinating center of human activity—in economic development, cultural achievements, or emancipation from group restraints, among others. In addition to conflicts fueled by established nationalist and ethnic groups, there are those arising among newer kinds of groups animated by an ever-expanding range of issues and interests, some even in evident opposition to territorial political systems. Many among these groups transcend national boundaries in the nature of their membership, the range of issues addressed, and their linkages to others. There exist also global political movements, interests in free trade, resurgent universalistic religious creeds, knowledge-based associations, understandings among local officials, not to mention regional arrangements, and international organizations linked to subnational ones, in addition to other configurations.

Territorial groups fighting for autonomy in South Asia, in Europe, in Central Asia, or in Africa never quite achieved their liberation in the great wave of newly independent states during the first half of the twentieth century. The coveted promise of self-determination in a world of independent states at once protective of group interests and supportive of others' rights never came to be a reality for them (Etzioni, 1994). Yet even as these groups acquire their independent states—with more than ten new states now recognized in Europe alone, in the space of a few years, and still more to come, including some in Africa and Asia—they will be losing control not only to a globalizing system but also to growingly independent localities, minority groups, organizations, and the individuals within them (Ziemowit, 1991). Thus their own autonomy can be assured only by linkages to broader systems. Affording political autonomy in hard space will require linkages to the outside world, if only to assure prosperity and political integrity, especially for those that are in greatest need of such.

With globalization, entities below the level of the nation-state that acquire sufficient autonomy are not only being freed from the control of a state but also enabled to bypass it and to deal directly with the state's neighbors and with the global system as a whole (Mlinar, 1992a). The state cannot continue to function as a monopolistic intermediary when groups and persons seek to gain comparable "standing" under "international" law. Where global norms are not available, international laws are most likely to continue to serve as guidelines for localities, persons, and organizations in lieu of the internal rules formerly imposed exclusively by the state through its coercive institutions.

Once, in many areas of the world, developmental processes would lead to the weakening of localities in favor of the nation-state and to the liberation of individuals from the tyrannical grip of local communities, tribes, and religious groups. Today, such processes are giving rise to new regions, thereby intra- and trans-nationally nurturing the preconditions for supra-national associations and organizations. Simultaneously, these processes have softened the strictly competitive nature of conflicts among the states, the localities and the organizations that control state trade, that have a say over the use of the military and an influence on the exchange of skilled workers and technologies.

A global system is characterized by the interdependence of its groups, organizations, and individuals, on a world scale, such that a change in one of them will have some probability of effectuating some changes in the others. As these changes spread, the familiar in one part of the world becomes recognizable as not dissimilar to what is known in others. And the wider diffusion of the world's social variety assures a given locality's integration into a world system, and its diversification from within, through permutations and combinations of the local and the global. From a physical perspective, the world remains a "total system." Even if it is hard for some to measure its social, economic, or political wholeness accurately, and irrelevant for others to try to fathom its meaning, its now-evident capacity to integrate diversity in a global human system constitutes one more assurance that the lives of all individuals and groups could be thereby favorably altered.

Among the attributes of global systemness, one may mention shared norms of behavior, as in the treatment of minorities; identifiable elements, such as multinational businesses; world institutions, such as world banks; common languages for instant communications, such as computer software; and universal privileges and obligations, including human rights. Controversial indicators would also exist. These might include the growing irrelevance of the United Nations in addressing local conflicts where no state is in the position of acting on its own; or, say, a weakening of the European Union's control over the economic activities of one of the organizations within it. After all, both of these bodies were founded on state obligations and agreements; thus, each remains limited by the incapacities or shortcomings of the weakest tier of its member states to take action where, when, and as needed.

DYNAMICS OF GLOBALIZATION

The developmental processes conducive to a world system are marked by increased differentiation at all levels of noted human aggregation, which also differentiate by sectors. The levels are mixed: A region for trade can be more encompassing in size than a space specific to political cooperation on flows of immigration or tourism. Levels may become fluid or fuzzy across sectors. Lags among sectors will become noticeable if one sector's integration leads to the integration of one but to the collapse of another. Some parts of universities—say, business education and cognitive science, to mention but two—will tend to become global, if only by integrating with communications corporations, for instance; even as others—remedial education, for example—may languish, if only for limiting reading and writing solely to one's own tongue. And yes, this may fragment universities into divergent spheres of activities, if one cannot fully integrate active adaptive change.

The unfolding of levels—imparting ever-greater autonomy, from the lowest levels, ultimately to the one with the greatest possible scale, the world as a whole—will continue to be driven by the very processes of integrating diversity. The integration of the world—the attainment of the highest level of diversity—currently at a low level of systemic cohesiveness when compared to most countries and regions, is the potential target of the global system. Enriched by the largest amount of diversity, an integrated world would provide the greatest quantity of novel variety the highest rates of increase in comparison to any of its components. An integrated world would be far more innovative as a whole than any one of its nationally definable centers or foci of innovation—as is already evident from the numerous breakthroughs accomplished in certain fields of physics, genetics, and medicine.

As systems develop through the augmentation in the diversity of their components and in the level of their integration to the whole, the relevance of intermediate structures will diminish. At relatively low levels of development, countries have weak central authorities; as said countries achieve some level of development, their central controls expand rapidly in such critical sectors as transportation, capital markets, and education, to list the most obvious ones. As even higher levels of development are attained, governments begin to decentralize and to divest themselves of initial controls as their countries, as well as their components, become increasingly integrated into greater encompassing systems.

For totalitarian governments, the choice is between control and development. To develop, they must open; to open to the world, they must relinquish control. Countries may channel penetrations by the global, but there is little choice about whether or not to be open. As a long-term alternative, closure will breed poverty and social regression. And yes, openness at its extreme will exact a price.

CONFLICTS IN THE GLOBALIZATION PROCESSES

The world may be a global system, but its components are far from attaining high integration. Its institutions are incipient; some of its groups and parts, not well incorporated; the younger political levels, the regions, are in conflict with the longer-established state interests; new local systems, new political groups and movements, conflict with their national governments—often in alliance with global organizations. And some among the established groups, with a determination to recapture a past that never was, can even transform confrontations into conflicts conducive to acts of violence.

The two main structural conflicts in developmental processes are across levels and across time. And both are generated by new variety; both feed on each other. No matter where it occurs, new variety has a tendency to "migrate upwards," to more encompassing levels of aggregation, which always dispose of greater variety. There, the new variety is less "disturbing"; it is only one more item in a large pool and, hence, more easily absorbable than at levels endowed with less variety. Immigrants to a country settle more easily in a large city or region than in a small town. As a variety comes to be established at more encompassing levels (say, a center), it can offer access to itself at lower levels (say, at a locality, for instance). This provides a basis for hierarchies, especially territorial ones. The center(s) will always have more variety than the localities. A center can control access to its space and use such selectivity to dominate. One outcome is direct conflict between the centers and localities. Another consequence may be conflict among centers claiming control over localities.

There are, however, limits to the amount and kind of variety that any level in a hierarchy can hold. This explains a tendency to dump such downward, on lower levels. In today's language, such off-loadings can be portrayed as restructurings, downsizings, or decentralizations. When this happens, clashes occur between the new and the old. Usually, localities and older organizations tend to have fixed structures, often deeply embedded in physical ecologies that may include buildings, roads, and other established uses of land. At least initially, locals are likely to resist. Yet ultimately, they may "trade up," by giving up some older kind of variety for a new one— say, a downtown shopping area for a mall. Indeed, cross-level shifting of variety is a necessary part of the dynamics of development in most settings.

Also, accumulations in the penetrations of the new, although welcomed by certain local groups for broadening their choices and autonomy, may spark strong resistance by some localities in most dramatic ways: riots against location decisions, or fury against foreign cultures—often with nationalistic and racial overtones. Over time, however modified to mitigate local destabilization, localities begin to reflect the variety of the global system. The global political economy becomes manifest in the locality, quite palpable inside the multinational corporations, most visible in entertainment, and even remarkable in food. In the years ahead, the local as an autonomous unit will, itself, eventually lose out to those among its own groups and individuals who entertain an intimate link to the world at large (Mlinar, 1995a).

The very first to adopt new items of variety in any locality will continue to constitute the "elites" who, more easily than "others," will be able to bypass local structures and qualified to deal directly with the world as a system. In the past, such practices were deplored for conducing to grave asymmetries in the relations of poor localities, by forcing them to become dependent on big exploitative centers. A counterperspective would now see in such penetration the seeds of freedom for some of the locals eager to build ties to the outside world.

The severe disturbances and conflicts characterizing such a process find their origin in the inequalities that occur between the time that these items of global variety initially penetrate a part of that locality and the time that the locality is at last fully saturated by them. As nothing new can be distributed to each and every component of a locality at once, the critical time here is the lapse needed for the first resentment to display an explosive expression.

Note that time interacts with conflicts among levels, inside developmental processes: New items continue to enter the evolving system at a discrete point in time, thereby disturbing it. As it begins to be distributed, variety becomes diversity and uses up linear time for requisite system-wide adaptation and integration. In the past, a classic example was the automobile. As cars began to enter a country or a community, service stations were built, and roads, parking spaces, and other adaptations followed. The resistance came from those seeing in the automobile a disruption to the city, for harming public transport and polluting the clean air, for disrupting solitude, and for requiring greater social control. Yet today, for most individuals, the automobile is a source of freedom, of autonomy from constraints on personal mobility. In the past, a slightly modified utilization of the automobile would be integrated into daily life, after intense political struggles over issues about road construction and public access to parking. In the future, the penetration of the world as a system, the proliferation and reconstitution of localities, and the rise of the individual as an autonomous actor may create a very different dynamic. Though such a long-term process may prove easy to delay, it may reveal itself as rather difficult to reverse once adopted (Strassoldo, 1992).

Note also that historical conditions tend to mix with these developmental conflicts: Globalization intensifies conflicts if two or more ethnic groups are entrapped within a locality under a single political system. If one of the groups is more developed or globalized, from having acquired variety from the "outside," then it will seek access to even more variety and make greater efforts to open the boundaries of the political system to that end. If another, less developed group controls the political system, however, it will seek to keep the boundaries as closely under control as possible. This will put the two groups in direct conflict, the globally conversant group tending to view the more exclusive ruling group as oppressive. Such was the problem in the case of the former Yugoslavia, in the conflicts pitting rich and poor republic and the respective nationalities against each other on issues of national policies concerning Europe and openness. This conflict was compounded by the differences in the population size of these groups as well as by the stark disparities in their respective political influence on the then-national center, the capital of Belgrade from where ex-Yugoslavia used to be governed.

The developmental processes that impact on group conflicts today are of a different makeup than the group antagonisms that used to be kindled in a world of fragmenting states, however. The developmental changes did to some extent weaken the capacity for territorial control of political centers. But they also rendered more viable the existence of smaller groups in a world political economy lacking the intermediation of a political center.

The big tales of tiny groups that have only recently secured independent states will soon end, however. To prosper as viable small political systems, these will have to open up to the global system. But that will undercut their integrity as a group when even tinier domestic entities and individuals begin to seek their own links to the global system—by skirting the hierarchies of their at-long-last formal political capitals (Mlinar, 1995b).

"Civil" wars have increased since the cessation of external infusions of control resources, once sent to political centers in an effort to marshall their capacities in support of the Soviet–U.S. confrontation. These are fought in the relatively less developed peripheries of the world: southern Europe, Central Asia, South Asia, and of course, Africa. Almost no violent conflicts in the years since the end of the Cold War have taken place between states; most are between groups within recognized countries or inside neighboring ones. The peacekeeping mechanisms of regional compacts, and those of the United Nations, were, however, designed for conflicts among nation-states within an international system of states. A global system would make such institutions obsolete, if only on grounds of their inability to deal with conflicts that are not strictly between warring state governments. The temporary absence of transnational institutions capable of mediating intranational group conflicts may increase the very probability of national and international violence.

IMPLICATIONS FOR A FUTURE WORLD ORDER

The foregoing holds serious implications for the structures of a world system in the coming years. Some of these are already apparent. Detractors argue that current conditions are temporary. Some have even concluded that, in the long run, another group of countries will become ascendant—that great powers and empires will ensue, regardless of whether it should take decades for them to emerge (Modelski, 1987). A contrary view is that the world will break up into a thousand or more conflicting tribes before varied "peaces" can be established by new empires that have "risen and fallen" since agriculture became a primary means of human output (Snyder, 1982).

The perspective here is that of a world transforming into a different kind of system, a few sketches of which will be offered under the caution that the rate of such changes depends on technology and on human will and purpose—the "know how" and the "know what" of the human condition. Technologies and human choice, however, can end up in catastrophes—a nuclear disaster, an uncontrollable war, or an epidemic. But in the future, such setbacks are likely to be remedied in years, not in decades: A global system would not only have greater capacities for response but also far faster responses than any one country or locality could ever single-handedly afford. What, then, do such contexts and perspectives bode for the future? We see at least six dimensions of change in the altered and evolving landscape:

1. The flow of goods, services, and ideas will accelerate on a global basis, for two main reasons: (a) reductions in the traditional territorial restraints on movement of goods and ideas across the selectively more permeable political boundaries of nation-states and (b) the weakening of the power and purview of the intermediate groups that exact tolls on exchanges and from transmissions. Note that the requisite technologies already are largely in place, and their evolution toward faster and more reliable flows has been predicted, especially by those in the telecommunications industries.

2. The units of human activity, including production, will get smaller. This again follows from the arguments about intermediate organizations, with a critical difference. The more encompassing the world becomes as a global system, the more viable its smaller unit components can afford to be. Smaller includes new forms of human organization, whether in production groups, in research teams, in the reorganization of the familiar in neighborhoods, in residential associations, or in lifestyle groups. Smaller, however, will come to require being linked to what is far larger, even to the point of becoming part of the largest-scale system.

3. The individual will gain autonomy. Not only will smaller units become more viable in a global system, but so will individuals be able to find their place as diversity is opened to them. Having access to variety requires knowing not only the alternatives but also the ways to access them. The lead sector in the processes of globalization will be that of information. Information follows from rationalization and standardization—the two necessary, if insufficient, conditions for integrating diversity, which are part of the same social cognitive processes of mapping social and physical objects and relationships. What is necessary for integrating diversity is the capacity to predict from the cognitive in order to access objects for exchange, conflict, or interaction on a selective basis.

4. The territorial imperative in human aggregation and societal organization will become fuzzy and fluid (see Zartman, this volume; cf. Buzan, this volume). Not only will there be many more territorial units, but most of them will be penetrated by elements of other systems, especially by exponentially expanding numbers of nonterritorial organizations (as Mansbach, too, seems to agree, in this volume). Already, the corporation can jump territorial boundaries easily. And where territory retains its importance in production—as in agriculture, today—requisite conditions could be reproduced by technologies located anywhere. Are not corporate relocations so replete with aging stories of detachment from place, already?

5. The variety present in the world will be distributed to almost all localities and organizations. Variety is to be discarded in exchange for access to that variety at some future time, at some designated place. In the language of space, that which is located in one place is accessible and can be present in every place. Low-cost access to variety at will is the key. One

consequence will be that destroying anything anywhere will destroy something of the destroyer as well—if only stock ownership, customers, future contributors, or potential use. Zero-sum situations will acquire fuzzy payoffs. If someone loses, the winner also loses something. This will be especially true within the context of environmental problems (see chapters by Pirages, also Zartman, this volume). Already, the globalization of distribution of variety makes wars more difficult to calculate in terms of sheer winners and losers.

6. The world centers will become nodes in global flows rather than control points. Put differently, centers will proliferate, and instead of just a few world centers, there will be hundreds, perhaps thousands of them. These nodes will be specialized, say, in trade, banking, fashion, and science. This is quite in keeping with the theoretical idea that variety disperses into diversity. A polycentric world will be made up of switching or clearing points, useful in reducing uncertainty, not designed to control and to dominate. It will be a world without empires. And theory building will have to account for the dynamics of this profound, if still incomplete but continuing, worldwide transformation.

Our sketch of this "future conditional" scenario should not be mistaken for a linear progression into a world system. Conflicts inherent to the process have been already presented. First, most of the violent situations being faced today are consequences of change in national political systems and in the state's reach within its borders. This is what now encourages groups to seek and to attain long-suppressed recognition. The wars of tomorrow will not rest on old antagonisms seeking reassertion. Not that fine distinctions of the sort would make violence necessarily less bloody. Second, the local incursions by global activities may well ruin the aesthetics of micro-environments. And that may precipitate ugliness. Third, the wanderings of the masses in search of their share of profit from a globalizing political economy will probably disrupt human relations to saddening levels. Fourth, the unleashing of certain elements from established norms will lead to crime, and that could be threatening.

Establishing new, integrative norms is a far slower process than the delegitimization of existing regulations. There is reason to develop a fuller appreciation of the dynamics of globalization and to foster a more pondered understanding of their negative and positive consequences. There is need to encourage novel approaches to theory-making that are not only open to "ecological" narratives but just as attentive to the caveats scrutinized in each and every chapter of this volume. Understanding, more than explanation, can help to make such more or less foreseeable outcomes tolerable for all and their globalizing inputs and impacts manageable by most. Without new mentalities and newer mind-sets, futures may be pasts.

REFERENCES

Albrow, Martin, and Elizabeth King (eds.) (1990). *Globalization, Knowledge, and Society: Readings from International Sociology.* London: Sage Publications.

Etzioni, Amitai (1994). The End of Self-determination. *Annals of the International Institute of Sociology* n.s., 4.

Featherstone, Michael (ed.) (1990). *Global Culture: Nationalism, Globalization, and Modernity.* London: Sage Publications.

Mlinar, Zdravko (1992a). European Integration and Socio-spatial Restructuring. *International Journal of Sociology and Social Policy* 12, 8: 33–58.

Mlinar, Zdravko (ed.) (1992b). *Globalization and Territorial Identities.* Aldershot, UK: Avebury.

Mlinar, Zdravko (1995a). Local Response to Global Change. *Annals of the American Academy of Political and Social Science* 540 (July): 145–59.

Mlinar, Zdravko (1995b). Territorial Dehierarchization in Emerging Europe. In Josef Langer and Wolfgang Pollauer (eds.), *Small States in the Emerging New Europe.* Eisenstadt: Verlag für Soziologie und Humanethologie.

Modelski, George (1987). *Long Cycles in World Politics.* Seattle: University of Washington.

Rummel, R. J. (1997). *Power Kills: Democracy as a Method of Non-Violence.* New Brunswick, NJ: Transaction Publishers.

Snyder, Louis L. (1982). *Global Mini-Nationalisms: Autonomy or Interdependence.* Westport, CT: Greenwood Press.

Strassoldo, Riamondo (1992). Globalism and Localism: Theoretical Reflections and Some Evidence. Pp. 35–59 in Z. Mlinar (ed.), *Globalization and Territorial Identities.* Aldershot, UK: Avebury.

Teune, Henry, and Zdravko Mlinar (1978). *The Developmental Logic of Social Systems.* Beverly Hills, CA: Sage Publications.

Wallerstein, Immanuel (1974). *The Modern World-System.* New York: Academic Press.

Ziemowit, Pietras (1991). The Role of Minorities in Transnational Europe. *La Communita Internazionale*, Quaderni, No. 4, Padova-Cedam. 11.

CHAPTER 7

Sustaining a Global Civilization: An Evolutionary Perspective

DENNIS PIRAGES

INTRODUCTION

The world's population is now approaching 6 billion and is projected to reach 8 billion by the year 2025. In that year, 6.8 billion people will live in the presently less developed countries, and only 1.2 billion, approximately the current population, will live in the more developed countries.[1] After tens of thousands of years of coevolution with millions of other species, Homo sapiens has emerged as the dominant one—now accounting for more than 40 percent of worldwide consumption of the products of photosynthesis.[2] But after this fabulous run of good fortune, numerous ecological, demographic, and technological challenges are now developing to human well-being. Throughout most of human history a balance has been maintained between the environmental demands of human beings and nature's capabilities to meet them through continuous adaptation processes. Principles of biological natural selection hold that such interactive processes have shaped the genetic package called Homo sapiens through differential reproduction. Whereas all species have been able to profit from such biological processes, Homo sapiens has had a distinct advantage over the competition. Human beings have been able to use spoken and written language to pass accumulated wisdom from one generation to the next. While there are many reasons for the adaptive success of Homo sapiens, development of complex communication skills and related cultures has been critical. A body of survival-relevant information now evolves in response to environmental and technological change, much as does the genetic information shaped by natural selection.

Nature has continually created difficult challenges for human societies, and some inflexible and maladapted civilizations have fallen by the wayside. But most human societies have been able to respond to such challenges through technological innovations, value changes, shifts in behavior patterns, and creation of new institutions.[3] At present, however, the pace of change is rapidly accelerating, and many human societies are approaching a turning point. It is now unclear whether many current development trends are sustainable. And as the pace and scale of human activity are increasing, so is the penalty for failure to live within the limits of nature.

The contemporary international system is rapidly evolving into a global one. Technological innovations, demographic changes, and environmental shifts are combining to accelerate change, create global environmental challenges, and merge previously isolated human societies into a global community. While these wrenching shifts are creating numerous global issues, there are as yet no coherent and reliable global political institutions to manage them. Rapid population growth in many parts of the world is taxing environmental services, numerous states are failing or on the verge of failure, and the gap between rich and poor within and among countries is increasing. Indeed, Homo sapiens has experienced centuries of social progress, but the successes of the industrial period are now challenging the capabilities of a nascent global polity to deal with the many dilemmas associated with the emergence of a global civilization.

THE PASSING OF INDUSTRIAL SOCIETY[4]

Human societies and their value systems have been transformed by at least two clearly identifiable revolutionary currents of change. The first of these pulses, the agricultural revolution, began gathering momentum around 8000 B.C. in the Middle East and slowly spread to encompass almost the entire world.[5] This revolution was driven largely by innovations in agricultural production, including the domestication of plants and animals, that greatly enhanced the available food supply. The sociocultural impact of this revolution was considerable. Hunting and gathering bands were transformed into sedentary populations, a much more refined division of labor emerged, human populations began to expand, and major psychological changes in the dominant social paradigm or "worldview" took place.

The more recent and relevant transforming pulse, the industrial revolution, began gathering momentum in fifteenth- and sixteenth-century Europe and is still expanding into the more peripheral areas of the world. Initially enhancing human productivity by harnessing energy from fossil fuels to do the work previously done by human beings and draft animals, industrial era technologies also have been instrumental in fundamentally changing the nature of the impacted societies. Agrarian cultures have been transformed into more secular and materialistic ones, villages have given way to cities, farmers have become factory laborers, and human psychological and physical mobility have been greatly enhanced. Most important, this revolution has created a secular, materialistic, rational, pragmatic, utilitarian belief system that has been strengthened by many decades of increasing material abundance.

These revolutionary changes have also had significant political consequences. The surplus produced by agricultural innovations paradoxically gave rise to fledgling democracies, such as ancient Greece, but also to large empires. The industrial revolution has also fostered large-scale political modernization reflected in the emergence of mass democracy and concern for universal human rights. And the integrated international system of sovereign states, another product of the industrial revolution, is now being transformed into a global one.

The evolutionary products of these two great transformations have been shared social paradigms—collections of beliefs, norms, values, institutions, and survival rules that provide a common frame of reference and make social life possible.[6] Many of the violent clashes that have accompanied the modernization process, even though often disguised as class or ethnic conflict, are clashes between agrarian and industrial paradigms, different ways of perceiving reality and defining a good life.

This industrial transformation, which is commonly called *development*, has been a very unsettling and revolutionary period in human history. It has been characterized by massive social upheavals and destruction of old value systems and social orders. Industrial development and modernization have been characterized by world wars, revolutions, and large-scale bloodshed.

But, on balance, the industrial transformation has been a positive experience, and few people would opt to return to agrarian circumstances. This materially productive epoch has yielded unprecedented abundance, rising living standards for much of the world's population, and increasing human mobility. While over a 400-year period the industrial revolution has offered material abundance and a different way of life as it has penetrated more remote areas of the planet, it has also created dilemmas, disparities, and discontinuities as related increases in population and consumption threaten the future course of industrial progress. There is increasing evidence that material-intensive industrial civilization may no longer be sustainable, and a third major transformation may well be under way.[7] But compared to the last revolution, there is greater understanding of the dynamics involved, and it is possible to make intelligent policy choices to smooth the period of transition.

As a new millennium opens up, the global system is once again undergoing a major transformation, moving from an era of intense resource-dependent growth to a new era of more sustainable development. The continuing spread of material-intensive industrialization is now beginning to yield mixed results. And it is clear that even if tremendous efforts were to be made by all involved parties to transfer enough capital to raise consumption levels in the less industrialized world and eliminate existing income gaps, it would still be impossible for the bulk of humanity to be sustained for long at material consumption levels reached by the early industrializers.

The rapid growth taking place in China is an obvious case in point. If China were to continue its rapid rate of growth and reach U.S. levels of consumption, an ecological disaster would be inevitable.[8] For example, energy consumption in this hypothetical China would be roughly 14 times current domestic consumption and 25 percent higher than present global energy consumption.[9] Obviously this hypothetical China with split-level homes and attached two-car garages could not be sustained by the resources and environmental services available on this planet.

THE ORIGINS OF SUSTAINABILITY CONCEPTS

Sustainability is at once simple and complex. In its simple form the concept denotes human populations living within the carrying capacities of the relevant environments and having no long-term negative impact on opportunities for future generations. Complexity is introduced because all industrial societies are, to some extent, living beyond the long-term carrying capacity of the territory that they occupy. The industrial modernization that began developing in Europe nearly 400 years ago has culminated in value systems, institutions, consumption patterns, and habits that are congruent with environments of resource abundance and unlimited opportunity but that are much less appropriate for the future, particularly for the dense and growing populations in many of the presently less industrialized areas of the world.

Numerous societies at different times and in different places have encountered local sustainability crises as demands on nature have exceeded system regenerative capabilities. But academic and policy concerns about global sustainability have been apparent only for about three decades. The impetus for such concerns lies in the combined global population explosion, industrial expansion, and rapid increase in demand for raw materials of the 1960s. While the reasons for this rapid expansion of human demand are many, the result has been an awareness that growth in raw material consumption and environmental despoliation could not long continue without serious consequences for the quality of life in a more densely populated world. Increasing numbers of human beings and higher levels of per capita consumption have set off alarm bells over the ability of the Earth to respond to the demands of future generations.[10]

Growing demographic and environmental concerns catalyzed the publication of *The Limits to Growth* and subsequent debates over the future of the human condition in the late 1970s.[11] One of several studies commissioned by the Club of Rome, the "limits" computer simulation led to conclusions that without significant reductions in rates of population growth and new resource efficiencies in industrial production, some sort of major ecological collapse would be inevitable. Publication of the book, the first oil crisis, and the 1972 Stockholm Conference on the Human Environment raised public awareness of environmental issues and sparked an extended debate over potential future limits to growth in resource consumption.

Sustainability emerged from these growth assessments as a way of continuing what is defined as socioeconomic progress without contravening the limits of natural systems.[12] While more sustainable societies would have to be materially somewhat more frugal, there would be possibilities for new efficiencies and satisfactions that could maximize human satisfaction while minimizing the throughput of raw materials.[13]

Many of these ideas were given an official seal of approval by the World Commission on Environment and Development in 1987. The Bruntland Commission, concerned with the many dilemmas and issues associated with the future development in the less affluent countries, defined *sustainable development* as "development that meets the needs of the present without compromising the ability of future generations to meet their own needs."[14] This statement marked a departure from previous development thinking in two ways. First, it prescribed meeting human needs rather than human wants. Second, it abandoned the assumption, championed by liberal economists, that successive generations would naturally be better off than their predecessors. The commissioners concluded that changes in access to resources and in the distribution of production costs and benefits necessitated a new concern for social equity between and within generations.

The sustainability movement gathered significant political momentum in the 1990s. The 1992 United Nations Conference on Environment and Development in Brazil produced Agenda 21, a 40-chapter action plan dealing with many aspects of sustainable development. National, regional, and local commissions on sustainability have been appointed in dozens of countries. Scholars and activists have also tried to create measures of sustainability. In reviewing these attempts, Walter Corson has identified more than 100 suggested indicators of sustainability that cluster along 12 dimensions.[15] What was once a straightforward response to perceived limits to growth has blossomed into a significant global movement.

SUSTAINABILITY AS PROCESS

Building a more sustainable world is thus best accomplished by moving from environmentally destructive industrial to postindustrial and postmaterialist societies.[16] This process involves more than changing how resources are used and allocated. It also means carefully evaluating values and institutions that have been molded by generations of increasing material affluence. There are thus two aspects of building a more sustainable world. The first concerns relationships between human beings and nature, addressing the requisites for maintaining a balance between environmental capabilities and material demands. The second focuses on assessing and preserving, where possible, many of the ideals and institutions that have evolved during an era of prosperity.

The global sustainability problematic is therefore a cluster of environmental, economic, social, and political paradoxes associated with resolving issues resulting from the waning of the traditional industrial way of life while simultaneously creating more sustainable societies that preserve nature, retain some socially acceptable vision of affluence, and preserve many of the hard-won freedoms derived from industrial modernization. Becoming more sustainable is also best thought of as a process rather than a condition to be reached because relevant constraints and possibilities differ over time and space. What is sustainable under one set of circumstances may well not be under others. For example, steps to create a more sustainable future for oil-rich Saudi Arabia would be quite different than those required for resource-poor Japan. Future sustainability will be influenced by patterns of population growth and decline, changing environmental constraints, and technological innovations. Thus, moving in an organized way toward a more sustainable world requires that diverse alternatives be explored with an emphasis on preserving the greatest possible flexibility.

There are two methods by which the world can become more sustainable. The first is through a painful process of muddling through, a process that is well under way. The second is through a process of design, whereby anticipatory thinking can be employed in creating policies that can mitigate some of the harshest aspects of the transition. But building more sustainable societies need not require mass ecological penance such as forced vegetarianism or fashion industries based on sackcloth. Rather, real intellectual excitement and a renewed sense of political purpose can be associated with devising new ways to enhance human satisfaction without substantially increasing the burden on nature.

FORCES FOR GLOBAL TRANSFORMATION

There are three kinds of forces that are now driving the structural transformation toward greater sustainability. The first is a widespread and growing perception of new types of environmental limits to traditional forms of industrial growth. The second is a series of demographic shifts, both population explosions and implosions, that are already limiting growth in consumption on a global scale. Finally, new types of postindustrial technologies are pulling global economic activities in new directions.

The perception of global limits has changed significantly in recent years. Fears of "running out" of key raw materials proved unfounded during the lengthy recessions that followed the energy crises. Instead, water, food, and the integrity of the Earth's environmental services (i.e., the atmosphere and the hydrosphere) are now of greatest concern. Scientific speculation about the decline of the Earth's protective ozone layer has been followed by observations that thinning has been taking place. A consensus on the severity of the problem has led to international agreements to reduce and eventually eliminate production of destructive chlorofluorocarbons and related chemicals. More recently, abundant evidence of global warming due to carbon dioxide buildup has given credence to earlier environmental fears and led to a flurry of diplomatic activity to restrict carbon dioxide emissions. Although the extent of the projected warming might be somewhat less than originally feared, perhaps only two degrees Celsius over the next century, decreasing carbon dioxide emissions has become a priority item in international negotiations and potentially a significant limit on traditional forms of transportation and industrial production.

Demographic changes are slowing industrial expansion and reshaping global consumption patterns, thus creating a somewhat unexpected force for greater sustainability. Rapid population growth and political instability in Africa, the Middle East and parts of Asia are dimming prospects for future industrial growth. But on the other side of the demographic coin, a population implosion is serving to dampen potential demand for consumer goods. Many European countries have reached or dipped below zero population growth. Taken as a whole, the population of Europe is now declining at 0.1 percent annually. And people in industrial countries are living much longer. The net result is that almost one in five Europeans is now over the age of 65; and that percentage will grow rapidly over the next two decades.[17] Economic growth of a traditional sort is highly unlikely in countries with shrinking, aging, and financially insecure populations.

The net result of these two kinds of demographic shifts is that demand for many kinds of consumer goods will likely increase much more slowly than historical norms in the future. In much of the less industrialized world, lack of purchasing power presages very slow development of new markets, whereas in many of the more industrial countries aging populations on pensions will hardly have the purchasing power or desire to become avid consumers. Thus, world demand for raw materials is presently growing much more slowly than originally forecast in the 1970s, dampening inflationary pressures but contributing further to the stagnation in resource-exporting countries.

Finally, in line with the projections made by Daniel Bell more than 20 years ago, present patterns of technological innovation and entrepreneurial activity indicate continuing momentum toward postindustrial conditions and greater sustainability.[18] Growth in non-resource–intensive industries, for example, is creating a shift from blue-collar to white-collar employment. While this type of structural transformation is taking place unevenly, just as fossil fuel–intensive technological innovations drove the industrial revolution and a growing burden on the environment, a broad range of biomedical and telecommunication technologies are slowly moving human preferences and economic activity in more sustainable directions.

CONTEMPORARY DILEMMAS

The economic successes of the advanced stages of the industrial revolution ironically have spawned a set of global problems that now cannot easily be resolved with traditional remedies. Central to these is a rapid acceleration of technological innovation and diffusion that threatens to undermine the efficacy of evolutionary processes. The body of biological and sociocultural wisdom that has been passed from generation to generation historically has changed very slowly. Thus, "traditions" have previously served human populations well because the physical and social environments in which they have lived have changed only rarely. But the current rapid shifts from industrial growth to a more sustainable world threaten both to make evolutionary processes obsolete and to erode the mechanisms by which they operate.[19]

The quickening pace of technological innovation is now overwhelming governmental capacity to direct it in socially useful ways. Thus, technology continually reshapes societies in ways that are often in conflict with existing value systems. Knowledge and values (operating rules) passed from parent to child quickly become outmoded in this rapidly changing world. And the influence of primary agents of socialization, the family, schools, and religious institutions, has been much reduced by global babysitters, satellite television, and MTV.

There are many manifestations of this discontinuity such as erosion of standards, lack of vision, and value relativity. In many countries the nuclear family is in disarray, drug use and violent crime are rising, and prisons are teeming with the social casualties. In emerging "winner-take-all" societies, people have no concept of equity or enoughness.[20] Corporate executives in the United States lavish salaries and bonuses on themselves nearly 100 times the wages of their average worker. A professional basketball player can earn $30 million dollars per year, or a boxer can earn that much for one fight. This is more than 100 times the salary of the president of the United States.

A second set of dilemmas and problems stems from the technology-induced growth of an increasingly interdependent global village that is without the services of a global village council. Economic interdependence continues to deepen. Chinese workers produce clothes for American markets. Middle Eastern oil fuels automobiles in Europe and Japan. Transnational corporations leap across boundaries, leaving heavy footprints as they move. And worldwide increases in industrial production in the face of tightening environmental constraints mean that significant pollution from any source is now of concern to all countries sharing an increasingly fragile global commons.

But in the face of deepening integration and a tightening web of interdependence, there is no political authority with the power to keep order in a world of semisovereign states. A jumble of "soft law" ad hoc consensual agreements maintains some semblance of order in this global village, but without stronger political institutions, the course of international economic and social development will continue to wobble forward (or backward), propelled by technological change and the whims of the market.

A third cluster of significant global problems is associated with the failure of industrial modernization to benefit substantially a large portion of the world's population in less industrialized nations. The diffusion of industrial technology and know-how, without a corresponding sociocultural transformation of traditional societies based on a positive vision of social progress, has had an environmentally destructive impact. For example, medical technologies have dramatically reduced infant mortality and lengthened the life span in many less industrialized countries. But there has been no corresponding shift in reproductive values in many of them, and rapid population growth now limits economic possibilities. In many cases the shared visions and ties that hold traditional societies together have been destroyed, but with the exception of secular materialism, no positive visions have been offered as replacements.

Patterns of technology diffusion and related economic growth have had a very mixed impact. There have been some winners, but many marginal countries have been left behind. Numerous economic prescriptions for development have been written over the years, but they have met with limited success. Nearly two decades ago, Mahbub Ul Haq pointed out that development planners have changed their prescriptions several times, moving from import substitution to export expansion, then to emphasis on self-sufficiency through domestic agriculture, then to family planning and to wealth redistribution, and finally to free markets, in an attempt to find a formula that works.[21] Each of these strategies worked for some countries for a short period of time, but in most cases, growth slowed and a development gap widened.

During the period 1980–1993, the bulk of less industrialized countries experienced a per capita decline in measured income. Of 121 countries for which World Bank data are available, 53 experienced an annual decline in per capita gross national product (GNP) for this 13-year period.[22] Nicaragua led the negative growth list with an incredible 5.7 percent annual decline, followed by Côte d'Ivoire with a decline of 4.6 percent. Assuming that at least a 1 percent per capita annual growth rate is needed to cope with increasing developmental complexity and to maintain the existing quality of life—that is, widening highways, installing traffic signals, fighting pollution—another 18 countries fell short of this target and failed to make any significant per capita economic progress.

More than one-third of the world's population lives in China and India, and a claim is often made that these two giants are poised for significant growth. But India has been plodding along with an annual per capita growth rate of 3 percent, adding a minuscule $9 per year to its $300 per capita GNP. The Chinese case is more interesting and raises some troubling questions about the future potential of the industrial model of progress. Recovering from decades of authoritarian political control and unleashing an associated pent-up dynamism, a liberalized China grew at an 8.2 percent per capita rate during this 1980–1993 period. Much of this per capita progress has been due to what some call draconian Chinese population policies, which have resulted in a manageable 1.4 percent annual rate of population increase.[23] But these policies are now under concerted attack by human rights groups and foreign governments. In addition, consumption growth in China will soon run up against domestic resource and global environmental constraints that will have a significant impact on growth rates.[24]

Long-term prospects for the poorest countries aren't likely to change significantly. Foreign assistance is increasingly under attack in donor countries as skyrocketing welfare costs are stressing budgets. And the meltdown of the East–West confrontation has significantly reduced strategic donor interest in a number of the less industrialized countries. Despite growing needs, official development assistance from OECD (Organization for Economic Cooperation and Development) countries has remained stagnant in the 1990s. More important, however, the United States, which gave 0.32 percent of GNP in aid in 1970, had cut back to 0.15 percent by 1993. Fortunately, other countries have taken up some of the slack, but the percentage of GNP devoted to official assistance never approached the targets set during the development decade and actually declined from 0.34 in 1970 to 0.30 in 1993. The total inflation-adjusted (1992 dollars) assistance only increased from $35 billion in 1970 to $57 billion in 1993 in the face of rapidly increasing populations and needs in the less industrialized countries.[25] The global AIDS epidemic has been exacting a tragic toll in many of the less industrialized countries, but the per patient cost of new AIDS therapies, now estimated to be in excess of $12,000 per year, places these pharmaceuticals well beyond the means of governments and patients in these countries.

Finally, one of the most important evolving dilemmas stems from the unpleasant reality that the resource-intensive core industrialization processes that support industrial change are not sustainable on a global scale and cannot be transferred to areas containing the bulk of the human race. Numerous persuasive arguments have been made elsewhere about basic flaws in the future of industrial progress, and they need not be repeated here.[26] Suffice it to say that, from an ecological point of view, traditional forms of industrial development feed on creating material expectations that cannot be met without unacceptable environmental destruction. An industrialized China or India would create tremendous amounts of carbon dioxide and hasten warming on a global scale. On a local scale, dozens of developing countries already face severe urban pollution problems that significantly impact human health.

Growing constraints on certain types of consumption need not herald the end of progress. But these constraints do indicate that the context for development has changed. This means that a number of fundamental ethical and political questions that have been eclipsed during several generations of rapid growth in material consumption now must be addressed. The political task has been put succinctly by William Ophuls: "The liberal paradigm of politics unleashed human will and appetite, but provided no countervailing source of moral principle strong enough to preserve society from their ravages over the long term. Liberalism is therefore based on intrinsically self-destructive principles."[27] Given that continued industrial growth on a global scale is no longer ecologically possible, future social progress can only occur by deliberately sorting out the aspects that are both desirable and sustainable in the more ecologically fragile world of the next century.

A SOCIOCULTURAL GENOME PROJECT

Resolving these problems must be part of a long-term process in which human values and institutions, the products of sociocultural evolution, adjust to changing demographic and ecological constraints and reassert control over the future direction of a currently autonomous technology.[28] Someone in favor of slowing the pace of technological change in order to redress the balance between technology and human values runs the risk of being branded a neo-Luddite. Realistically, in the existing competitive international system, an attempt by one country to control the pace of technological change would only bolster the fortunes of economic competitors.

Existing imbalances can't be redressed by constraining technology, but they can be addressed by reinvigorating sociocultural evolutionary processes and strengthening the values and institutions that should guide investments in new technologies. A first step is to recognize the urgency of an analysis of the origins of the problem. In biology and genetics, scientists have embarked on a human genome project aimed at developing a better understanding of the physical product of evolution, the human body. A great effort is under way to identify the genes responsible for passing various traits from one generation to the next. A major goal of the project is to develop a comprehensive understanding of these processes and to identify genes that may be responsible for inherited diseases so that remedial actions may be taken to repair them.

The human genome project offers an appropriate model for similar efforts in the social sciences aimed at identifying and assessing the utility of the norms, values, and beliefs that are being transferred from one generation to the next through sociocultural evolution. Just as certain dysfunctional human genes are responsible for passing on harmful physical traits, many aspects of the dominant industrial paradigm are now equally threatening to the long-term persistence of many human societies. The purpose of such a sociocultural genome project, or research paradigm, would be to develop a better understanding of these evolutionary processes and to isolate and deal with destructive and nonsustainable patterns of human behavior.

This effort might initially focus on the primitive way that social progress is now defined and measured. The technology-driven materialistic growth path taken to this point in the industrial revolution was only one of many that could have been, and still could be, chosen. But the consequences of choices and nonchoices already made are obvious in the statistics detailing increases in social disintegration. Basic needs of large numbers of human beings are not, and will not be, met without redefining the direction of progress. On the south side of the planetary industrial divide, basic needs for food, clothing, and shelter are no longer adequately being met. While the wealthy on the north side are, for the most part, adequately sheltered, higher-level needs for affiliation and self-actualization seem no longer to be optimally fulfilled.

The benchmark measure of progress developed and used by economists over the years is gross domestic product (GDP), an undifferentiated indicator of economic activity. Its continuing use has been lambasted by critics over the years, but it is still officially sanctioned by almost all governments as a primary indicator of social progress. But it makes little sense to do so since GDP makes little distinction between social progress and social regress. Assume, for example, that the current crime wave in the United States, and many other parts of the world, continues to intensify. More police would be required in order to arrest criminals, more judges would be required to sentence them, and more prisons would be required to hold them. In addition, frightened citizens would buy more home "defense" weapons, thus quickening the pace of arms production. Insurance premiums would increase in order to pay growing stolen property claims. And all of this would show up in the relevant countries as an impressive addition to GDP.

There are many sensible alternatives that are better indicators of social progress. One of these is the Genuine Progress Indicator (GPI).[29] The GPI totals the value of goods and services produced and then subtracts defensive expenditures, social costs, and the depreciation of environmental assets and natural resources. Calculations done for the United States indicate that while the measured annual per capita GDP grew steadily from $8,000 in 1950 to $16,000 in 1995 (in 1982 dollars), the Genuine Progress Indicator rose from $6,000 per capita in 1950 and peaked at about $7,500 in 1975. It declined steadily over the next 20 years, dropping to $4,000 per capita in 1995. The Genuine Progress Indicator is just one example of numerous suggestions that could lead to much more refined measures of social progress.[30]

GOVERNING A GLOBAL VILLAGE

The worldwide spread of the industrial revolution has forged human populations into ever larger political and economic units. The early stages of industrialization were associated with the emergence of large states from the consolidation of city-states and small kingdoms. The middle stages of the industrial revolution were characterized by the development of colonial empires and eventually a world system. In the latter stages of this revolution an interdependent global economy and society has emerged. But this global economy and nascent community face complex problems of growing interdependence without any significant political guidance.

The origins of the contemporary state contain lessons for political development and economic redistribution in the new global community. In the history of contemporary industrial states the pressures for integration came from the top down. Consolidation of smaller populations into a larger whole, the process of nation building, was usually accomplished through military force. Authoritarian rule was often the norm, and mass democracies emerged only after long and often bitter struggles over the right to vote. In the emerging global system, pressures for deeper integration are being driven by autonomous technological, ecological, and demographic forces. But there is no higher political authority, and a system for authoritatively allocating values must be built from the bottom up.

In all social systems, including the nascent global system, privilege can be allocated by a mixture of public and private (political and market) mechanisms.[31] Recently, the collapse of socialism has given added impetus to long-term trends toward market-based allocations. But markets are favored by the powerful and privileged because they serve to reinforce an existing structure of prejudices and preferences. And markets are seen to be useful because they dampen potential conflicts over unequal distribution. Marketplace winners can justify their privileges by praising the market, and losers can lick their wounds and find solace by blaming Adam Smith's invisible hand. Markets are very readily embraced during periods of rapid growth, as even the welfare of the least fortunate usually increases. But markets are looked upon with increasing suspicion as growth slows.

The bias toward heavy reliance upon markets within industrial societies is mirrored in the global system. The United States, exerting hegemony over the postwar world economy, stressed a free trade system as a "natural" way to increase gross world product. The failure to establish an effective international trade organization after World War II obviated possibilities for asserting political control over international economic processes. The postwar global economic expansion provided a fertile environment in which markets could operate. It has only been over the last 15 years, when the global expansion has slowed, that the efficacy of markets has been challenged.

Markets do a credible job of keeping the peace where a structure of preferences is well established, leads to ethically acceptable outcomes, and is not subject to serious challenge by the disenchanted. Markets clearly can help maximize global production of goods and services. But markets have little foresight capability and have no internal mechanism for altering privileges or preferences. Thus, they cannot address two of the greatest challenges of the new century: Markets cannot arrest a devastating human assault on the physical environment, nor can they address the growing gap between the rich and poor within and among countries.

Current market-oriented trade policies seek to increase individual consumption of material goods, encourage resource-intensive economic growth, promote global specialization, and insulate trade officials from political pressure.[32] Even though a quasi-political World Trade Organization has been created to referee global trade disputes and to give lip service to environmental issues, the organization is staffed largely by lawyers and economists, not environmentalists. Similarly, there is no dynamic in the existing global market that operates to improve the lot of the poor, and a small trickle of charitable aid to the poorest countries currently makes little developmental difference.

Thus, international political governance is required to handle the complexities of interaction in an increasingly interdependent global village and to facilitate the evolution of political, social, and economic rights for all villagers. But ceding more power to international organizations seems to be a utopian idea at present because the United States, the present global hegemon, sees no reason to upset a system that it dominates. The United States has withdrawn from the United Nations Educational, Scientific, and Cultural Organization (UNESCO) and has been repeatedly in arrears meeting financial obligations. Although the United Nations itself is now a somewhat rusty bureaucratic product of the industrial era and certainly can be profitably restructured, the antipathy of the United States toward a wider distribution of global power stems mostly from self-interest and a desire to squelch a discussion of distributional issues.

AUTHENTIC SUSTAINABLE DEVELOPMENT

Traditional visions of progress indicated that industrialization and related economic growth were to diffuse throughout the world and that all countries would eventually share the material fruits of industrial progress. During the heyday of rapid worldwide economic growth, laissez-faire approaches were buttressed by claims that a rising tide would lift all ships. In the present era of significant population growth and slower industrial expansion, however, it is uncertain how rapidly the tide is rising. And it is clear that the tides lift some boats far higher than others; and many remain mired in the mud.

The shortcomings and failures of old prescriptions for development are well known and the subject of numerous studies and books.[33] From an evolutionary perspective, there are several basic flaws in these traditional approaches. First, they have not led to significant material or ethical progress for the bulk of the human race. The laissez-faire approach provides no method, other than cheap and often oppressed labor, by which poor countries can overcome the huge technological edge possessed by early industrializers and become economically competitive. Although there is now significant economic growth reported in China, for example, new factories financed by foreign capital are often organized along paramilitary lines, with workers living in barracks and working 12-hour shifts.[34] These old approaches to development also involve the destruction of traditional cultures. Processes of change are themselves often a major cause of spiritual decline and social dislocation. Finally, there is little possibility that past patterns of resource-intensive industrialization can be replicated by the bulk of the human race. Put concisely, the existing prescriptions for social progress haven't worked for most of the human race, often lead to social decay and destruction when materialism replaces traditional values, and cannot be replicated in countries that are already pressing close to ecological carrying capacity.

The World Commission on Environment and Development helped to clarify the dialogue on future prospects by defining *sustainable development*. Some have claimed that *sustainable development* is a contradiction in terms, and others have appropriated the terminology for less-than-laudable causes. But this definition contains realistic guidelines for a new planetary bargain for authentic development, a process that Denis Goulet defines as one that promotes justice within and among societies while respecting traditional cultures and the forces of nature.[35] Sustainable authentic development means focusing on meeting existing human needs rather than on creating more human wants. It means respecting the evolutionary product represented by the cultures of less industrialized societies. Sustainable authentic development also contains an element of stewardship reflected in the imperative to preserve opportunities for future generations to meet their own needs. And it leaves the door open for the development of appropriate and environmentally benign technologies that could play a role in increasing welfare in the less affluent countries.

Sustainable authentic development also implies a new relationship between affluent industrialized and poorer, less industrialized countries. Attempts to transfer the existing industrial growth model should be rethought by all parties. Reducing commercial advertising and "want-creation" activities in societies where there is little possibility of meeting rising expectations should also be a priority. And leaders of less industrialized countries should focus on remedying demographic and ecological problems that pose a serious threat to future generations.

A new approach to financing sustainable authentic development is also necessary. Meeting future entitlement demands in OECD countries will inevitably shrink the flow of bilateral aid, and the World Bank has yet to make a real transition to alternative lending practices.[36] A new international development authority, staffed by social scientists, environmentalists, and perhaps a few economists, might be necessary to facilitate "postindustrial" development. This authority could play a significant role in defining new patterns of development if it were supported by measures such as a 1 percent tax on exports from industrial countries.

ECOLOGICALLY SUSTAINABLE PROGRESS

Creating a more sustainable world while maintaining social progress are long-term processes requiring extensive research, dialogue, political will, and bargaining. Future social progress requires compromises and new approaches within the framework of an evolving global society facing challenges to its ecological security. Nature's limitations can no longer be ignored, nor can the deeper integration of the global system be reversed. The Western European industrial experience may have been an appropriate response to the material abundance of the time, but it cannot, and should not, be replicated by the bulk of the human race. A new postmaterialist definition of progress and development, stressing qualitative, rather than quantitative, growth, should guide this evolutionary process.

In a world of complex interdependence, there is little prospect of constructing a protective moat between northern and southern neighborhoods in the global village. The countries of the Global North, having exploited the planet's commons in building secular, materialistic societies, can take the lead in deliberately transforming a way of life that cannot and should not be emulated. In fact, elements of such a transformation to a postmaterialist world are already visible there.[37] A new development dialogue must be opened if all parties to a new planetary bargain are to avoid the harsh consequences of continued environmental deterioration and social injustice.

Foresight and compromises are also essential in the Global South. The most obvious one is the need to address resolutely the issue of rapid population growth. Substantial progress cannot take place in regions, such as Sub-Saharan Africa, where population growth rates average 2.9 percent annually and populations are doubling every 24 years.[38] Such reproductive excesses, based on the persistence of pro-natalist values in a much-changed world of limits, are leading to the collapse of local ecosystems and are destroying the potential for meeting basic human needs, building education, and enhancing other forms of sustainable authentic development. And leaders in the Global South could themselves play a more assertive role in creating and disseminating new models of social progress based on qualitative development rather than quantitative growth. There is no reason that China, India, or a number of other countries need to repeat the environmental and social mistakes of rampant industrialization, only to find themselves in a sustainability quandary in the course of this new century.

Future social progress can, in the end, only take place in an ecologically secure environment. Many of the current challenges to human well-being can be traced to Homo sapiens acting and organizing in an ecologically imprudent manner. Sustainable, authentic, ecologically secure development means anchoring social progress in a conception of human well-being stressing a balance among human populations, between them and the nurturing capabilities of the physical environment, and between them and the other organisms with which the earth is shared.

NOTES

1. Figures taken from Population Reference Bureau, "1997 World Population Data Sheet" (Washington, DC: Population Reference Bureau, 1997).

2. Peter Vitousek et al., "Human Appropriation of the Products of Photosynthesis," *Bioscience* 36 (1986): 6.

3. On the collapse of human civilizations, see Clive Ponting, *A Green History of the World: The Environment and the Collapse of Great Civilizations* (New York: Penguin Books, 1991); Joseph Tainter, *The Collapse of Complex Societies* (Cambridge: Cambridge University Press, 1988); J. Donald Hughes, *Ecology in Ancient Civilizations* (Albuquerque: University of New Mexico Press, 1975).

4. Borrowed from Daniel Lerner, *The Passing of Traditional Society: Modernizing the Middle East* (Glencoe, IL: Free Press, 1963). It is interesting that it has taken only 35 years to move from the passing of agrarian societies to the transformation of industrial ones.

5. For more information on the origins, impacts, and rate of spread of world agriculture, see Jared Diamond, *Guns, Germs, and Steel: The Fates of Human Societies* (New York: W. W. Norton, 1997), ch. 10.

6. The dominant social paradigm concept is derived from the work of Thomas Kuhn, *The Structure of Scientific Revolutions* (Chicago: University of Chicago Press, 1962). See also Dennis Pirages and Paul Ehrlich, *Ark II: Social Response to Environmental Imperatives* (New York: Viking Press, 1974).

7. Willis Harman, *An Incomplete Guide to the Future* (New York: W. W. Norton, 1979).

8. These calculations yielded similar conclusions in the early 1970s. See Dennis Pirages and Paul Ehrlich, "If All Chinese Had Wheels," *New York Times*, March 16, 1972.

9. Derived from World Resources Institute, *World Resources 1996–97* (New York: Oxford University Press, 1996), table 12.2.

10. Paul Ehrlich, *The Population Bomb* (New York: Ballantine Books, 1968). A good account of the course of environmental activism is provided by John McCormick, *Reclaiming Paradise: The Global Environmental Movement* (Bloomington: Indiana University Press, 1989).

11. Donella Meadows et al., *The Limits to Growth* (New York: Universe Books, 1972).

12. Dennis Pirages, *The Sustainable Society* (New York: Praeger, 1977).

13. Herman Daly, *Steady-State Economics: The Economics of Biophysical Equilibrium and Moral Growth* (San Francisco: W. H. Freeman, 1977), ch. 1.

14. World Commission on Environment and Development, *Our Common Future* (New York: Oxford University Press, 1987), p. 43.

15. Walter Corson, "Measuring Sustainability: Indicators, Trends, and Performance," in Dennis Pirages (ed.), *Building Sustainable Societies* (Armonk, NY: M. E. Sharpe, 1996).

16. Postmaterialism is explored in Paul R. Abramson and Ronald Inglehart, *Value Change in Global Perspective* (Ann Arbor: University of Michigan Press, 1995).

17. Figures taken from Population Reference Bureau, "1996 World Population Data Sheet" (Washington, DC: Population Reference Bureau, 1996).

18. Daniel Bell, *The Coming of Post-Industrial Society* (New York: Basic Books, 1973).

19. See Gerard Piehl, *The Acceleration of History* (New York: Knopf, 1972).

20. Robert H. Frank and Philip J. Cook, *The Winner-Take-All Society* (New York: Free Press, 1995).

21. See Mahbub Ul Haq, *The Poverty Curtain* (New York: Columbia University Press, 1976), p. 20.

22. World Bank, *World Development Report 1995* (New York: Oxford University Press, 1995), table 1.

23. Ibid., table 25.

24. Lester Brown, *Who Will Feed China?* (New York: W. W. Norton, 1996).

25. World Bank, *World Development Report 1995*, table 18.

26. See, for example, Lester Milbrath, *Envisioning a Sustainable Society* (Albany: State University of New York Press, 1991); Joel Jay Kassiola, *The Death of Industrial Civilization: The Limits to Economic Growth and the Repoliticization of Advanced Industrial Society* (Albany, NY: SUNY Press, 1990).

27. William Ophuls, *Requiem for Modern Politics* (Boulder, CO: Westview Press, 1998), ch. 1.

28. See Jacques Ellul, *The Technological Society* (New York: Knopf, 1964); Langdon Winner, *Autonomous Technology* (Cambridge, MA: MIT Press, 1977).

29. Clifford Cobb, Ted Halstead, and Jonathan Rowe, "If the GDP Is Up, Why Is America Down?" *The Atlantic Monthly* (October 1995).

30. See Hazel Henderson, *Building a Win-Win World* (San Francisco: Berrett-Koehler Publishers, 1996), ch. 10.

31. Charles E. Lindblom, *Politics and Markets: The World's Political-Economic Systems* (New York: Basic Books, 1977), ch. 1.

32. Thomas A. Wathen, "Trade Policy: Clouds in the Vision of Sustainability," in Dennis Pirages (ed.), *Building Sustainable Societies* (Armonk, NY: M. E. Sharpe, 1996), p. 71.

33. See, for example, S. C. Dube, *Modernization and Development: The Search for Alternative Paradigms* (London: Zed Books, 1988); Richard B. Norgaard, *Development Betrayed: The End of Progress and a Coevolutionary Revisioning of the Future* (London: Routledge, 1994).

34. See Anita Chan, "Boot Camp at the Shoe Factory," *Washington Post*, November 3, 1996.

35. Denis Goulet, "Authentic Development: Is It Sustainable?" in Dennis Pirages (ed.), *Building Sustainable Societies* (Armonk, NY: M. E. Sharpe, 1996).

36. See Bruce Rich, *Mortgaging the Earth: The World Bank, Environmental Impoverishment, and the Crisis of Development* (Boston: Beacon Press, 1994).

37. See Abramson and Inglehart, *Value Change in Global Perspective.*

38. Figures taken from Population Reference Bureau, "1996 World Population Data Sheet."

REFERENCES

Abramson, Paul R., and Ronald Inglehart (1995). *Value Change in Global Perspective.* Ann Arbor: University of Michigan Press.

Bell, Daniel (1973). *The Coming of Post-Industrial Society.* New York: Basic Books.

Brown, Lester (1996). *Who Will Feed China?* New York: W. W. Norton.

Chan, Anita (1996). "Boot Camp at the Shoe Factory." *Washington Post,* November 3.

Cobb, Clifford, Ted Halstead, and Jonathan Rowe (1995). "If the GDP Is Up, Why Is America Down?" *The Atlantic Monthly* (October).

Corson, Walter (1996). "Measuring Sustainability: Indicators, Trends, and Performance." In Dennis Pirages (ed.), *Building Sustainable Societies.* Armonk, NY: M. E. Sharpe.

Daly, Herman (1977). *Steady-State Economics: The Economics of Biophysical Equilibrium and Moral Growth.* San Francisco: W. H. Freeman.

Diamond, Jared (1997). *Guns, Germs, and Steel: The Fates of Human Societies.* New York: W. W. Norton.

Dube, S. C. (1988). *Modernization and Development: The Search for Alternative Paradigms.* London: Zed Books.

Ehrlich, Paul (1968). *The Population Bomb.* New York: Ballantine Books.

Ellul, Jacques (1964). *The Technological Society.* New York: Knopf.

Frank, Robert H., and Philip J. Cook (1995). *The Winner-Take-All Society.* New York: Free Press.

Goulet, Denis (1996). "Authentic Development: Is It Sustainable?" In Dennis Pirages (ed.), *Building Sustainable Societies.* Armonk, NY: M. E. Sharpe.

Harman, Willis (1979). *An Incomplete Guide to the Future.* New York: W. W. Norton.

Henderson, Hazel (1996). *Building a Win-Win World.* San Francisco: Berrett-Koehler Publishers.

Hughes, J. Donald (1975). *Ecology in Ancient Civilizations.* Albuquerque: University of New Mexico Press.

Kassiola, Joel Jay (1990). *The Death of Industrial Civilization: The Limits to Economic Growth and the Repoliticization of Advanced Industrial Society.* Albany: State University of New York Press.

Kuhn, Thomas (1962). *The Structure of Scientific Revolutions.* Chicago: University of Chicago Press.

Lerner, Daniel (1963). *The Passing of Traditional Society: Modernizing the Middle East.* Glencoe, IL: Free Press.

Lindblom, Charles E. (1977). *Politics and Markets: The World's Political-Economic Systems.* New York: Basic Books.

McCormick, John (1989). *Reclaiming Paradise: The Global Environmental Movement*. Bloomington: Indiana University Press.

Meadows, Donella et al. (1972). *The Limits to Growth*. New York: Universe Books.

Milbrath, Lester (1991). *Envisioning a Sustainable Society*. Albany: State University of New York Press.

Norgaard, Richard B. (1994). *Development Betrayed: The End of Progress and a Coevolutionary Revisioning of the Future*. London: Routledge.

Ophuls, William (1998). *Requiem for Modern Politics*. Boulder, CO: Westview Press.

Piehl, Gerard (1972). *The Acceleration of History*. New York: Knopf.

Pirages, Dennis (1977). *The Sustainable Society*. New York: Praeger.

Pirages, Dennis, and Paul Ehrlich (1972). "If All Chinese Had Wheels." *New York Times*, March 16.

Pirages, Dennis, and Paul Ehrlich (1974). *Ark II: Social Response to Environmental Imperatives*. New York: Viking Press.

Ponting, Clive (1991). *A Green History of the World: The Environment and the Collapse of Great Civilizations*. New York: Penguin Books.

Population Reference Bureau (1996). "1996 World Population Data Sheet." Washington, DC: Population Reference Bureau.

Population Reference Bureau (1997). "1997 World Population Data Sheet." Washington, DC: Population Reference Bureau.

Rich, Bruce (1994). *Mortgaging the Earth: The World Bank, Environmental Impoverishment, and the Crisis of Development*. Boston: Beacon Press.

Tainter, Joseph (1988). *The Collapse of Complex Societies*. Cambridge: Cambridge University Press.

Ul Haq, Mahbub (1976). *The Poverty Curtain*. New York: Columbia University Press.

Vitousek, Peter et al. (1986). "Human Appropriation of the Products of Photosynthesis." *Bioscience* 36: 6.

Wathen, Thomas A. (1996). "Trade Policy: Clouds in the Vision of Sustainability." In Dennis Pirages (ed.), *Building Sustainable Societies*. Armonk, NY: M. E. Sharpe.

Winner, Langdon (1977). *Autonomous Technology*. Cambridge, MA: MIT Press.

World Bank (1995). *World Development Report 1995*. New York: Oxford University Press.

World Commission on Environment and Development (1987). *Our Common Future*. New York: Oxford University Press.

World Resources Institute (1996). *World Resources 1996–97*. New York: Oxford University Press.

CHAPTER 8

Probing the Unknown: Changing Visions of International Relations

RICHARD W. MANSBACH

INTRODUCTION

Can international relations theory make sense of the immense changes that have transformed the world around us in recent years? And if current theory fails to do so, how should those theories be revised? The aim of theory is to make sense of what happens in an apparently complex universe by highlighting those features of that universe that are necessary for us to understand it. The failure of international relations theory to predict the end of the Cold War or to explain it except in an ad hoc fashion, when combined with the profound changes in the world confronting us, may finally provide the impetus to move beyond Europe's "great tradition" of Realpolitik.

FROM INTERNATIONAL TO POSTINTERNATIONAL

Even a superficial review of today's world reveals that there is much more to global politics than an interstate system of unitary actors delineated by sovereign frontiers that set off "domestic" politics (whose stability and peace are assured by the state's monopoly of the means of coercion) from the "anarchy" of international politics. Yet the formal study of international relations as an autonomous discipline or subfield rests on three fundamental concepts: state, power, and anarchy.

This highly limited and limiting portrait of global politics is the fruit of the European tradition of power politics that stretches back to Thucydides and comes to us through readings of Machiavellian tradition in Western political thought. The first of the three concepts—the sovereign state—is the most important, as without it there is no foundation on which to construct the other two. Power and anarchy become logically central only after we assume a political arena dominated exclusively by a system of independent, legally equal, and self-sufficient entities. And it is hardly coincidental that this great tradition flowered at a time when princely territorial states were throwing off the complex property arrangements that characterized feudal Europe. International politics, as Martin Wight observes, is "the untidy fringe of domestic politics"; Western political thought "is the tradition of speculation about the state," and international politics is "a tradition of speculation about the society of states."[1]

Although some of America's Founding Fathers, most notably Alexander Hamilton, were in the power politics tradition, that tradition had to compete in American thought with a powerful English liberal current until the end of World War II, when it was disseminated by European emigrants like Hans Morgenthau and Henry Kissinger.[2] And the "scientists" who seized control of the discipline from the late 1960s until the 1990s were realists with slide rules, led by greater concern for method than theory and by a vested interest in a state-centric model facilitating data collection and comparison. The "great debate" of that era was less about epistemology than about funding and promotions.

In consequence, the advocates of realism/neorealism, having dismissed their critics as naive "idealists" and "utopians," stood largely unchallenged until the end of the Cold War. Although the state "black box" was gingerly opened by a few theorists in decision making and economic phenomena, too, were permitted entry through the back door under the rubric of international political economy, realism's basic premises continued unabashedly to govern international relations theory and practice.

Efforts to criticize realist norms were dismissed as a sorry confusion of "is" with "ought" even as a powerful predisposition toward favoring stability dominated realist analysis. To this day, mainstream critics of realism go to great lengths to avoid this charge by disguising or diluting the very real normative commitments on which their criticisms are based. Suggestions that power-based analyses explain everything, and therefore nothing, are repeatedly and vigorously dismissed as assaults on parsimony, as though parsimony were an end in itself.

The great tradition, however, has begun to give way to new ideas as the Westphalian era during which that tradition evolved and prospered comes to an end. States are no longer able to take citizens' loyalties for granted as new identities are formed and old ones reemerge (see Zartman, this volume).

Throughout the developing world, states are competing (often unsuccessfully) with popular loyalties to a variety of political forms that were largely suppressed during the colonial era. And states everywhere enjoy less and less control over their very own affairs, owing to forces that transcend sovereign frontiers. The "retreat of the state"[3] is evident everywhere as governments find themselves paralyzed by a variety of forces from above and below, ranging from currency speculation to street demonstrations.

The state, with origins in exclusive control over territory, finds it difficult to deal effectively with deterritorialized authority made possible by the revolution in telecommunications. It was the state's link with territory as a source of wealth and power that enabled it to emerge from the untidy overlap of messy medieval patterns of authority. Paradoxically, that same link is increasingly a source of weakness as states compete with other targets of loyalty such as transnational corporations or currency speculators. Amid simultaneous processes of fragmentation and integration of political structures (see chapter by Teune and Mlinar, this volume), many of which occupy the same political and territorial space, global politics is again assuming some of the features of the medieval era.

The ending of the Westphalian era as a chapter in human history is now encouraging fissiparous tendencies not only in political structures but also in theorizing about international relations. The discipline is hopelessly divided into tracts of theory whose champions often speak only to one another and prefer to write only in highly specialized journals. What, then, should theories of global politics emphasize? In seeking an answer, this chapter reconsiders the emerging features of international or, as James Rosenau calls it, "postinternational politics."[4]

ON THEORY

The breakdown of theoretical coherence in the field and the absence of any paradigmatic authority raise the specter of a renewal of conflict among competing "schools." Many of us recall firsthand from collisions among earlier disciplinary theologians how efforts to achieve authoritative recognition can conduce to discriminatory labeling and fierce infighting and how such ugly collisions may ruin an academic department.[5] These quarrels may involve real "spoils" such as public funding, academic hiring and promotion, and the destiny (and well-being) of graduate students. Tolerance of theoretical diversity (see Holsti, this volume) has become more critical than in the past, as immense changes shake the very foundations of the political world in which we live.

Theory entails strategic simplification of that universe. In other words, theory tells us what is important to investigate by shrouding everything else. Theorists seek to tease meaning from a mass of factual and normative information. They do so by ordering that information in ways that conform to underlying beliefs about what is important and what is unimportant and how the important facts and values are related to one another. The order that the theorist perceives is not necessarily inherent in the phenomena being observed. Rather, it is usually imposed by the theorist whose perceptions are founded on unproved, and almost certainly unprovable, assumptions.

And more often than we care to admit, it reveals a theorist's attitudes about phenomena that are innately subjective (see Krippendorff chapter, this volume). Consequently, processes of selecting and organizing facts often reflect powerful (if not always articulated or even conscious) epistemological, normative, and even political commitments and premises.[6] As Robert Keohane and Joseph Nye put it: "One's assumptions about world politics profoundly affect what one sees and how one constructs theories to explain events."[7]

Put differently, the way in which theory conditions us to see certain facts and values while ignoring others is logically prior to and more important than theory's function of imposing order on the field. By the time order begins to emerge out of disorder, we are already conditioned to "see" some phenomena while (almost) deliberately overlooking others.

Recognition of these commitments and premises (or prejudices and predispositions, if the reader prefers) should make us leery of seductive claims by "scientists" who promise to lead us from the dark realm of subjectivity to the sunny uplands of objective and systematic truth.[8] If, as Alan Ryan insists, the paradigms that set our research agendas and guide our enquiries "do not so much confront the facts as tell us what we should see in the facts,"[9] our efforts to simplify reality demand sustained self-consciousness, lest we end up altering our perceptions of reality to fit the premises of the paradigm. We must also beware of pursuing parsimony as an end in itself rather than as one of the numerous desirable features of theory—a propensity that, critics of positivism might argue, has led to many errors.

Today, technology conspires to make the sheer accretion of facts a more serious obstacle to understanding. By telling us what to look at and allowing us to infer what we may safely ignore, theory preselects (at the risk of creating) the very facts on which we are trying to impose order.

It is no exaggeration to suggest that ordinary citizens who follow the news may have a better picture of how the world works actually than many a blinkered international relations theorist. Happily, failure does provide healthy incentives to reconsider concepts and theories on which we might have leaned for too long. The most important of these are *nation-state, domestic politics,* and *territory.* However, if we abandon the concepts and theories that we have, we will need substitutes. Since we may not replace something with nothing, we should not merely criticize. Where we destroy by plan, we must rebuild by design.

This is no simple matter. Constructing theory demands more than a dispassionate recitation or a reconciliation of partial truths in search of a larger truth. As theory not only reflects reality but also helps to shape it, it may lend itself to serve, defend, or assail a particular version of reality as well. While foes of realism have sought to replace concepts such as "state" and "national interest" with "international organizations" and "international law," realists from Jean Bodin to Kenneth Waltz have either advocated the virtues of the "sovereign state" or defended its status in global politics.

Although often unstated, such analyses are infused with normative commitment. As Frank Wayman and Paul Diehl remind us, "[R]ealist scholarship . . . reemerged in the West at the time of the Renaissance in Italy. Not entirely coincidental, this reemergence corresponded with and helped justify the inception of the modern state system."[10] Thereafter, the leaders and bureaucrats who led and managed states wanted no competitors. In Hendrik Spruyt's version of events: "The state system, or rather the state actors who made up that system, . . . recognized or denied certain forms of organization as legitimate international actors." Today, as in the past, "sovereign actors" themselves tend to recognize only "particular types of actors as legitimate players in the international system."[11]

THE KEY ISSUES BEFORE US

If there ever was a theoretical consensus about the nature of global politics, that consensus was shattered long ago. Just as the theorists and practitioners of Realpolitik could simply not understand or predict the French revolution nor the explosion of nationalism that was its companion, and not even the Russian revolutions of 1917, so were contemporary theorists of war and peace taken unawares by the Russian revolution of 1991, by the demise of the Soviet empire, and even by the end of the Cold War. These theorists seem also at a loss in addressing the political fragmentation of such states as the Soviet Union and Yugoslavia in Europe or of Zaire and Somalia in Africa. Let us now turn our attention to some of the key issues that continue profoundly to divide international relations theorists.

THE TWO WORLDS OF GLOBAL POLITICS

Part of the difference arises out of what part of the world one is analyzing. Organized violence is only a remote contingency within the advanced world of Europe and North America. The sort of theory that can capture the essential features of the advanced world is greatly different than that which can extend and deepen our understanding of the developing world. The former has become a pluralist security community in which societies are linked by an ever thickening web of interactions and shared fates. In that world, governments are disciplined by the iron logic of a global market, and monetary and trade issues have become the stuff of "high politics" that was once reserved for war and peace. The problem confronting states is less their fragmentation into tiny islands of self-identity[12] than the task of establishing the sort of transnational and international institutions that will enable societies to cope with globalization and allow them to limit its worst consequences.

By contrast, violence remains a significant, even a growing, problem in much of the developing world, especially in South Asia and Africa. Even here, however, the nature of war has changed in ways that diminish the relevance of state-centric approaches to international relations. The Gulf War of 1991 notwithstanding, theory has yet to account for the declining levels of *interstate* violence in these regions and the increasing levels of *intrastate* conflict.[13] It is the changing face of war that compelled British military historian John Keegan to begin his history of warfare by starkly denying Clausewitz's Eurocentric idea of state-sponsored violence: "War is not the continuation of policy by other means." Arguing that Clausewitz's idea "implies the existence of states, of state interests and of rational calculation about how they may be achieved," he observes that war "reaches into the most secret places of the human heart, places where self dissolves rational purpose, where pride reigns, where emotion is paramount, where instinct is king."[14]

In addition, the fragmentation of states in the developing world is a consequence of the growing incapacity to meet even minimal demands of citizens. Notwithstanding their Westphalian borrowings, today a growing number of states in the developing world cannot maintain order at home, let alone manage the large-scale economic and social forces determining their fate. At best "quasi-states," they embody "a parody of statehood indicated by pervasive incompetence, deflated credibility, and systematized corruption."[15] They are "failed states." "From Haiti in the Western Hemisphere to the remnants of Yugoslavia in Europe, from Somalia, Sudan, and Liberia in Africa, to Cambodia in Southeast Asia, a disturbing new phenomenon is emerging: the failed state, utterly incapable of sustaining itself as a member of the international community."[16]

In Africa, the failure of many states to cope with explosive socioeconomic problems intensifies and deepens the tribal identities that their postcolonial leaders had tried so hard to shed. In consequence, a number of African governments are little more than an extension of the dominance of some tribes over others. Rwanda and Burundi exist only in atlases; in reality, the organizing key words are *Hutu* and *Tutsi*. The Liberian state is dead; the country is little more than a shooting ground for the Krahn, Mende, and Gbande. And in South Asia, Afghanistan still is a murderous arena for Pathans, Tajiks, Uzbeks, Hazarags, and Turkmens.

Two very different worlds meet in East Asia, as reflected by the West's relations with a seemingly schizophrenic leadership in China. On the one hand, China seeks to join the world of advanced societies by gaining admission without further delay to the WTO, the World Trade Organization. On the other hand, Beijing's strong military modernization program, its insinuated threats to annex Taiwan, and the continued harsh repression of Chinese dissidents and Tibetan separatists reflect China's obsession with military security and preoccupations with preemptive closure and control.

ON STATES AND THE STATE SYSTEM

No one seriously questions the continuing relevance and the basic importance of sovereign states. Of greater concern here is whether and to what extent a state-centered perspective may risk omitting facts or even distorting reality. As suggested earlier, the world's nearly 200 sovereign states, especially those in the developing world outside of Europe, include entities of remarkably different parentage and status. At one extreme are states with tribal roots and soft frontiers; at the other are states with strong national foundations, a geographically rationalized territory, and hard frontiers.[17] Was the triumphant expansion of Europe's territorial states and their conquest of older political forms not the source of what scholars have called the global state system? But neither the state system nor statism as an ideology could eliminate older identities and contingent forms of loyalty and authority. Today, some states, for example in Europe, have deeply penetrated their societies. In contrast, the governments of many states elsewhere represent little more than the institutionalized dominance by a few ethnic, tribal, or kinship fragments of the many not-so-lucky.

State-centric theory (a term less loaded than "realism" or "neorealism") owes its dominance and durability to the leading role that Europeans and their descendants have played in global politics for over three centuries. In its various guises, this body of theory chooses to relegate to the margins of history the competition among political forms other than sovereign states, thereby implying, in Stephen Krasner's words, "that sovereignty has a taken-for-granted quality."[18]

Such a theory is ahistorical, in that it universalizes a set of facts that actually characterized a mere few hundred years of human experience pervasive only in regions inhabited or governed by Europeans. So there is a timelessness to state-centric theory that makes it seem as though a particular political form based on exclusive control of a defined territory, which took root, shape, substance, and direction in a specific context (Europe) at a very particular time (post-Westphalia), is of universal relevance.

For theorists in the European tradition, states are not the cause of violence in global politics but part of the solution to that violence, and their erosion is to be deplored. For Rosenau, this flies in the face of a profoundly altered reality: "Given the profound transformations in the nature and location of authority, legitimacy, and compliance, and . . . the emergent roles and structures of the modern state, transnational organizations, social movements, common markets, and political parties, the basis for extensive re-examinations of government and governance in an increasingly interdependent world is surely compelling,"[19] and many of these are "boundary-spanning forms of control."[20]

We are in the midst of one of the very infrequent historical epochs that feature dramatic shifts in identities and loyalties and attendant political forms. One such, was the sixth century A.D. in the Near East, when an existing clan system (Arabic) and an aspiring universal religious community (Islam) competed for loyalties and in the course of doing so brought about the utter collapse of two great empires. Another such was the sixteenth and seventeenth centuries in Europe and Latin America, when the Westphalian state was "ratified" by the international community and when Spain and Portugal imposed European political forms on old tribal systems in the New World. A third such was the late eighteenth and nineteenth centuries, when "nation" and "state" were married, nationalist self-consciousness brought an explosive new element to global politics, and Europeans consolidated their control over much of Africa and Asia. Yet another momentous epoch was ushered in by World War II and its aftermath, which saw the emergence of two superpowers.

In such times when incompatible identities, split loyalties, and political forms fiercely compete, scholars and practitioners are forced to rethink the tools of their trade. Andrew Linklater describes the tension between West-phalian polities and the larger conception of Christendom (see the chapter by Lipschutz in this volume), which confronted Europeans during an earlier era of rapidly changing loyalties and political forms:

The modern European state emerged within the confines of a single civilization united by the normative and religious power of Christendom. During its rise the state sought to free itself from the moral and religious shackles of the medieval world. But while it pursued this aim the state was aware of the dangers of totally under-mining earlier notions of an international society. . . .

Quite clearly, the state set out to employ the notion of a wider society of states for the explicit purpose of maintaining international order.[21]

In all such epochs, rapid change in political institutions and behavior creates a yawning disjunction between theory and practice. In recent years, this disjunction was made apparent in our collective failure to predict or explain adequately, even in retrospect, the end of the Cold War; in the difficulties faced by experienced scholars and practitioners alike in understanding the meaning of foreign policy dilemmas, including ethnic violence in Bosnia and Rwanda and the secession of Chechnya from Russia. As in similar historical periods, today the collapse, erosion, or evolution of some political forms and the emergence of others as well require us to correct what Rosenau identifies as scholars' failure to focus attention "on the conditions whereby authority is created, legitimacy sustained, and compliance achieved."[22]

Much of the statist tradition in international relations evolved after an earlier era of great change, the Thirty Years War, and was modified by "nations" and "nationalism" after the French Revolution. During the brief period between world wars, the statist tradition was challenged—albeit far less than is often claimed (as sheer "idealism," "utopianism," and "legalism")—by the liberal tradition, which had flourished in the United States and Great Britain during the last half of the nineteenth century. World War II reconfirmed the dominance of statists (now called "realists") both in academic and policy-making circles.

ON THE FUTURE: CHANGE IN CONTINUITY OR CONTINUITY IN CHANGE?

The contrast between the developed and developing regions returns us to the question of change and to the processes of expanding/contracting authority.[23] It is almost impossible to know with any certainty whether events augur fundamental change or simply more of the same. Ultimately, the answer depends on the theoretical framework that we choose to employ. Do the changes in global politics in recent years point to much more than a mere reshuffling of interstate relations? Rosenau explains how easy it is to reach opposite conclusions from observing the same events:

> [T]he question remains of whether the emergent, successor order rests on new systemic foundations or whether it derives from the reconstitution of the existing system. . . . Much depends . . . on how the characteristics of the global system are perceived and identified. If they are conceived in broad terms which stress the continuing competence and dominance of states and their anarchical system which accords them sovereignty and equality, then the end of the Cold War and the replacement of its superpower rivalry with a more dispersed, less militaristic competition among many states can be seen as merely a new form of the existing order. . . . If, on the other hand, emphasis is placed on the diminished competence of states, the globalization of national economies, the fragmentation of societies . . . the advent of transnational issues that foster the creation of transnational authorities . . . then the end of the Cold War and the emergent arrangements for maintaining global life are likely to be viewed as the bases for a wholly new order.[24]

Thus, realists, whose vision of global politics is that of a frozen world of insecurity, anarchic conflict, and struggles for power, remain comfortable with the persistence of violence in the developing world.[25] Their theoretical premises lead them to pay attention to the conflictual side of global politics, ignoring the rest of it. They are decidedly less comfortable with a world of declining military budgets, growing economic interdependence, and autonomous and influential interstate and transnational nonstate institutions—altogether a world ill-suited to the metaphor of anarchy. For the most part, power theorists deal with change in a superficial way, assuming that what endures far outweighs what is altered.

Kenneth Waltz exemplifies the difficulties experienced by many power theorists when confronted by the issue of change. Waltz identifies a number of "ordering principles" that he calls variables, but of which he actually permits only one to vary—the redistribution of power. As a result, there is little scope in Waltz's world for *fundamental* change, be it in the patterns of conflict and cooperation, the relationship between the domestic and interstate arenas of politics, the types and functions of leading actors, or the hierarchical nature of relationships among actors. For Waltz, global politics is, by definition, interstate politics in a world neatly divided into territorial compartments. And even though he declares that states "never have been the only international actors," his view of the prospects for any erosion of their dominant role is clarified when he rhetorically asks whether the Soviet Union or IBM is more likely "to be around 100 years from now."[26] It took a bit more than a decade to find out.

Liberals, in contrast, cite the striking differences in the developed world from the Hobbesian universe of their realist foes as proof of likely change and ignore the endemic violence in much of the developing world. If realists ignore change in general, liberals have a propensity to believe that the world is "going someplace" that is presumably better than where it had been. They confuse change with progress and, like realists, often pick and choose what they want from history.

Neither realists nor liberals have approached the question of change with the seriousness that it merits. The emergence, decline, and disappearance of political communities was a central concern to Aristotle and Machiavelli. Hobbes's metaphoric "state of nature" and Rousseau's "contract" were central to their effort to reconstruct the conditions of political birth and maturation. Expansion and contraction of authority are linked. On the one hand, economic interdependence pushes states into larger regional or global regimes and institutions in which they can voluntarily surrender autonomy. On the other hand, smallness and rediscovery of ethnicity and religion provide psychological refuge for those individuals and groups bewildered by the pace of change and quite fearful of cultural annihilation as a consequence of worldwide homogenization.

The enlargement of a polity by conquest or coalescence also will tend to create the conditions for its own fragmentation. As some polities enlarge, old loyalties, identities, and political forms rarely vanish completely. Instead, they are nested, and they remain partly or completely embedded within the larger polities. The extension of central authority to more territory or persons may entail bureaucratic growth that, at the periphery, engenders interests different from those at the center. As a polity grows, bureaucrats tempted to govern with even greater autonomy find greater opportunity to do so. But a polity's expansion usually gives rise to greater economic and social complexity, thereby further complicating the task of governance from the center. The process comes full circle when a large polity disintegrates into smaller fragments, each of which proves incapable of satisfying citizens' security or economic needs. Pressures may then build for selective reunification or even toward fuller reintegration.

Variation in size is only one aspect of these processes. Equally important is their embodiment of multiple conceptions of the self. It is because of this aspect of change that emerging international relations theory is likely to feature, with some emphasis, the politics of identity.

ON THE NORMATIVE NATURE OF THEORY

Whatever the claims of our discipline's "scientists" that facts and values can be kept apart, there is a critical normative dimension—whether articulated or not—in all our theories. That dimension is implicit in the questions we ask, and unlike the (often false) image of practitioners of natural science, social scientists seek more than the truth; they seek to change reality by finding a "solution" to the problem they have identified. In effect, this produces a peculiarly potent sense of indeterminacy, if only because the observer's research is intended to make it impossible to falsify the very claims it makes.

For liberals who view the state as a fundamental impediment to collective action, the solution to many problems of global politics lies in transnational linkages, international regimes, and all the rest of those instruments that are thought to erode state power and authority. For realists, rather, the state is our best defense against the problems that threaten to overwhelm us. Kalevi Holsti, for one, argues that the problem of contemporary war is best met by "the strengthening of states." "This will not be good news," he suggests, "to many contemporary analysts who believe that it is the state itself which is the source of so many of our current problems."[27]

And although *explicit* "prescription" need not necessarily flow from diagnosis, the desire to confront and overcome social problems is virtually universal among social scientists.[28] Of course, the identification of something as a "problem" entails a subjective choice that defies empirical justification. Sometimes such choices stem from identifiable national or class identities (examples abound: Indian analyses of nonalignment, Latin American claims about core and periphery in trade, French evaluations of nuclear strategy,[29] and, of course, contending U.S. and Soviet versions of the Cold War). In some cases, problem identification and even proffered solutions may seem self-interested. More often than not, they most certainly reflect deeply held beliefs.

Thus, neoliberal economists start with an overriding belief in efficiency, often paying little attention to distributive "fairness." Those norms are institutionalized in organizations such as the International Monetary Fund and the World Bank and are forced upon developing societies regardless of their value preferences.[30] For their part, realists have traditionally favored order and stability, in contrast to *dependencia* and to world systems theorists, who start with a belief in the primacy of equality and justice. There is a tension between the quest for order (or hierarchy), on the one hand, and justice (or equality), on the other, and theorists could not bridge this difference even if they wanted to. Interestingly, such differences do not rest on competing empirical claims, although competing claims may arise from those differences.

Thus, as states weaken and lose their autonomy in the face of regional and global economic forces, they also lose a capacity to define, rank, and protect the values of citizens. As a result, entire peoples have lost or will lose the benefit of democratic accountability for which they had struggled in past centuries and that they believed they had secured.

ON EMERGING THEORY AND CHANGING CONCEPTIONS OF SPACE AND TIME

The essence of the sovereign state and of the state system is the belief that territory is the source of identity and power. Yet territory is only one of many ways in which we can describe our "location" in global politics. Moreover, whereas control of territory virtually defined wealth and military power during those centuries in which the state emerged from a feudal past, neither intercontinental missiles nor investment capital is anchored to territory. Distance in a geographic sense no longer provides physical security, and territorial dimensions tell us little about wealth. Unlike past centuries, geography no longer limits communication nor the exchange of goods over great spans. Nor does physical distance entail, to the degree that it once did, erosion of political influence.[31] As a result, leaders at the center no longer need to delegate significant authority to surrogates overseas, just as ambassadors and local rulers no longer exercise the sort of absolute authority once so necessary owing to episodic, unreliable communications and transportation.

As we escape the tyranny that territory has exercised over our intellectual imagination, it becomes possible to think about global politics in new and creative ways. It is still true that "individuals are enmeshed in a complex web of relationships" and that their multiple identities may entail competing loyalties to a variety of political associations.[32] The end of the Cold War and the collapse of the Soviet Union have encouraged theorists to focus on changing identities, on conflicting loyalties and their legitimating ideologies, as well as on nested political forms that, as far as we know, have played a major role in political change since the dawn of history. In some instances, clashing identities and loyalties may constitute a genuine reawakening of earlier ideas and political forms; in others, they may represent a reinvention of the past; while, on a few occasions, they may even produce an altogether new identity or novel ideology.

The nature of "space" may be quite different for different polities, and the way in which space is defined and distributed undergoes continuous change. The Golden Horde had its range; Sony and General Motors have their markets; the United States and Burkina Faso, their territory; and Islam and Catholicism, their spiritual reach. As the boundaries of polities rigidify or erode, we witness the mixing and remixing of identities and consequently the "we–they" relationships that dominate global politics.

Far from enjoying exclusive control of a territory with hard boundaries, as is ascribed to Westphalian states, political units often share the loyalties of the same individuals and as a result common political space as well.[33] Conceptualizing space only as territorial domain, contemplating time as though it were distinct from space shows "close genealogical links between the 'Cartesian coordinates' of space and time and the discrete, sovereign state. . . . These links include relations of mapping, boundary setting, inclusion, and exclusion."[34] As the European state emerged and matured, political and economic power were tied to landed holdings. Today, by contrast, "land" is only one of several ways to define the space occupied by a polity. The telecommunications revolution, among other phenomena, is redefining space and time and, in so doing, also "our possible experiences of 'proximity' and 'simultaneity.' "[35]

Like Europe toward the end of the Middle Ages—when "the international system went through a dramatic transformation in which the crosscutting jurisdictions of feudal lords, emperors, kings, and popes started to give way to territorially defined authorities"[36]—polities today typically layer, overlap, or nest. And this is why the distinction between interstate and intrastate politics is becoming so tenuous.[37] In some instances, identities reinforce one another, as "state" and "nation" after the French Revolution roused the political consciousness of the bourgeoisie in Europe. Where identities are compatible, they may reinforce each other, thereby hardening the boundary between in- and out-groups. Thus, nested Islamic identities have been aroused from dormancy in a variety of societies, not only to reinforce citizen identities but state and cultural boundaries as well. The potency of Islamic fundamentalism lies in the fact that it "is an amalgam of religion and politics" that "fuses politics, religion and violence."[38]

In other cases, identities will crosscut, thereby softening or attenuating boundaries. In much of Sub-Saharan Africa, tribal and state identities overlap, and state frontiers have become more porous since decolonization. In the belt of Muslim states, which was formerly a part of the Soviet Union, citizenship, ethnicity, and religion crosscut in their own particular ways.

Recognizing the potential challenge of nested identities, leaders may try to harness them by reinforcing shared loyalties through the promotion of religion, literature, dialect, poetry, or ritual.[39] The European Union gains legitimacy by identifying with the medieval idea of "Europe" and linking Europe's shared history and culture with its more recent social, economic, and political symbols. Europe's territorial states thus coexist with "transnational microeconomic links," viewed as "a nonterritorial 'region' in the world economy—a decentered yet integrated space-of-flows, operating in real time, which exists alongside the space-of-places that we call national economies."[40]

Like space, time entails boundaries between people, based in this case not on geographic but on generational location. And as for space, the nature and role of time in global politics have been transformed in recent decades by a variety of factors that include technology, increasing life expectancy, and perhaps more important, the accelerating rate of social and political change. Our ancestors had reason to expect that the world into which they were born and the world in which they would die would remain much the same. In traditional societies, it was widely assumed that conditions were "givens" and that destiny—as in Machiavelli's "fortuna"—had to be meekly accepted. Generational "gaps," to the extent they existed at all, would be relatively modest and, by and large, the consequence of age itself.

By contrast, children born today may anticipate not one but several generation gaps—tantamount to boundaries separating generations—based on psychological, not geographical, distance. Such boundaries make themselves visible in dissimilar cognitive frameworks, through different value hierarchies, expectations, and interpretive lenses. Thus, belief systems vary as much, if not more, over time as over space.[41] The greater the cultural or temporal psychological distance, the more we can expect conflict based on misperceptions or misunderstandings.

In addition, at any historical moment, different societies and many segments within societies are at different evolutionary points. Even the European states themselves evolved at different rates: England and France created centralized bureaucratic and political structures and institutions earlier than, for example, Russia or Italy. And the clashes between European state polities and the tribal polities of the Americas and Africa represent in a real sense a collision between peoples situated at very different historical stages. Since the rate of speed at which societies are evolving is perhaps greater today than in the past, psychological distance may be increasing even as physical distance becomes less and less important.

Thus, many Africans remain traditional in outlook compared to most citizens in the West and even to the urbanized elites in their own countries. Because different societies and different sectors within the same society are changing at different rates, the psychological distances rooted in time, separating modernized urban elites from traditional agrarian peasants wherever they may reside, are probably growing. The resultant clash between the more traditional and the modernized social segments can be seen in a country like Afghanistan, where a movement based on traditional village values has seized power. Intergenerational conflict is every bit as central to contemporary global politics as Samuel Huntington's "clash of civilizations."[42]

CONCLUSIONS

There exist at least three serious intellectual impediments to constructing new theory in global politics. The first is the persistent dichotomy that is said to divide international and domestic politics. The second, as suggested earlier, is the static nature of much of our theorizing about global politics. And the third, and perhaps most daunting, is the dominance of an obsolete territorial conception of the world and the absence of a vocabulary and grammar that might get us beyond our obsession with a strictly territorial definition of space.

Beginning with the first, the wall between the international and intranational arenas, so central to the definition of the sovereign state, has been reduced to rubble in many parts of the world. The contrast between an "inside" pacified by the benign power of the state and an anarchic "outside" populated by enemies and opportunists is underplayed even by those who remain staunch statists in other respects. The role of state frontiers as walls between "us" and "them" continues to erode. And identities other than "citizenship"—ethnicity, religion, race, and so forth—are proving to be even more formidable sources of conflict.

As regards the second, it is high time for theory to come to terms with the disintegration of some political communities even as others integrate into larger polities. We live in a world that is, at once, old and new—a museum of old political forms, aging identities, and tired ideas, as well as a laboratory for nascent identities and unborn loyalties. This complex reality calls for a genuinely historical perspective to be adopted in our scholarly research and theory building in international relations.

Finally, to the extent that political configurations overlap, it becomes necessary to redefine "territory" in nontraditional ways—whether production and customer networks for corporations, cyberspace for investors, or virtual epistemic communities across state borders. In doing so, we have to reconceptualize space and think of time as creating or abolishing distance between peoples. New theory will recognize that the interstate system of exclusive territorial authorities, which has defined the Westphalian era of world history, now is yielding pride of place to an increasingly deterritorialized present. Today, a future has become imaginable in which geographic boundaries are being eroded by the logic of economic markets and by megalopolistic agglomerations of people. Demarcated by a variety of identities, people reconfigure within the same geographic space, in the manner of religion and caste.

For over 300 years, theories of global politics have been dominated by a model of the world that, in Robert Kaplan's words, was "an invention of modernism" at a time when "[p]eople were suddenly flush with an enthusiasm to categorize, to define." That model "offered a way to classify new national organisms, [by] making a jigsaw puzzle of neat pieces without transition zones between them," and as Europe kept expanding, "cartography came into its own as a way of creating facts by ordering the way we look at the world."[43]

For "postinternational politics," we need a map that allows for the collapse of states; accounts for kinship groups, tribes, transnational corporations, religious faiths, and regional and global markets; and represents nonstate political forms that attract loyalties, constitute sources of rewards and punishments, and condition the ways in which people behave in global politics.

Many of our theories about global politics are incompatible with such a world. Ad hoc conceptualizations or adjustments to existing theories will not suffice. Instead, what is now called for is a practice of dynamic theorization that makes a decisive break with the static models of the past and with a state-centric tradition of power politics that—like successive generations of international relations scholars before us—we inherited from our Westphalian past and dutifully and loyally sustained for so long.

NOTES

1. Martin Wight, "Why Is There No International Theory?" in Herbert Butterfield and Martin Wight (eds.), *Diplomatic Investigations: Essays in the Theory of International Politics* (Cambridge, MA: Harvard University Press, 1968), pp. 21, 18.

2. Kalevi Holsti observes that "[a]lmost all of what we call international theory today has been developed by observers from only two countries, Great Britain and the United States." *The Dividing Discipline: Hegemony and Diversity in International Theory* (Boston: Allen & Unwin, 1985), p. viii. Kissinger, of course, wrote his doctoral dissertation on the architects of the Concert of Europe, all of whom were the "realists" of their era.

3. Susan Strange, *The Retreat of the State: The Diffusion of Power in the World Economy* (Cambridge: Cambridge University Press, 1996). This highly readable analysis examines a variety of forces that limit the autonomy of the state in global politics.

4. James N. Rosenau, *Turbulence in World Politics* (Princeton, NJ: Princeton University Press, 1990), p. 9.

5. During the height of the disciplinary wars over "science" and "tradition," a graduate student in political philosophy contacted me to ask me if he could transfer from the university where he had passed his qualifying exams. He explained that after he had discussed his proposed thesis topic with his examiners, they informed him that they no longer considered Hobbes (about whom he wished to write) part of political science. That committee consisted of zealots of science, for whom the authoritative "text" was Morton A. Kaplan, "The New Great Debate: Traditionalism vs. Science in International Relations," in Klaus Knorr and James N. Rosenau (eds.), *Contending Approaches to International Politics* (Princeton, NJ: Princeton University Press, 1969), pp. 39–61.

6. I first began to doubt the triumphal march of science when, as a young academic undertaking a factor analysis of event data, I asked a senior colleague how one

"named" the factors. He peered at me quizzically over his spectacles and remarked: "It depends on what you want to find!"

7. Robert O. Keohane and Joseph S. Nye, *Power and Interdependence: World Politics in Transition* (Boston: Little, Brown, 1977), p. 23.

8. Many postmodern critics of positivism have a political and normative agenda that remains hidden unless one knows where to look. What compounds the search is that some postmodernists couch their criticisms of existing theory in unabashed relativism. Most would heatedly deny this, but their unwillingness to allow others to make counterclaims or to render aesthetic or normative judgments makes it difficult to avoid the slough of relativism.

9. Alan Ryan, *The Philosophy of Social Sciences* (New York: Pantheon Books, 1970), p. 72.

10. Frank W. Wayman and Paul F. Diehl, "Realism Reconsidered: The Realpolitik Framework and Its Basic Propositions," in Frank W. Wayman and Paul F. Diehl (eds.), *Reconstructing Realpolitik* (Ann Arbor: University of Michigan Press, 1994), p. 6.

11. Hendrik Spruyt, *The Sovereign State and Its Competitors* (Princeton, NJ: Princeton University Press, 1994, pp. 16, 178–79). This is a superb analysis of how the sovereign state triumphed over its competitors as Europe emerged from the Middle Ages. Historical contingency and context and institutional change are at the heart of Spruyt's analysis. (Cf. Lipschutz's chapter in this volume.)

12. Although many of these conflicts are in the developing world, there are, of course, exceptions, such as the cases of Canada's Québecois and Britain's Scottish and Welsh nationalists. What is different about these cases than the sort of tribal atomism that characterizes so many countries in the developing world is that the logic of regionalism and globalism allows advocates of localism to argue that the state is no longer necessary for their well-being.

13. "As in 1994, all the major conflicts in 1995 were internal, or intrastate, rather than between states." Margareta Sollenberg and Peter Wallensteen, "Major Armed Conflicts," in *SIPRI Yearbook 1996* (New York: Oxford University Press, 1996), p. 15. (Cf. Buzan's chapter in this volume.)

14. John Keegan, *A History of Warfare* (New York: Knopf, 1993), p. 3. Keegan is greatly influenced by Martin van Creveld's distinction between "war" and "crime" and, like van Creveld, believes that the distinction is eroding. See Van Creveld, *The Transformation of War* (New York: Free Press, 1991), p. 204.

15. Robert H. Jackson, "Quasi-States, Dual Regimes, and Neoclassical Theory: International Jurisprudence and the Third World," *International Organization* 41, 4 (Autumn 1987): 526–27.

16. Gerald B. Helman and Steven R. Ratner, "Saving Failed States," *Foreign Policy* 89 (Winter 1992–1993): 3.

17. Traditionally, states of comparable pedigree bestowed sovereignty on one another while withholding it from others. See, for example, Robert H. Jackson and Alan James, "The Character of Independent Statehood," in Robert H. Jackson and Alan James (eds.), *States in a Changing World* (New York: Oxford University Press, 1993).

18. Stephen D. Krasner, "Westphalia and All That," in Judith Goldstein and Robert O. Keohane (eds.), *Ideas and Foreign Policy* (Ithaca, NY: Cornell University Press, 1993), p. 235.

19. James N. Rosenau, "Governance, Order, and Change in World Politics," in James N. Rosenau and Ernst-Otto Czempiel (eds.), *Governance without Government: Order and Change in World Politics* (New York: Cambridge University Press, 1992), p. 4.

20. James N. Rosenau, "Governance in the Twenty-first Century," *Global Governance* 1, 1 (Winter 1995): 20.

21. Andrew Linklater, cited in Michael N. Barnett, "Sovereignty, Nationalism, and Regional Order in the Arab States System," *International Organization* 49, 3 (Summer 1995): 496.

22. Rosenau, *Turbulence in Global Politics*, p. 117.

23. James N. Rosenau refers to these two processes as "fragmegration." See "New Dimensions of Security: The Interaction of Globalizing and Localizing Dynamics," *Security Dialogue* 25 (September 1994): 256. (See Teune and Mlinar's chapter in this volume.)

24. Rosenau, "Governance, Order, and Change in World Politics," pp. 22–23.

25. Realists are prepared to revise their definitions of power to take cognizance, for instance, of the shift from what Joseph Nye calls "hard" to "soft" power. Joseph S. Nye, Jr., *Bound to Lead: The Changing Nature of American Power* (New York: Basic Books, 1990), p. 188.

26. Kenneth N. Waltz, *Theory of International Politics* (Reading, MA: Addison-Wesley, 1979), pp. 93, 95.

27. Kalevi J. Holsti, *The State, War, and the State of War* (Cambridge: Cambridge University Press, 1996), p. xii.

28. Thus, data-based analyses routinely recite the mantra "correlation is not causation" to assert that their high statistical correlations do not prove causality. Nevertheless, in the silent depths of their hearts, they celebrate the one true answer they *know* to have discovered.

29. In the 1960s, French commentators like Raymond Aron argued that U.S. strategic theory *consciously* aimed to perpetuate America's nuclear dominance.

30. See Graham Bird, "The IMF and Developing Countries," *International Organization* 50, 3 (Summer 1996): 477–511.

31. See Kenneth E. Boulding, *Conflict and Defense* (New York: Harper & Row, 1962).

32. Yale H. Ferguson and Richard W. Mansbach, *Polities: Authorities, Identities, and Change* (Columbia: University of South Carolina Press, 1996), p. 43.

33. It is useful in this regard to distinguish between "hard" and "soft" identities and hard and soft boundaries. (See Zartman's chapter in this volume.)

34. Jonathan Boyarin, "Space, Time, and the Politics of Memory," in Jonathan Boyarin (ed.), *Remapping Memory: The Politics of TimeSpace* (Minneapolis: University of Minnesota Press, 1994), p. 4.

35. Ibid., p. 13.

36. Spruyt, *The Sovereign State and Its Competitors*, p. 3.

37. See Yale H. Ferguson and Richard W. Mansbach, "Political Space and Westphalian States in a World of 'Polities': Beyond Inside/Outside," *Global Governance* 2 (1996): 261–87.

38. Johannes J. G. Jansen, *The Dual Nature of Islamic Fundamentalism* (Ithaca, NY: Cornell University Press, 1997), p. xiv.

39. E. J. Hobsbawm, *Nations and Nationalism since 1780* (New York: Cambridge University Press, 1990), pp. 46–79.

40. John Gerard Ruggie, "Territoriality and Beyond: Problematizing Modernity in International Relations," *International Organization* 47, 1 (Winter 1993): 172.

41. See Ofira Seliktar, "Identifying a Society's Belief Systems," in Margaret G. Hermann (ed.), *Political Psychology* (San Francisco: Jossey-Bass, 1986), pp. 320–54.

42. See Samuel P. Huntington, "The Clash of Civilizations," *Foreign Affairs* 72, 1 (Summer 1993): 22–49; and Huntington, "The West Unique, Not Universal," *Foreign Affairs* 75, 6 (November–December 1996): 28–46.

43. Robert D. Kaplan, "The Coming Anarchy," *The Atlantic Monthly* (February 1994): 69.

REFERENCES

Barnett, Michael N. (1995). Sovereignty, Nationalism, and Regional Order in the Arab States System. *International Organization* 49, 3 (Summer).

Bird, Graham (1996). The IMF and Developing Countries. *International Organization* 50, 3 (Summer): 477–511.

Boulding, Kenneth E. (1962). *Conflict and Defense*. New York: Harper & Row.

Boyarin, Jonathan (1994). Space, Time, and the Politics of Memory. In Jonathan Boyarin (ed.), *Remapping Memory: The Politics of TimeSpace*. Minneapolis: University of Minnesota Press.

Ferguson, Yale H., and Richard W. Mansbach (1996). Political Space and West-phalian States in a World of "Polities": Beyond Inside/Outside. *Global Governance* 2: 261–87.

Ferguson, Yale H., and Richard W. Mansbach (1996). *Polities: Authorities, Identities, and Change*. Columbia: University of South Carolina Press.

Helman, Gerald B., and Steven R. Ratner (1992–1993). Saving Failed States. *Foreign Policy* 89 (Winter).

Hobsbawm, E. J. (1990). *Nations and Nationalism since 1780*. New York: Cambridge University Press.

Holsti, Kalevi (1985). *The Dividing Discipline: Hegemony and Diversity in International Theory*. Boston: Allen & Unwin.

Holsti, Kalevi (1996). *The State, War, and the State of War*. Cambridge: Cambridge University Press.

Huntington, Samuel P. (1993). The Clash of Civilizations. *Foreign Affairs* 72, 1 (Summer): 22–49.

Huntington, Samuel P. (1996). The West Unique, Not Universal. *Foreign Affairs* 75, 6 (November–December): 28–46.

Jackson, Robert H. (1987). Quasi-States, Dual Regimes, and Neoclassical Theory: International Jurisprudence and the Third World. *International Organization* 41, 4 (Autumn).

Jackson, Robert H., and Alan James (eds.) (1993). *States in a Changing World*. New York: Oxford University Press.

Jansen, Johannes J. G. (1997). *The Dual Nature of Islamic Fundamentalism*. Ithaca, NY: Cornell University Press.

Kaplan, Morton A. (1969). The New Great Debate: Traditionalism vs. Science in International Relations. In Klaus Knorr and James N. Rosenau (eds.), *Contending Approaches to International Politics*. Princeton, NJ: Princeton University Press.

Kaplan, Robert D. (1994). The Coming Anarchy. *The Atlantic Monthly* (February): 69.

Keegan, John (1993). *A History of Warfare*. New York: Knopf.

Keohane, Robert O., and Joseph S. Nye (1977). *Power and Interdependence: World Politics in Transition*. Boston: Little, Brown.

Krasner, Stephen D. (1993). Westphalia and All That. In Judith Goldstein and Robert O. Keohane (eds.), *Ideas and Foreign Policy*. Ithaca, NY: Cornell University Press.

Nye, Joseph S., Jr. (1990). *Bound to Lead: The Changing Nature of American Power*. New York: Basic Books.

Rosenau, James N. (1990). *Turbulence in World Politics*. Princeton, NJ: Princeton University Press.

Rosenau, James N. (1992). Governance, Order, and Change in World Politics. In James N. Rosenau and Ernst-Otto Czempiel (eds.), *Governance without Government: Order and Change in World Politics*. New York: Cambridge University Press.

Rosenau, James N. (1994). New Dimensions of Security: The Interaction of Globalizing and Localizing Dynamics. *Security Dialogue* 25 (September).

Rosenau, James N. (1995). Governance in the Twenty-first Century. *Global Governance* 1, 1 (Winter).

Ruggie, John Gerard (1993). Territoriality and Beyond: Problematizing Modernity in International Relations. *International Organization* 47, 1 (Winter).

Ryan, Alan (1970). *The Philosophy of Social Sciences*. New York: Pantheon Books.

Seliktar, Ofira (1986). Identifying a Society's Belief Systems. Pp. 320–54 in Margaret G. Hermann (ed.), *Political Psychology*. San Francisco: Jossey-Bass.

Sollenberg, Margareta, and Peter Wallensteen (1996). Major Armed Conflicts. In *SIPRI Yearbook 1996*. New York: Oxford University Press.

Spruyt, Hendrik (1994). *The Sovereign State and Its Competitors*. Princeton, NJ: Princeton University Press.

Strange, Susan (1996). *The Retreat of the State: The Diffusion of Power in the World Economy*. Cambridge: Cambridge University Press.

Van Creveld, Martin (1991). *The Transformation of War*. New York: Free Press.

Waltz, Kenneth N. (1979). *Theory of International Politics*. Reading, MA: Addison-Wesley.

Wayman, Frank W., and Paul F. Diehl (1994). Realism Reconsidered: The Realpolitik Framework and Its Basic Propositions. In Frank W. Wayman and Paul F. Diehl (eds.), *Reconstructing Realpolitik*. Ann Arbor: University of Michigan Press.

Wight, Martin (1968). Why Is There No International Theory? In Herbert Butterfield and Martin Wight (eds.), *Diplomatic Investigations: Essays in the Theory of International Politics*. Cambridge, MA: Harvard University Press.

Epilogue

JOSE V. CIPRUT

Theorists in the social sciences may be *against* interpretation (Sontag, 1966), method (Feyerabend, 1975), or theory (Furrow, 1995); *for* "the myth of total reason" (Albert, 1976); *aloof* to "feelings and emotions" (Arnold, 1970); or *torn between* a positivist's great expectations from value-free knowledge (Popper, 1972; Bryant, 1985) and a critical theorist's value-laden conception of social theory as "critique" (Horkheimer, 1972; Habermas, 1974). Whatever their proclivities, theorists in the social sciences will go on serving as *conduits* for the politics of social theory (Keat, 1981) for as long as they covet unsuspected meanings in rereadings conditioned to discover untapped understandings.

The socioeconomic and geopolitical realities around citizens are changing ever faster as a result of advanced communications. Their sense of spatiotemporal locus and perceptions of the tenor and implications of their relevant social relationships with the rest of the world are continually being challenged. Many national decision makers are becoming increasingly active participants in transnational issues of governance, be these on the free movement of people, goods and services; on revenue sharing from expanding exchanges; on multilateral security; or on the terms of continued peace and order. The crisscrossing causeways that thereby multiply deplete the checkpoints and gates prepositioned along the state's geographic boundaries, and can only abate the function of the walls once raised to shut off the citizenry from the outside world. The day is imaginable when the citizen may become the measure of all things—again. As global exchanges develop, bureaucracies and hierarchies will need to reconfigure themselves if states seek to adjust to the globally changing landscape. Such reconception and reorientation could contribute to a convergence of what used to be strictly internal and

menacingly external in the affairs of state. Interpenetrations may also enhance the gradual elimination of the prime sources of anarchy contaminated
with misunderstandings and misperceptions conducive to generalized wars.
The changed scenery may provide incentives for the residual zones of conflict, self-servingly to transform themselves into zones of peace and order.
Next, the rule of law could also help speed up their development and their
peaceful reintegration of the world community at large.

The emergence of virtual communities and their development via self-
styled traditions, the increasing participation in the world's advanced industries, and innovative product flows by globally local venture capital and
locally globalizing skilled labor cannot but transform everyday life for the
educated while spurring even more those with newly discovered reasons
swiftly to emulate the skilled and the emancipated.

Issues, actors, relations, structures, functions, processes, and contexts in
adaptive modes of continual self-respecification will redefine and redirect the
meaning and purpose of civic life on earth and in outer space. The institutions that embody order and culture and the social forces that shape communities and sustain good governance will accordingly also transform
themselves, creating a global system based on units of analysis designed to
acknowledge the micro in the macro and to distinguish the enveloped from
the overlapping.

In that world, "socially instituted forms of communications" will more
or less "facilitate the production of the universal." And the broadened and
widening inclusive common spaces may well provide a "visible manifestation
of the communality of the problematic as an agreement on the grounds of
disagreement with which no genuine discussion—as distinct from parallel
monologues—can dispense." Only

a point of view that perceives itself as such, that is, as a view taken from a point in
a space of contending positions, is in a position to overcome particularity. It can do
this in particular by entering into a rational exchange capable of effecting, through
a regulated confrontation of differences of vision (which includes an awareness of the
social determinants of these differences), a departicularization of particular points of
view. (Bourdieu, 1991: 384)

In this volume, we emphasized the importance for social and political
theory of history (time) and narrative (space) on which retrospectives and
pursuits continue to depend. We examined some of the corrigible proclivities that impede sound theory making. We considered the changing tenor
and tenets of theoretical building blocks such as the self, the other, the state,
territory, power, boundaries, development, and milieu, at a time when the
vistas of international relations are transforming at remarkable speed.

What will future theory be inspired by? Platonic elitism, Aristotelean caution, Machiavellian opportunism, Hobbesian spunk, Rousseauesque con-

tractarianism, Kantian optimism, Marxist strife, Waltzish realism? An esoteric mix, or yet another fix? We came neither to bury Caesar nor to praise him. The theories that mortals "do" live after them, their truths oft buried with their bones. New eras create worlds in their image. If this is a new era, why not let it become what it is meant to be?

REFERENCES

Albert, H. (1976). The Myth of Total Reason. Pp. 163–67 in G. Addey and D. Frisby (eds.), *The Positivist Dispute in German Sociology*. London: Heinemann. [Trans. in English from T. W. Adorno's original in German.]

Arnold, M. B. (ed.) (1970). *Feelings and Emotions*. New York and London: Academic Press.

Bourdieu, Pierre (1991). On the Possibility of a Field of World Sociology [trans. L.J.D. Wacquant]. In J. S. Coleman and P. Bourdieu (eds.), *Social Theory for a Changing Society*. Boulder, CO: Westview Press.

Bryant, Christopher G. A. (1985). *Positivism in Social Theory and Research*. New York: St. Martin's Press.

Feyerabend, Paul (1975). *Against Method*. Rev. ed. 1998. London and New York: Verso.

Furrow, Dwight (1995). *Against Theory: Continental and Analytic Challenges in Moral Philosophy*. New York: Routledge.

Habermas, Juergen (1974). *Theory and Practice*. Trans. J. Viertel. London: Heinemann.

Horkheimer, M. (1972). *Critical Theory*. Trans. M. O'Conell et al. New York: Herder & Herder.

Keat, Russell (1981). *The Politics of Social Theory: Habermas, Freud, and the Critique of Positivism*. Chicago: University of Chicago Press.

Popper, Karl, R. (1972). *Objective Knowledge*. London: Oxford University Press.

Sontag, Susan (1966). Against Interpretation. In *Against Interpretation, and Other Essays*. New York: Dell.

Name Index

Subject Index

About the Contributors

BARRY BUZAN is Research Professor of International Studies at the University of Westminster, England, and a Project Director at the Copenhagen Peace Research Institute. Up to September 1995 he was Professor of International Studies at the University of Warwick; from 1988 to 1990 he was Chairman of the British International Studies Association; from 1993 to 1994 he was Vice President of the (North American) International Studies Association; and in 1993 he was Visiting Professor at the International University of Japan. His recent books include *People, States, and Fear* (1991); *The Logic of Anarchy: Neorealism to Structural Realism* (1993, with Charles Jones and Richard Little); *The Arms Dynamic in World Politics* (1998, with Eric Herring); and *International Systems in World History: Remaking the Study of International Relations* (2000, with Richard Little).

JOSE V. CIPRUT is an independent researcher. His postdoctoral work dealt with Near-/Middle-Eastern security problems. His subsequent research focused on the political economies of East and Southeast Asia. He specializes on international geopolitical issues in socioeconomic perspective and strategic context. He is an industrial technologist trained in the United Kingdom and Germany. He returned to academe as a social scientist following a tricontinental executive career in international industrial development. He has been named Fellow at the Middle East Center of the University of Pennsylvania. His recent writings include refereed journal articles—"Demand for Defense in East Asia" (co-authored, 1995) and "Rethinking East Asian Security in an Evolving Global Political Economy" (1996); a book chapter ("East-Southeast Asian Security in Context," 1997); a critical strategic reestimate ("Macau SAR: A Space in Search of Its Place," 1999); an edited volume, *Of Fears and Foes: Security and Insecurity in an Evolving Global Political Economy* (Praeger, 2000); and two current projects on indeterminacy, uncertainty, and risk.

KALEVI J. HOLSTI is Professor of Political Science at the University of British Columbia, Vancouver, Canada. He has taught at universities in Canada, the United States, Japan, and Israel, and he was a Visiting Fellow at the Australian National University. He is a former editor of the *International Studies Quarterly* and of the *Canadian Journal of Political Science*. He was president of both the International Studies Association and the Canadian Political Science Association, and elected a Fellow of the Royal Society of Canada in 1983. He has authored an extended essay on International Theory, *The Dividing Discipline* (1985), *War and Peace: Armed Conflicts and International Order, 1648–1989*, and other volumes, including *The State, War, and the State of War* (1996).

KLAUS KRIPPENDORFF is Professor of Communication at the University of Pennsylvania's Annenberg School for Communication. He is former President and Permanent Fellow of the International Communications Association, Fellow of the American Association for the Advancement of Science, of the Netherlands Institute for Advanced Studies, and of the East-West Center in Hawaii. He has taught at universities in the United States and abroad, is on the editorial boards of numerous journals of communication, has organized international conferences, and also consults with industry, governmental institutions, and the courts. He has edited *Communication and Control in Society* (1979); authored books—*Content Analysis* (1980) and *Information Theory* (1986); reported on *Design in the Age of Information* (1997) for the National Science Foundation; and published over 80 articles in scientific journals and books on communication theory, cybernetics, systems theory, design, constructivist epistemology, and methodology in the social sciences.

RONNIE D. LIPSCHUTZ is Associate Professor of Politics at the University of California, Santa Cruz (UCSC), where he teaches courses on foreign policy, international politics, and the politics of global environmental protection. He is also Director of the Stevenson Program on Global Security at UCSC. He has worked on the scientific staffs of the Union of Concerned Scientists, the Massachusetts Audubon Society, and the Lawrence Berkeley Laboratory. He has been a Research Fellow of the Institute of International Affairs at the University of California at Berkeley, a Visiting Research Fellow at the Royal Institute of International Affairs in London, and a Postdoctoral Fellow of the MacArthur Interdisciplinary Group in International Security Studies and the Energy and Resources Group at Berkeley. He is the author of *Radioactive Waste: Politics, Technology and Risk* (1980); coauthor of *The*

Energy Saver's Handbook for Town and City People (1982); author of *When Nations Clash—Raw Materials, Ideology and Foreign Policy* (1989); coeditor (with Ken Conca) *The State and Social Power in Global Environmental Politics* (1993); editor of *On Security* (1995); coeditor (with Beverly Crawford) of *The Political Economy of Cultural Conflict* (1998); and author of *Global Civil Society and Global Environmental Governance* (1996) and *After Authority* (1999).

RICHARD W. MANSBACH is Professor of Political Science at Iowa State University. He is the author, coauthor, or editor of numerous articles, chapters, and books, including *In Search of Theory: Toward a New Paradigm for Global Politics* (1981, with John Vasquez); *The Elusive Quest: Theory and International Politics* (1988, with Yale H. Ferguson); *Changing Order in North Eastern Asia and the Korean Peninsula* (1993, with Manwoo Lee); and, more recently (with Yale H. Ferguson), *Polities: Authority, Identities, and Change* (1996).

ZDRAVKO MLINAR is Professor of Sociology at the Faculty of Social Sciences, University of Ljubljana, Slovenia. He was a researcher at the Institute of Sociology and Philosophy, later Professor and Dean at the Faculty of Social Sciences. He is Head of the Centre for Spatial Technology. He was the first president of the Slovenian Sociological Society (1965–1969), the president of the Yugoslav Sociological Association (1971–1972), an officer of the International Sociological Association, and co-founder of its group, Sociology of Local and Global Relations. He is a member of the Academy of Science and Arts of Slovenia and heads its section on historical and social sciences. One of his three recent award-winning books, *Individuation and Globalization in Space* (1994), is being translated into English. His 400 volumes include *The Developmental Logic of Social Systems* (1978, with Henry Teune); *Contradictions of Social Development* (1986); *Globalization and Territorial Identities* (ed., 1992); and *Autonomy and Connectedness in the European Space* (ed., 1995).

DENNIS PIRAGES is Professor of Government and Politics and Director of the Harrison Program on the Future Global Agenda at the University of Maryland. He is one of the pioneers in the study of issues of global sustainability. His book, *The Sustainable Society*, was published in 1977. He has authored or edited 12 books and nearly 40 articles, among which *The New Context for International Relations: Global Ecopolitics* (1978), *Global Technopolitics: The International Technopolitics of Technology and Resources* (1989), and *Building Sustainable Societies: A Blue Print for a Post-Industrial World* (1996) provide his contextualized perspectives and insights. *Ecological Security in Northeast Asia* (1998), edited with Miranda A. Schreurs, exposes the complexities of a case in point.

HENRY TEUNE joined the Department of Political Science at the University of Pennsylvania in 1961. He has held many visiting academic appointments at home and abroad since. He is a member of the editorial boards of *Comparative Political Studies* and *The Journal of Theoretical Politics*. He served as President of the International Studies Association (1981–1982), and until 1994 as a member of the Executive Committee of the International Sociological Association. Since 1990, he has directed the Project of Democracy and Local Governance, an international research program involving local political leaders and governments in 26 countries and backed by the NSF and other agencies and foundations. He is the author or coauthor of many articles. He coedited *The Logic of Comparative Social Inquiry* (1970), *The Developmental Logic of Social Systems* (1978), and *The Social Ecology of Change* (1978), and is the author of *Growth* (1988). He wrote in and coedited *Democracy and Local Governance: Ten Empirical Studies* (1993) and is the editor of *Local Governance Around the World* (1995).

I. WILLIAM ZARTMAN, the Jacob Blaustein Professor of International Organization and Conflict Resolution at the School of Advanced International Studies (SAIS) of the Johns Hopkins University at Washington, D.C., is also Director of African Studies. He is the author, coauthor, and editor of numerous works on North Africa and on negotiation analysis—a scholarly field that he has helped to develop into a widely practiced international specialty. He was the Project Director of the Case Studies on Negotiations at SAIS and the editor of the SAIS–Praeger African Studies Publications series. He has filled many executive positions in a variety of professional organizations and remains a consultant to the U.S. Department of State and to the U.S. Information Agency. His recent works include *Collapsed States: The Disintegration and Restoration of Legitimate Authority* (1995), *Elusive Peace: Negotiating an End to Civil Wars* (1995), *Power and Negotiation* (1998–1999) with Jeffrey Z. Rubin, and *Preventive Diplomacy: Averting Violence and Escalation* (1999).